THE WORLD IN CONFLICT

Over the course of a journalistic career that began in the Middle East, **John Andrews** became *The Economist*'s most experienced foreign correspondent, with postings in Europe, Asia and America. Before joining *The Economist*, he wrote from and about north Africa and the Middle East for the *Guardian* and NBC News, interviewing personalities such as Muammar Qaddafi, Yasser Arafat and Ezer Weizman. He is the author of two books on Asia, co-author of a book on Europe and co-editor of *Megachange: The World in 2050* (Profile Books, 2012).

THE WORLD IN CONFLICT

Understanding the world's troublespots

JOHN ANDREWS

THE ECONOMIST IN ASSOCIATION WITH
PROFILE BOOKS LTD

Published by Profile Books Ltd
3 Holford Yard
Bevin Way
London WC1X 9HD
www.profilebooks.com

Typeset in EcoType by MacGuru Ltd
info@macguru.org.uk
Maps by Martin Lubikowski, ML Design
www.facebook.com/makingmapswork

Printed in India by Manipal Technologies Ltd, Manipal

A CIP catalogue record for this book is available from the British Library

ISBN 978 1 78125 368 7
eISBN 978 1 78283 115 0

To Mika and Sam, in the vain hope that they will grow up in a world without conflict.

Geographical regions covered by individual chapters

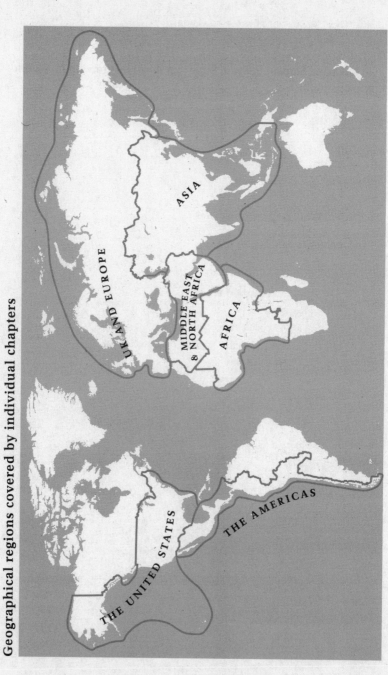

UK AND EUROPE

ASIA

MIDDLE EAST & NORTH AFRICA

AFRICA

THE UNITED STATES

THE AMERICAS

Contents

An explanation

THE WORD "CONFLICT" can be applied to everything from a playground squabble to the second world war. For this book it means a difference of opinion – between nations, peoples or political movements – that involves the use of deadly violence. My criterion is that the conflict, no matter how distant its origins, should still be happening today (which is why, for example, there is only a passing reference to the wars that broke up Yugoslavia at the end of the last century).

There is a sobering number of conflicts that satisfy my criterion, from the unresolved civil wars in Iraq and Afghanistan to the secessionist violence in India and the Philippines. Does the violence meted out by "organised crime" meet my criterion? Not when the criminals are the Russian mafia. But in the case of Latin America, conflicts involving the drug cartels threaten the state itself – and the violence by both cartels and state is easily extreme enough to qualify.

Nonetheless, on the basis of cause and effect, I have tried to place every conflict in its historical context. I have also tried not to "take sides": violent conflicts arouse passions, certainly among the participants and often among outsiders (the Arab–Israeli conflict is an obvious example), but I hope I have been impartial.

As Chapter 1 makes clear, conflicts can have many, often overlapping causes, which makes it difficult to catalogue them by categories such as religion, race, territory, resources or ideology. The simplest solution is surely to categorise them by geography and country, even though many conflicts, especially in Africa and the Middle East, cross national boundaries.

The best example of this defiance of national frontiers is the rise of violent Islamism. Much of this can be traced back to the cold-war era in which the West supported Muslim *mujahideen* from the Arab world in their ultimately successful fight to expel Soviet troops from Afghanistan. As is clear from this book's chapters on the Middle East, Africa and Asia, the Islamist movements of today – whether in Algeria and Mali or Pakistan and the Philippines – often have their roots in the Afghanistan of the 1980s.

Violent Islamism also marks an upward tick in the otherwise downward trend of conflict in the wake of the second world war and, especially, the cold war. As wars between states almost disappear, civil wars and insurgencies – many with an Islamist flavour – are taking their place and so mocking our recent fantasies of universal peace and the triumph of democracy.

Should we therefore surrender to a fatalistic gloom? This guide to the world's conflicts may well bring to mind the view of Mahatma Gandhi:

> What difference does it make to the dead, the orphans and the homeless, whether the mad destruction is wrought under the name of totalitarianism or in the holy name of liberty or democracy?

But Gandhi was speaking in an age horribly scarred by the first and second world wars. Though his words are still relevant, at least – as Chapter 8 shows – today's many conflicts are creating fewer corpses and fewer orphans.

Lastly, Arabic transliteration is fraught with difficulties (see Appendix 3). I hope I will not offend purists by frequently deviating from classical correctness.

John Andrews
October 2015

1 The reason why

"IF EVERY EIGHT-YEAR-OLD in the world is taught meditation, we will eliminate violence from the world within one generation." Or so the Dalai Lama has claimed in one of those comforting quotations that go viral in a world of social media. There is, of course, no possibility that His Holiness's condition will be fulfilled. If the present is a guide to the future, it will be one of frequent conflict – confirmation that violence is part of the human condition and that men and women will continue to take up arms in pursuit of their goals. As Carl von Clausewitz, a Prussian general with a more realistic view of humanity than the Tibetan leader, put it: "War is an act of force to compel our enemy to do our will."

The evidence is everywhere. During the 21st century, which is not even two decades old, the US and its allies have invaded Iraq and Afghanistan; Russia has been at war with Georgia; the UK and France have combined to help topple a regime in Libya – which then succumbed to fratricidal anarchy. These are just a few of the more bloody conflicts pitting nations against nations. Others are less bloody, but still dangerous: for example, the nervous stand-off between India and Pakistan in Kashmir, where troops from both sides threaten each other – occasionally with fatal results – across the line of control drawn as long ago as 1972 in the snow-bound Himalayan and Karakoram mountains. In East Asia, North and South Korea may not be in direct conflict, but the nuclear-armed totalitarian north and the capitalist, democratic south have yet to conclude a peace treaty to put a formal end to a war that began in 1950. Elsewhere in the Pacific region, maritime and territorial disputes entangle China, Taiwan, Japan, the Philippines, Malaysia, Vietnam and Brunei, and no one can be truly confident that these arguments, over bits of rock or expanses of ocean, will not lead to armed conflict – whether by design or by human error.

One school of thought holds that democracy and peace go together. The American neoconservatives around President George W. Bush believed that toppling Saddam Hussein in 2003 would bring democracy first to Iraq and then to the rest of the Middle East, which would in turn lead to a genuine acceptance of democratic Israel in the Arab neighbourhood. After all, Rudolph Joseph Rummel and other political scientists have persuasively argued that democracies do not wage war on each other. Sadly, the aftermath of the Iraq war – be it sectarian bloodshed in Iraq itself or civil war in adjacent Syria – has mocked the neoconservatives' naive predictions.

But if democracies are loth to attack other democracies, they are hardly immune from armed conflicts from within, be it a case of Basque separatists in Spain or republican extremists in Northern Ireland in the UK. Nor can democracies be immune from imported violence. The attack on the Twin Towers of New York's Manhattan and on the Pentagon just outside Washington, DC, on September 11th 2001 shattered the complacent illusion that the US – the world's economic and military hyperpower – could be untouched at home by the consequences of its policies abroad. It is a bitter irony that the US-style date matches the country's emergency telephone number. It was 9/11 that provoked President Bush's global war on terror and the invasions of Afghanistan and Iraq, and it was the same 9/11 that has engraved Osama bin Laden's al-Qaeda in the global consciousness.

Does al-Qaeda (which means the base in Arabic) introduce a new form of conflict to the world? Its choice of weapons is actually quite conventional: terrorism against civilians, 9/11 being the supreme but far from only example; light arms, notably AK-47 assault rifles and rocket-propelled grenades; and improvised explosive devices (IEDs). In other words, it is the normal resort of the relatively weak against the technologically mighty in what is now called asymmetric warfare. Nor is al-Qaeda's use of suicide bombers new: as long ago as the 1980s the Tamil Tigers were carrying out suicide attacks in Sri Lanka in their bloody and eventually abortive attempt to create an independent Tamil state in the north of the island.

But there are two areas where al-Qaeda has broken new ground. One is in its use of social media, notably videos on YouTube, to spread its message beyond the Middle East. An example was enlisting Anwar al-Awlaki, an American of Yemeni extraction, to use his fluent English to preach Islamic extremism over the internet to non-Arabophone Muslims wherever they might be in the world (Awlaki was killed by a CIA-directed drone strike in Yemen in 2011). The other innovation is to franchise the al-Qaeda name. Just as McDonald's lends its name and recipes to independent managers around the globe, so too with al-Qaeda, whose offshoots range from Iraq to Mali.

Al-Qaeda has in some ways been eclipsed by the Islamic State in Iraq and Sham (ISIS), whose other acronym is ISIL – the Islamic State of Iraq and the Levant (Sham is the Arabic name for greater Syria or the Levant). Whereas al-Qaeda has concentrated much of its efforts on attacks outside the Muslim world, ISIS has proclaimed a new caliphate in the Middle East, and has recruited thousands of fighters from Europe and the rest of the Arab world by an internet presence, complete with slickly produced videos of beheadings and martial gore, that is far more sophisticated than that of al-Qaeda.

The force of the faithful

In the case of the violence wreaked by al-Qaeda and ISIS, religion is an obvious factor. The invocation of a pure form of Islam; the division of the world between the *dar al-islam* (the house of Islam) and the *dar al-harb* (the house of war, populated by those yet to submit to Islam); the determination to establish a new caliphate transcending the borders of modern states: all these are as if the world had not changed in the 13 or so centuries since the Muslim faith first spread, by conquest and conversion, from the Arabian peninsula to the Atlantic in the west and the Himalayas in the east. The fundamentalist Sunni zealotry of al-Qaeda and the Islamic State, scorning all other forms of Islam, especially Shi'ism, alarms even the stern Wahhabis of Saudi Arabia, but excites those who yearn for the straightforward strictures of Islamic *sharia* law and an end to corruption and decadence.

At least in terms of headlines, and quite possibly in terms of bloodshed too (for instance the 1980–88 war between Shia Iran and the secular but Sunni-led regime of Saddam Hussein in Iraq), the world's gravest source of conflict is this Muslim divide between Sunni and Shia. It provokes and threatens violent upheaval throughout the Middle East and beyond, from Lebanon in the west to Afghanistan and Pakistan in the east and south to parts of east Africa.

Yet ironically, though some scholars dispute this, the original schism had no ideological or theological cause. Instead, it was a political disagreement over who should be caliph (successor) of the Muslim community (*umma* in Arabic) on the death of the Prophet Muhammad in 632 AD. The Shia, meaning party or faction in Arabic, were the partisans of Ali, the prophet's cousin and son-in-law, and they believed that he should have been the first caliph. Instead, it was Abu Bakr, the prophet's father-in-law, who first succeeded, nominated by the Sunnis (the word *sunna* refers to the customs and habits of Muhammad) on the grounds that what mattered was a man's worthiness, rather than his lineage to the prophet. There were two further caliphs, Umar and Uthman, before the Sunnis in 656 AD accepted Ali as the fourth of the *rashidun* (rightly guided) caliphs.

But peace between Sunni and Shia was short-lived. In 661 AD Ali was attacked at prayer and died within days. His son Hassan was almost immediately forced to surrender the caliphate to Muawiya ibn Abi Sufyan, a long-time opponent of Ali and also a brother-in-law of the prophet. When Muawiya died in 680 AD, his son Yazid assumed the caliphate, only to be challenged by Hussein, another son of Ali. In a brief battle in Karbala, in modern-day Iraq, Hussein and his followers were defeated – and, to the lasting anger of the Shia, their corpses mutilated.

In subsequent centuries, politics has become both theological and cultural. For the Shia, Ali was the first imam or leader of the community's worship, and all later imams were his direct descendants. But how many descendants? The Shia are themselves divided into seveners (the Ismaili followers of the Aga Khan), fivers (the Zaydis of Yemen) and twelvers (the majority faction), depending on how many imams they recognise before the disappearance of the final imam – who will later emerge as the Mahdi (the guided one) to redeem the world. The similarity to the Christian and Jewish concept of the Messiah is obvious, and the Sunni, too, accept the idea of a Mahdi.

What they reject is the mysticism and philosophical flexibility that has come from the Shia heartland of what was the Persian empire. Whereas Sunni doctrine is essentially simple and straightforward (Sunni imams are local leaders in the mosque, with none of the almost papal power given to their Shia counterparts), Shi'ism has been influenced by Persian Zoroastrianism and Manichaeism – a development that serves only to deepen the traditional antipathy between Arabs and Persians and thus between the Arab world today and Iran.

Beyond religion

Religion is hardly the sole factor in creating conflict. Nations and individuals come to blows over ideology, territory and the quest for resources. They fight each other over their perceived identities. Demographic pressure, too, can play a part, when an increasing population seeks more space to live. In the 1990s Samuel Huntington, an American political scientist, famously outlined a "clash of civilisations". The underlying cause of conflicts present and future, he argued, was the tensions between cultures: Western; Latin American; Islamic; Confucian; Hindu; Slavic-Orthodox (the Christianity of Russia and eastern Europe); Japanese; and, possibly, African. It remains a controversial theory, dismissed as simplistic by some critics, who attacked it for paying too little attention to economic pressures and the tensions within cultures. Conversely, the anti-West, especially anti-US, sentiment in much of the Muslim world and the confrontations between China and Japan have given pause to Huntington's critics. Perhaps, they reluctantly concede, there is something in the notion of cultural conflicts that transcend the conflicts brewed so often in history by bellicose nationalism.

If cultures are not confined to national frontiers, the same is also true of ideologies. The 20th century was marked by four great contests: between fascism and communism; democracy and totalitarianism; capitalism and socialism; imperialism and decolonisation. The confrontations included the bloodiest in history: the death toll from the first world war (ironically termed the war to end all wars) was at least 16 million; some experts, by including war-related deaths from disease and famine, put the total death toll from the second world war at over 80 million. And then there was the cold war, pitting the US and the West against the Soviet Union for the following four decades.

The confrontation was cold in the sense that in this ideological struggle neither the West nor the Soviet Union came directly to blows (thankfully, given the nuclear warheads on both sides); instead, their conflict expressed itself by proxy, notably in the third world, where the colonies of the Western powers were demanding (and eventually obtaining) their independence. In the Middle East the cold-war division was almost a caricature: the US supported Israel and the conservative monarchies of Jordan, Saudi Arabia and the Gulf; and the Soviet Union supported the socialist republics of Syria, Egypt and Iraq. Traces of that caricature survive even today – an example is Russia's refusal to countenance the US call for a change of regime in Syria after the winds of the Arab spring provoked first a popular uprising in 2011 and then full-scale civil war.

The ideological stand-off divided Europe, too: the iron curtain, as Churchill termed it, separated the continent between Western and Soviet camps, and even on the western side of this curtain there were strong pro-Soviet communist parties, particularly in France and Italy. Following the collapse of the Soviet Union and the unification of Germany at the end of the 1980s and start of the 1990s, Francis Fukuyama, an American political scientist, famously declared "the end of history", writing:

> What we may be witnessing is not just the end of the cold war or the passing of a particular period of post-war history, but the end of history as such: that is, the end point of mankind's ideological evolution and the universalisation of Western liberal democracy as the final form of human government.

If only that were so. Fukuyama has since modified his views, acknowledging that American neoconservatives, in whose camp he had been a leading figure, had been proved wrong by the tragic reality of the war in Iraq. Sadly, the triumph of Western liberal democracy might have to wait.

Just how long, if not for ever, is a tricky question. As Freedom

House, a US think-tank, has noted, though democracy (rather broadly defined) spread impressively in the late 20th century, it has now stalled. The wonks at Freedom House reckoned that by 2000 there were 120 democracies in the world – an impressive gain on the 11 that could be counted in 1941 – but 2014 was the ninth year in a row in which they also calculated that global freedom had declined.

The basic building blocks of democracy – free speech, free assembly, free elections and an independent judiciary – might seem at first glance a perfectly adequate deterrent to violence. In practice, they fail time and time again. The US, which often asserts it is the world's oldest continuous democracy (Iceland's claim is weakened by a 45-year break in its parliamentary sessions in the 19th century), has regularly had to confront domestic dissidents who have preferred terrorism to the ballot box. Groups such as the Black Panthers, the Symbionese Liberation Army, the Aryan Brotherhood and the Weathermen have all carried out violent attacks on the federal government; and dozens of militia groups today emphasise their willingness, if need be, to take up arms against a tyrannical government. Europe's democracies have had similar problems: Germany, for example, with the Baader-Meinhof group (also known as the Red Army Faction); Italy with the Brigate Rosse; France with Action Directe. So too has democratic Japan: in the 1970s and 1980s the Japanese Red Army carried out deadly attacks in both Japan and – in support of Palestinian groups – abroad; in 1995 the Aum Shinrikyo cult carried out a sarin gas attack on the Tokyo subway.

Those groups, be they in the US, Europe or Japan, were all motivated by a fervent ideological determination to change some of the world's richest societies. The same impulse exists in poor countries, too. Corruption in politics and business, usually allied to extreme disparities in wealth, is almost certain to lead to social unrest – and so to violence with an ideological flavour. Al-Qaeda in the Arab world is an obvious example; so too the Marxist FARC guerrillas in Colombia or the Maoist Naxalite insurgents in India.

In many developing countries, however, ideology tends to rest on the foundations of demography and the quest for resources. In 1950 the population of Egypt was just over 21 million, but by 2015 it had grown to more than 84 million – and the projection for 2025 is that another 10 million will by then have been added to the total. Cairo has become a choking megalopolis with some of Africa's biggest slums, while the countryside, relying on the Nile for its fertility, can no longer feed all the hungry mouths. Given that demographic reality, even the most efficient and benevolent government in the world (and Egypt's is neither) would find it hard to provide enough education, health care, housing and jobs to cope with such a population increase. It is hardly surprising, then, that in 2011 the famed docility of the Egyptian people gave way under the pressure of the so-called Arab spring to revolution, with both the regime and its opponents resorting to deadly violence.

The situation in Yemen is perhaps even worse. The country had around 4.3 million people in 1950, but by 2015 it had 26 million. As the population has increased, so has its need for water. Yemen's aquifers are draining at such an alarming rate that its capital, Sana'a, could soon run out of water. When aquifers are depleted, farms go dry, leaving the ground fertile only for rebellion. One of al-Qaeda's strongholds is in the Radaa Basin, the site of one of Yemen's most vulnerable aquifers. Near the northern border with Saudi Arabia, jobless workers have forsaken the now-arid fruit farms and taken up arms with the pro-Iran Houthi rebels. The Houthis are Zaydi Shia, which means that there will always be a sectarian element, originally latent but in 2015 increasingly overt, in their rebellion against the Sunni central government – which can rely on Sunni Saudi Arabia for support against its Shia adversaries.

Demographic pressure affects much of sub-Saharan Africa, too. Lagos now has more residents than Cairo and Kinshasa is catching up. But it is not so much demographic pressure as greed that fuels some of Africa's conflicts. Blood diamonds is an evocative term (rather more so than the alternative conflict diamonds) for the trade that both finances conflicts and, all too often, causes them. The list of African countries that have suffered conflicts fuelled by the quest for diamonds is depressingly long: Angola, Côte d'Ivoire, the Democratic Republic of Congo (formerly Zaire under a dictatorial president, Mobuto Sese Seko), the Republic of Congo, Liberia, Sierra Leone and Zimbabwe. Nor are diamonds the only bounties of nature to attract violence. There are plenty of conflict minerals too, from the gold that will adorn fashionable women from New Delhi to New York, to the columbite-tantalite (coltan) that goes into hearing aids and laptop computers. Their value is such that they have condemned millions in central Africa to years of vicious wars in which children are forced to carry out killings and women are raped with impunity.

The deadly combination

It is futile to ascribe any single cause to a conflict. Invariably, it is a combination of factors that leads to violence. Al-Qaeda and ISIS are motivated by a particular religious zealotry, but their fighters may also have other incentives: an ideological antipathy to the imperialist West, for example; or a desire to avenge a friend or relative already lost in battle; or in some cases an urge to escape poverty – or even boredom. There is no doubt that the Pakistan Taliban have gained recruits because US drone attacks in north-western Pakistan have all too often killed and injured the innocent. The Naxalites in eastern India are conventionally described as Maoist, yet it is clear that local grievances over tribal rights, landownership, mining and forest management are as important as any Marxist doctrine in attracting support. In Nigeria the Islamist militants of Boko Haram ("Western education is forbidden" in the Hausa language) are motivated not just by an extreme interpretation of Islam but also by their frustration with their own poverty and with corrupt authorities allegedly favouring their Christian neighbours.

By contrast, the fighters of the Free Papua Movement (Organisasi Papua Merdeka) are reacting to a less complicated impulse: their war is an attempt to secede from an Indonesia that is culturally and ethnically quite different from what used to be called Western New Guinea. Yet Indonesia is one of the world's most diverse nations, and the doctrine of *pancasila* (five principles), formulated by President Sukarno when the country gained its independence after the second world war, is a deliberate attempt to create unity from diversity. Arguably, if Indonesia had lived up to its principles, the Free Papua Movement would have disappeared. Instead, it is encouraged by the example of East Timor, a former Portuguese colony which resisted a quarter-century of Indonesian occupation before, in 2002, becoming the first new sovereign nation of the 21st century.

One other factor in conflict that often gets overlooked is the clash in developing countries between modernisation and tradition. Akbar S. Ahmad, a Pakistani anthropologist, has argued that the real cause in many conflicts in the developing world (he cites examples such as Pakistan, Myanmar and Yemen) is the tension in an increasingly globalised economy between modernisation and the traditions of tribal cultures, with their codes of honour and revenge. In these conflicts, religion is secondary – but is incorporated into the conflict to help justify the resistance to change.

Given General von Clausewitz's dictum, it is hardly surprising that conflict is both so frequent and so prevalent. There are groups that will feel stifled or frustrated in even the freest of democracies. When they realise that their aims can never be achieved by persuasion, one logical response is to resort to violence (for instance, the Red Army Faction in West Germany in the 1970s or the Real Irish Republican Army in the UK today). As this book will demonstrate, there are precious few areas of the world that are immune from conflict. Switzerland's dedication to political neutrality kept it out of the world wars of the 20th century (once the Congress of Vienna in 1815 recognised the country's independence, the only blip in its tranquillity was a brief civil war in 1847 with fewer than 100 casualties). But even Switzerland cannot be totally protected from the conflicts that originate beyond its borders: in 1969 Zurich airport was the scene of an assault by the Popular Front for the Liberation of Palestine on an El Al airliner en route from Amsterdam to Tel Aviv.

Ironically, the countries most protected from violence are the most repressive. A classic example is North Korea, where the cruelty of the regime mocks the country's official title of Democratic People's Republic of Korea. It sponsored several terrorist attacks abroad in the 1970s and 1980s, and in 2010 sank, without provocation, one of South Korea's navy ships. But within its own territory violence against the regime is unknown: state control is simply too absolute for dissidents to reveal themselves. And South Korea has no desire to attack – with unknown consequences – its unpredictable northern neighbour.

No country has the same level of state control as North Korea, and where such control is not absolute, dissent will find a way to express itself, often violently. The People's Republic of China, for example, has to cope with the secessionist demands of the Muslim Uighurs in the autonomous region of Xinjiang (which means new province); and those demands are on occasion expressed violently, from bomb attacks in Xinjiang's capital, Urumqi, in the 1990s to a suicide attack in Beijing's Tiananmen Square in 2013 and a knife attack in Kunming's railway station in 2014 that killed 33, including four of the assailants. Since 1975 communist Laos has been dogged by a low-level insurgency by the Hmong minority (who had sided with the US during the era of the Vietnam war). Myanmar, which is only slowly emerging from military dictatorship, continues to be beset with various ethnic conflicts. Indeed, it is host to the world's longest-running civil war, owing to the efforts by the Karen people to carve out their own state.

However, divining a correlation between state control and the presence or absence of conflict is a futile exercise. Rummel's argument that democracies do not fight each other is a strong one. Yet, given their reasonable pretensions to be termed democracies, Russia's invasion of Georgia in 2008 is a notable rebuttal of that particular theory. Where the conflicts are internal, the nature of the state and the extent of its power often seem irrelevant. In the Philippines, for example, both the communist New People's Army and various Muslim separatist groups have fought against the central government in Manila regardless of whether it was the Marcos dictatorship or the post-Marcos democracy. The same is true in Pakistan, where sectarian and separatist militants have taken up arms regardless of whether the regime of the day was democratic or military.

Some internal conflicts are just that, confined – as in the case of the Philippines and its communist insurrection – to the territory of a particular country. But frequently, and increasingly, the world's conflicts take on an international dimension. In part this is because the global economy, with trade linking virtually every part of the world, implies global politics, too. Because oil and gas are international markets, who controls the oil fields of Libya, for example, matters to consumers of oil everywhere. This in turn means that those consumers are anxious observers of the internecine conflict that has followed the toppling in 2011 of Muammar Qaddafi – and to go from observing to intervening is an obvious temptation.

The best example of internal disputes entangling outside players is Pakistan. The secessionist demands of Baluchistan; the anti-government assaults by the Pakistan Taliban in North and South Waziristan and the Swat Valley; the sectarian violence between the Sunni majority and the Shia minority: all condemn Pakistan to perilous instability. But because Pakistan is sandwiched between India and Afghanistan, outside powers are inevitably involved. The Pakistan Taliban provide a safe haven for the Afghan Taliban, and so the US, the Taliban's greatest enemy, launches drone attacks on the territory of its supposed ally, Pakistan, which is simultaneously meddling – as are India, Iran and Russia – in the politics of Afghanistan in ways that threaten American interests.

Media might

Economic concerns, with their political consequences, are not the sole reason for the internationalising of internal conflicts. There is also the so-called CNN effect: a conflict that captures the attention of the international, especially Western, media frequently compels vote-hungry politicians to react. This was the case in Libya. The British and French governments, reluctantly joined by that of the US, decided that the rebels seeking to topple Qaddafi could not be massacred in front of the TV viewers of Peterborough, Paris and Portland. "Something has to be done" is a powerful slogan in a democracy.

But it is powerful, too, in countries where democracy is absent or at best fragile. The television images of the Syrian civil war, for example, attracted young Saudi men, in defiance of a government edict, to travel to Syria to join the rebels against the Bashar al-Assad regime. Similarly, the TV images of Israeli assaults on Gaza consolidate anti-Israel sentiment throughout the Muslim world; and there is no doubt that Arab TV coverage of the Iraq and Afghan wars has led to the US being considered an enemy of Islam in much of the Muslim world. Indeed, American officials and commentators in the wake of 9/11 accused Al-Jazeera, a state-funded broadcaster based in Qatar with both Arabic and English channels, of being anti-American and anti-Semitic, especially in its Arabic-language broadcasts. The irony is that Qatar is a long-standing ally of the US, as are all the traditional kingdoms and sheikhdoms of the Arabian peninsula.

Clearly, in times of conflict, bias is an easy charge to make against virtually any media outlet – and on occasion the charge is doubtless justified. As Hiram Johnson, an isolationist American senator, is reported to have said in 1918: "The first casualty when war comes is truth." But the aphorism is hardly the product of the first world war; Aeschylus said as much some two millennia earlier.

Whether there can be an objective or absolute truth when men are fighting each other is, however, irrelevant: in pursuit of victory, media coverage and blatant propaganda are means to achieve that end. Jomo Kenyatta was a bogey figure in the British press when leading (at least according to the courts) the Mau Mau struggle for Kenyan independence; later, that same press treated him as an African statesman. As the cliché has it: "One man's terrorist is another man's freedom fighter." And, of course, vice versa.

The examples are legion: Nelson Mandela, who went from vilification to veneration; Yasser Arafat, for many years a terrorist in Israeli eyes, accepted the Oslo accords with Israel and won the Nobel peace prize; Che Guevara, executed in 1967 in Bolivia as a Marxist revolutionary (and so, by the regime's definition, automatically a terrorist), has posthumously become a celebrity icon on T-shirts around the world; Martin McGuinness, denounced by the British media as an Irish republican terrorist, has become a leading member of the UK government in Northern Ireland.

Perhaps the most impressive example of the fickle nature of public opinion is that of Qaddafi. In Western eyes he was first an idealistic young revolutionary, then a deranged tyrant exporting terrorism, and next (having given up his quest for weapons of mass destruction) a statesman worthy of the public embrace of a British prime minister, Tony Blair. Finally, as he sought to hold back the winds of the Arab spring, he was once again a brutal tyrant who had to be toppled. The Arab view of Qaddafi was equally schizophrenic: at first he was the new Nasser, a dynamic leader who could unite the Arab world; but soon he was an insulting and irrational ruler whose antics could be dangerous. When he was overthrown, few Arabs, whether high or humble, shed any tears.

In all conflicts, civilians suffer and are conveniently termed innocent victims – though US officials in the Vietnam war came up with the cynical euphemism "collateral damage". In describing terrorism, the common definition is that civilians are being deliberately targeted in contravention of what most people regard as civilised behaviour. But in practice the definition is a matter of choice: in the second world war the victors did not define as terrorism the fire-bombing of Dresden (up to 135,000 dead) or the atomic bombs launched on Hiroshima and Nagasaki. Israel argues that targeted assassinations are a legitimate means of self-defence, even if they take place thousands of miles from Israeli territory. Palestinian fighters argue that any Israeli, in or out of military uniform, is a legitimate target.

Salah Khalaf, better known by his *nom de guerre*, Abu Iyad, and the man who, as leader of Black September, was responsible for the killing of Israeli athletes at the 1972 Munich Olympics, explained:

> By nature, and even on ideological grounds, I am firmly opposed to political murder and, more generally, to terrorism. Nevertheless, unlike many others, I do not confuse revolutionary violence with terrorism, or operations that constitute political acts with others that do not.

In other words, a political motive will justify what others will deplore as terrorism.

The truth is that armed conflicts take their place on a broad spectrum, from conventional wars between states to violence by small groups of individuals beholden to no state at all. In between is a range of guerrilla movements, some rural (such as the Moro National Liberation Front in the Philippines) and some (such as Greece's Militant Popular Revolutionary Forces) urban. To use Huntington's definition:

> Guerrilla warfare is a form of warfare by which the strategically weaker side assumes the tactical offensive in selected forms, times and places. Guerrilla warfare is the weapon of the weak.

The supposedly weak can, however, become stronger with outside assistance. During the cold war a great many activists and guerrilla groups were supported – with money, weapons and, often, planning – by the rival superpowers. The same is true of today's conflicts, with the US and members of the European Union each happy to denounce state-sponsored terrorism by countries they are at odds with. Indeed, since 1979 the US has had an official list of the states involved, beginning with Libya, Iraq, South Yemen and Syria. But the list adapts to the geopolitical climate: North Korea was added in 1988 but removed in 2008 when it agreed to allow inspections of its nuclear activity; South Yemen left the list in 1990 when it united with North Yemen to become simply Yemen. In 2014 there were just four states on the list: Cuba, Iran, Sudan and Syria. But in 2015 Cuba was taken off it as President Barack Obama, to the applause of Latin America, moved finally to normalise US–Cuba relations.

Yet again, judgment depends on the eye of the beholder: in the Syrian civil war the Bashar al-Assad government argues that it is the victim of state-sponsored terrorism, since the rebel groups (many of which can certainly be as barbaric as the regime's followers) are financed and armed by Saudi Arabia, Qatar and the United Arab Emirates – with the US and others also providing support. Iran, too, has a counter-argument. It certainly supports Hizbullah, the militant Shia organisation in Lebanon (its name translates as Party of Allah), which in turn attacks Israel and the rebels in Syria, but it accuses the US of secretly aiding the Mujahedin-e Khalq (MEK), whose members were on the State Department's official list of terrorist organisations from 1997 to 2012 and who vow to overthrow the Iranian regime.

The usefulness or otherwise of the US list is a matter of debate. Categorising Hamas, the democratically elected government of Gaza, as a terrorist organisation obviously adds complexity to the already torturous search for an Israeli–Palestinian peace agreement. Similarly, in putting Hizbullah on the list, the US is saying that part of the government of Lebanon, by tradition a pro-Western nation, is in the hands of terrorists since Hizbullah has a presence in the cabinet. But what stands out from the list of more than 50 organisations is that the majority are Muslim – a reflection, perhaps, of the Huntington thesis of the clash of civilisations.

This book will avoid the temptation to place organisations, or indeed countries, into a convenient terrorist box, even when their actions satisfy any reasonable definition of terrorism: as, for example, was the case with hostage-taking and deadly bombings by Chechen and Dagestani separatists in Russia in the late 1990s. Instead, it will remind readers, in the words of General von Clausewitz cited at the start of this chapter: "War is an act of force to compel our enemy to do our will." Sadly war, in one form or another, touches us wherever we are.

2 Middle East and north Africa: connected by Islam

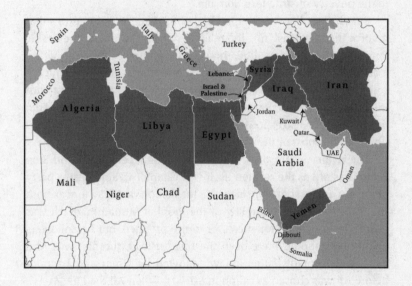

THE ARAB WORLD, stretching from the Arabian peninsula in the east to the Atlantic Ocean in the west, with a population of over 400 million, is divided by its politicians and the legacy of colonialism into a score of countries (22 by the count of the Arab League; 23 if the Saharan Arab Democratic Republic – rather than Morocco – is recognised as sovereign over the former Spanish Sahara). Its governments range from autocratic monarchies, as in the Gulf states, to supposedly socialist republics, as in Syria and Algeria. Its economies range from the petrodollar-fuelled wealth of Saudi Arabia and Qatar to the poverty of strife-torn Somalia.

But almost all are tormented by political and social tensions that involve the role of Islam – the religion which, along with the Arabic language (regardless of differences in dialect), gives the Arab world a coherence surmounting the national boundaries drawn by the old colonial powers. Moreover, they must coexist in the Middle East with Iran, a Persian nation that is not just traditionally at odds with its Arab neighbours but also espouses Shia Islam as a rival to the Sunni brand dominant in most of the Muslim world.

The rivalry – and often the warfare – between Sunni and Shia Islam is as old as the religion itself (see Chapter 1). Shia means party or faction and is short for *shiatu-Ali*, the faction of Ali, who was both the cousin and the son-in-law of the Prophet Muhammad. Ali was Islam's fourth caliph (or successor to the prophet), but his followers believed he should have been the first. Instead, the first was Abu Bakr, Muhammad's father-in-law, followed by Umar and Uthman before Ali was chosen as caliph in 656 AD. When Ali died in 661 AD, following an attack on him at prayer, the violent dissent that had already scarred Islam's early years evolved into war between Ali's opponents and followers, and the defeat and killing of Ali's son, Hussein, in the battle of Karbala in 680 AD in what is now Iraq.

In crude terms the Shia had been vanquished at Karbala by the Sunni, those who follow the *sunna*, or tradition, of the prophet. But Shia Islam has, of course, survived, notably in Iraq and Iran, and one legacy over the centuries has been a divergence in theology: Sunni doctrine is in essence straightforward; Shia teaching is more flexible and nuanced, having been influenced by the Zoroastrian and Manichean beliefs that pre-date the arrival of Islam in the old Persian empire. A crucial difference is that whereas Shia Islam gives great authority to its imams, with Iran's ayatollahs wielding almost papal power, Sunni Islam has no real clerical hierarchy.

In modern, post-colonial times there has been a second legacy of the original division: destructive Sunni–Shia wars for regional influence that resemble the proxy battles of the cold war between the United States and the Soviet Union. The 1980–88 war between Shia Iran and the secular – but Sunni-led – Iraq of Saddam Hussein is one example, but others are Iran's support for the regime in Syria of Bashar al-Assad, a member of the heretical Alawite Shia community, and Iran's support for Lebanon's Hizbullah (Party of Allah), a Shia party with an armed militia that is arguably at least as powerful as Lebanon's official army.

Yet ironically the Sunni wave of fundamentalist Islam now sweeping the Arab world owes much of its inspiration to Iran. The ousting of the pro-American Shah, Muhammad Reza Pahlavi, in 1979 by the followers of Ayatollah Khomeini led to the creation of today's Islamic Republic of Iran, and so serves as an example of how the Arab world's own supposedly invulnerable regimes might also be toppled. This explains their nervous reaction to the Muslim Brotherhood, founded by Hassan al-Banna, an Egyptian schoolteacher, in 1928 and influential throughout the Arab world, despite often being a banned organisation.

The message of the mosque does not in itself explain the so-called Arab spring, sparked by the self-immolation in December 2010 of a Tunisian vegetable vendor, which spread dissent and revolution throughout most of the Arab world. Initially, the dissent involved purely secular demands for greater freedom, and for economic growth, from regimes that had failed to provide either. But inevitably Islam, furnishing a sense of shared identity separate from the failed prescriptions of Arab socialism or traditional monarchies, became a rallying cry. In Cairo, for example, the liberal and educated Egyptians who flocked to Tahrir Square (Liberation Square) to denounce President Hosni Mubarak found their revolution hijacked by their more numerous illiberal (but more devout) compatriots. The result was the election of a Muslim Brotherhood government in 2012, followed in 2013 by a military coup that has banned the Brotherhood and taken Egypt back to the practices of the Mubarak era.

But why has Arab spring proved such an inapt phrase, with so many Arab countries, from Yemen to Somalia and from Iraq to Libya, descending into fratricidal chaos? One reason, of course, is that the social, economic and political challenges are too great to be settled overnight – or indeed within a generation.

Another is that the wars in Afghanistan (first against the Soviet invasion and then by the US and its allies against the Taliban) and the war this century in Iraq have spawned Islamist groups, such as al-Qaeda. These are willing to use extreme violence to attack the supposedly anti-Muslim West and to bring about a fundamentalist Muslim society that is often called Salafist (the *Salafis* were the companions or contemporaries of the Prophet Muhammad).

The most notorious al-Qaeda exploit was the 9/11 attack in 2001 on the United States, but in recent years al-Qaeda has been overshadowed by the organisation known variously as ISIL (the Islamic State in Iraq and the Levant) or ISIS (the Islamic State in Iraq and Sham – Sham being the Arabic name for greater Syria). Whereas al-Qaeda has used suicide bombers and improvised explosive devices (IEDs) to create terror, ISIS has used these tactics and more conventional military means to create what it calls the Islamic State (IS), with its leader, Abu Bakr al-Baghdadi, proclaiming himself the new caliph of the *umma*, the Muslim community. ISIS has also used social media with a slickness and professionalism that al-Qaeda has never matched. For example, its videos of almost ritualistic beheadings, designed both to terrify and to entice, have had a far greater impact than the cassette-taped recordings of Osama bin Laden could ever manage.

If the Islamic State survives, it will have erased the lines drawn on the map of the Middle East in 1916 by the UK's Sir Mark Sykes and France's François Georges-Picot when the European powers divided the territory of the defeated Ottoman empire. More ominously, the continued existence of the Islamic State will threaten Arab regimes everywhere, including the monarchy in Saudi Arabia, whose efforts to propagate a similarly fundamentalist (though peaceful) interpretation of Islam have perversely helped create al-Qaeda and ISIS.

That threat to the existing order in September 2014 drew ten Arab countries – Saudi Arabia, Bahrain, Egypt, Iraq, Jordan, Kuwait, Lebanon, Oman, Qatar and the United Arab Emirates – into a US-organised coalition against ISIS. All promised to do their share, but in practice this meant not ground troops but aerial sorties by the UAE, Jordan, Saudi Arabia and Bahrain against ISIS targets in northern Syria and Iraq – and after a Jordanian jet was shot down in December 2014 (the pilot was later burned to death by his captors in a cage) the UAE suspended its attacks. The UAE and its fellow Arab governments were only too well aware that many of their citizens regard the war against the Islamic State as yet another American war against Muslims. They are also aware that their own citizens, especially in Saudi Arabia and the Gulf states of Kuwait and Qatar, have willingly donated money to al-Qaeda and ISIS, seeing them as worthier recipients of support than the supposedly moderate rebel groups that get governmental aid.

Keep the faith – whatever the cost

But if Saudi Arabia, protector of the holy places of Mecca and Medina, is reluctant to wage war against fellow Muslims and indeed welcomes Shia Muslims to make their pilgrimage to Mecca, how can al-Qaeda and ISIS justify the Muslim blood they so willingly shed? The answer lies in a theological nicety of the kind first developed in the early 14th century in a *fatwa* (a ruling on Islamic law) by Ibn Taymiyya, a leading jurist. His edict declared that any Muslim ruler who did not enforce *sharia* law or follow strict Islamic practice was no longer a Muslim but was, in fact, an apostate and an unbeliever; and since the punishment for apostasy is death, such an infidel should be the target of *jihad*. This is the doctrine of *takfir* (excommunication, or literally "to call someone an infidel"), which allows ISIS and fellow Islamist extremists to slaughter Muslims and non-Muslims with barbarous enthusiasm.

One consequence has been a wave of attacks on Shia targets, in defiance of government attempts to repress all signs of dissent (in Saudi Arabia, for example, ISIS in May 2015 announced that "soldiers of the caliphate" were responsible for a suicide bomb at a Shia mosque in the kingdom's Eastern Province that killed more than 20 and injured more than 80).

Another consequence is the flight of Christians from a Middle East that was the birthplace of Christ. In one sense the phenomenon is not new: the Lebanese civil war of 1975–90 impelled thousands of Lebanese – particularly Christian Lebanese – to seek a better or safer life abroad. But whereas the Lebanese Christians then were not being targeted for their faith, all Christians in the Arab world today justifiably fear they are the potential victims of the *takfiri* ideology of ISIS and al-Qaeda. Though accurate figures are hard to come by, it is clear that the Christian communities of Iraq and Syria have suffered an extraordinary exodus. In Iraq, for example, the number of Christians before the American invasion was about 1.4 million, and by 2010 it had fallen to around 270,000; in Syria, the Christian population of 1.1 million in 2010 had fallen to around 400,000 by 2015. By one reckoning, Christians made up about 20% of the population in the Middle East at the start of the 20th century, but only 5% in 2015.

Such numbers make a mockery of the Quranic injunction – ignored by ISIS and al-Qaeda – that "there is no compulsion in religion". But the ideological extremism that targets Christians, Yazidis, Jews, Bahais and Shia Muslims (basically anyone who is not a confirmed Sunni) also targets rulers viewed as unworthy of the trust and support of the faithful, hence the violent two-week seizure of the Grand Mosque (Masjid al-Haram) in Mecca during the *hajj* (pilgrimage) season of 1979, with the insurgents criticising the corruption and Westernised ways of the ruling Saud family. That siege ended with at least 250 soldiers, pilgrims and insurgents dead and – in tacit recognition that the insurgents had a point – was followed by a stricter enforcement of the fundamentalist Wahhabi code of Islam practised in Saudi Arabia.

The absolutism of *takfiri* thought is ill suited to the modern world. Some historians see a similarity between ISIS and the Khawarij (or Kharijites), a fanatical sect in the 7th century that first supported Ali but then broke away (Khawarij comes from the verb to leave or go out) from both Sunni and Shia Islam. The Khawarij had more or less disappeared by the 9th century (though the Ibadis of Oman trace their ancestry to a Khawarij faction), and ISIS and its peers will doubtless also be defeated at some point, perhaps by economic and social pressures more than by military action.

Yet as long as governance in the Middle East and north Africa remains corrupt and inept, Islamist fundamentalism is likely to remain powerful in the minds of disaffected young men – and, in many cases, women – both in the Muslim world and beyond. Moreover, it is a fact of geography that north Africa provides vast areas of sanctuary in which extremists can both hide and prosper: in 2015, for example, fighters from ISIS, al-Qaeda and Boko Haram were reported to be training together in the deserts of Mauritania. This is precisely the kind of activity that is supposed to be prevented by "Opération Barkhane", the 3,000-strong counter-terrorism force dispatched by France to the Sahel region in August 2014.

ISIS and the Islamic State

The roots of ISIS lie with the 2004 merger between al-Qaeda and the Jordanian-born Abu Musa al-Zarqawi's Jama'at al-Tawhid wal-Jihad (Group for Belief in One God and Jihad) to become al-Qaeda in Iraq, which then became the Islamic State of Iraq (ISI) after al-Zarqawi's death in 2006. ISI became ISIS in 2013 when the new leader of ISI, Abu Bakr al-Baghdadi (a man who had apparently spent four years in an American detention camp during the Iraq war), attempted an alliance with Jabhat al-Nusra (the Support Front), al-Qaeda's affiliate in Syria.

One hope is that the brutality of al-Zarqawi and his successors and followers towards fellow Muslims will eventually diminish its popularity. Indeed, it was this extreme violence that led Ayman al-Zawahiri, Osama bin Laden's successor as leader of al-Qaeda, to more or less disown them as early as 2006 (the formal break with al-Qaeda came in 2014). In the meantime, ISIS can claim to be the most successful insurgency in history. By dint of kidnapping ransoms, the seizure of banks in Mosul in Iraq, the looting of pre-Islamic artefacts and the export of some of Syria's oil, it is extremely well financed. Iraqi intelligence said in mid-2014 that ISIS had assets worth some $2 billion, and the US Treasury reckoned oil sold illegally in Turkey was earning ISIS around $1 million a day. In early 2015 one Iraqi government adviser reckoned ISIS's assets were worth $8 billion. Whatever the true figure of its wealth, ISIS is certainly well armed, having captured huge amounts of equipment, some from the Syrian armed forces and others from the shattered Iraqi forces.

The most effective ISIS weapon, however, may turn out to be its use of social media. Its professionally produced online videos of its battles inspire plenty of young Muslims, within and beyond the Middle East (in late 2014 the CIA reckoned up to 30,000 foreign fighters from some 80 countries, including in Europe and North America, had gone to join ISIS in Syria and Iraq). The total number of ISIS fighters was estimated by a senior Kurdish official in late 2014 at more than 200,000 – a figure that contrasts with earlier CIA estimates of around 30,000 but which seems possible given that by the end of 2014 ISIS controlled a third of both Syria and Iraq and could therefore easily gain more recruits.

Meanwhile, equally slick videos, often narrated in English with Arabic subtitles, have shown the grisly, almost ritualistic beheadings of ISIS captives – including Western journalists and aid workers – and the burning alive of a captured Jordanian pilot. Such videos may well be designed to terrify, yet perversely they may also recruit impressionable and disaffected young men and women. When Abu Bakr al-Baghdadi on June 29th 2014 proclaimed himself amir al-mu'mineem (commander of the faithful) and caliph of the Islamic State – a worldwide caliphate, hence the change from ISIS to IS – the announcement revived rosy-hued memories of Muslim greatness before the colonial powers divided the *umma* (community) into separate countries.

As caliph, Abu Bakr al-Baghdadi claims the loyalty of Muslims everywhere; and several jihadist groups, for example Ansar al-Sharia in Libya and Boko Haram in Nigeria, have pledged themselves to the Islamic State. But by his announcement he risks fatally overreaching himself: existing regimes in the region, especially Saudi Arabia, Egypt and Jordan, are bound to join the West in seeing the Islamic State as an entity that has to be defeated.

Algeria

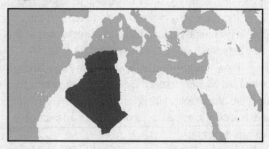

Ever since its brutal war, from 1954 to 1962, to wrest Algeria's independence from France, the People's Democratic Republic of Algeria has suffered periods of savage conflict. The war with France, marked by atrocities by both the Algerian Front de Libération Nationale (FLN) and the French armed forces, led to a death toll of anywhere between 400,000 on both sides (the French estimate) and 1.5 million Algerians (the Algerian version).

The resort to extreme violence by the state (*le pouvoir* – the power – as the political and military establishment is known) and its opponents reappeared three decades later after the government in 1988 brought in a multi-party system. In a December 1991 election the Islamic Salvation Front (Front islamique du salut, or FIS) was in the lead after the first round of voting, and this led the secularist-minded government to postpone the second round and the army to crack down on the FIS. The result was a violent confrontation during a "black decade" between the government's forces and both the Islamic Salvation Army (Armée islamique du salut, acting as the FIS's armed wing, with some 4,000 fighters) and the much more extreme Armed Islamic Group, better known by its French abbreviation GIA (Groupe islamique armé), with perhaps 3,000 fighters. Many of the GIA fighters had learned their trade as *mujahideen* in Afghanistan in the war against the Soviet occupation of the 1980s; they returned with the concept that any secular government was, by definition, illegitimate in a Muslim country.

The death toll of this civil war may have reached over 150,000 before the conflict petered out (the government offered an amnesty in 1999 and the Islamic Salvation Army declared a ceasefire in 2002). The GIA was always a more violent group, targeting Algerian journalists who wrote in French, killing women who did not wear a headscarf and assassinating some 120 foreigners. But by the start of the 21st century the GIA had been supplanted by the Salafist Group for Preaching and Combat (GSPC), founded by a former GIA commander who had disagreed with the GIA's practice of slaughtering civilians. The importance of the GSPC is that in January 2007, after talks with al-Qaeda's leader, Ayman al-Zawahiri, it announced that henceforth it would operate as al-Qaeda in the Islamic Maghreb (AQIM).

The threat from AQIM is not the sole preoccupation of the Algerian government. Relations with neighbouring Morocco have historically been tense. One reason as the post-colonial era began was the cultural and political antipathy between the conservative monarchy of Morocco and the revolutionary socialist regime of Algeria. A more concrete factor was a border dispute (the French had not been precise in their cartography) over the Tindouf region. This led to the so-called Sand War of 1963. After a military stalemate the Organisation of African Unity arranged a ceasefire in early 1964, but it took another eight years before the dispute was settled, with Algerian sovereignty over Tindouf finally being recognised.

The legacy of the Sand War is the long-drawn-out conflict in the former Spanish Sahara, annexed by Morocco after the Spanish withdrawal in 1975. In the resulting war – now in abeyance thanks to a 1991 ceasefire – against Morocco by the Polisario Front guerrillas in their quest for an independent Saharan state, Algeria offered both aid and refuge for Polisario and for Sahrawi refugees, notably in several camps in Tindouf. Algeria also, in 1976, recognised Polisario's establishment of the Sahrawi Arab Democratic Republic (SADR), which is now recognised by 82 states (though, of course, not by Morocco). For its part, the UN refers to the former Spanish colony as the Western Sahara and recognises neither SADR nor Morocco's sovereignty over the area.

Nonetheless, whatever the tensions with Morocco, it is clear that AQIM is the main threat to Algeria's stability. Militarily, any confrontation between the two should be no contest. Algeria, with a population of 39 million, has active frontline personnel of 512,000. By contrast, the GSPC may have had as many as 4,000 fighters before it evolved into AQIM. However, in its new guise it has introduced a tactic familiar to all al-Qaeda groups: suicide bombing. In April 2007 three suicide attacks killed 30 in Algiers, and then in December a double suicide attack on the UN headquarters in Algiers and the Algerian Constitutional Court claimed more than 30 dead.

Like many guerrilla movements, AQIM has suffered defections from its ranks. The Movement for Belief in One God and Jihad in West Africa (MUJAO, its French abbreviation) broke away in 2011, perhaps with the goal of spreading *jihad* farther south into Mali, though differences with the AQIM leader, Abdelmalek Droukdel (also known as Abu Musab Abdel Wadoud), were just as likely. Another defection, in late 2012, was that of Mokhtar Belmokhtar, a founding member of AQIM.

Belmokhtar, a one-eyed veteran of the war against the Soviet troops in Afghanistan, named his faction variously al-Mulathamun (The Masked Ones) and al-Muwaqqi'un bi-d-Dima (Those Who Sign in Blood). Collaborating with the MUJAO, Belmokhtar's followers specialised in kidnapping Westerners for ransom. Their greatest exploit came in January 2013 when they seized control of the Tigantourine gas facility near the town of In Amenas, south-east of Algiers and close to the border with Libya. Given that the gas field, operated by state-owned Sonatrach along with the UK's BP and Norway's Statoil, supplies 10% of Algeria's natural gas, the Mulathamun attack had implications for the economy as well as for the 800 hostages, including around 130 foreigners.

The group's demands included an end to French military attacks on Islamists in Mali (Algeria was allowing French planes to use its airspace) and the release of Islamist prisoners in Algeria. The reaction of the government was redolent of Algeria's long experience of extreme violence. Heedless of the concerns of foreign governments for their citizens, Algerian special forces launched an assault on the facility just a day after its seizure and a second, final attack just two days later. By the time the plant was fully under government control some 67 people had been killed, including 29 of the Mulathamun.

It is unclear whether Belmokhtar was present at the In Amenas attack or merely commanding it from afar. But he certainly survived it – hence the $5 million bounty put on his head by the US government. Even without him and his fighters, Algeria will still face the threat of Islamist extremism from groups such as AQIM. One reason is the sheer size of the country, with expanses of desert – dotted with oil and gas fields – that are too vast to police effectively against Islamist groups taking control of the Sahel region to Algeria's south. Another reason is the influx of arms from Libya in the chaos that followed the 2011 overthrow of Muammar Qaddafi. A third reason is the persistent inability of the state – blessed though it is with ample petroleum revenues – to offer jobs and opportunity to young Algerians.

Egypt

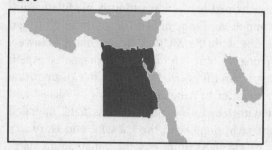

On January 29th 2015 simultaneous bomb attacks on Egyptian security installations in the Sinai peninsula killed more than 35 military personnel and wounded another 70. A senior army officer declared on Egyptian television:

> *Those who carried out the recent fierce operations are military forces [affiliated with] Hamas and coming from Afghanistan, Pakistan, Libya, Iraq and Syria, under the leadership and planning of the West and the CIA.*

The finger-pointing at the West and the CIA smacks of a reflexive resort to conspiracy theories only too common in the Arab world – and at odds with the support given by the United States to the regime of President Abdel-Fattah al-Sisi, who ousted the Muslim Brotherhood government of Muhammad Morsi in a military coup in July 2013. President Sisi's comment on the Sinai attacks was to blame the Brotherhood, and argue that the 87 million citizens of the Arab Republic of Egypt – the most populous in the Arab world – were paying the price for ending the Brotherhood's brief and ineffectual rule.

The reality, however, is that the militants who claimed responsibility for the Sinai assaults were from Ansar Bayt al-Maqdis (Supporters of the Holy House), extremist Islamists whose Sinai contingent in November 2014 swore allegiance to Abu Bakr al-Baghdadi and declared that Sinai was now part of the Islamic State. Though President Sisi, like presidents Hosni Mubarak, Anwar Sadat and Gamal Abdul Nasser before him, believes the Muslim Brotherhood is

Egypt's greatest political and security challenge, in terms of violence the greater threat in the late 20th and 21st centuries has come not from the Brotherhood – which has always claimed to want democratic and peaceful change towards a more Islamic Egypt – but from extreme Islamist groups willing to use terrorism as a weapon in their war against the state.

In 1997, for example, half-a-dozen militants from al-Jama'a al-Islamiyya (the Islamic Group), which is linked with al-Qaeda, slaughtered 58 tourists at the Temple of Hatshepsut near Luxor. In 2004 bomb attacks on resort hotels in Sinai – aimed at Israeli tourists and said by the authorities to have been carried out by Palestinian infiltrators – killed 34. In April 2005 there were bomb blasts, but with few casualties, in Cairo, with the Mujahideen of Egypt and the Abdullah Azzam Brigades claiming responsibility. Two months later the Abdullah Azzam Brigades claimed responsibility for bombings in the Sinai resort of Sharm al-Sheikh that killed 88 and injured over 170. (The Brigades take their name from a Palestinian, killed in a car bomb in Pakistan in 1989, who had been a founding member of al-Qaeda and one of the first *mujahideen* to fight Soviet troops in Afghanistan.)

Moving beyond Egypt is Takfir wa'l-Hijra (Excommunication and Flight – the flight being by the Prophet Muhammad from persecution in Mecca to safety in Medina). This Islamist group began in Egypt in the 1970s as Jama'at al-Muslimin (the Group of Muslims), an offshoot of the Muslim Brotherhood. However, it has since spread throughout the Middle East and even beyond (Russian security forces arrested 14 alleged members of Takfir wa'l-Hijra in Moscow in 2013). Rather like al-Qaeda, its activities take little account of borders or nationalities.

Within Egypt, the state and the economically crucial tourism sector are not the only targets of the Islamist groups. Also under threat are Egypt's Coptic Christians, who comprise around 10% of an otherwise almost entirely Sunni Muslim population. In recent years the Copts have suffered from many outbreaks of sectarian bloodshed. In 2011, for example, a suicide bomber killed 23 Copts and wounded almost 100 as they left a church in Alexandria. That particular attack was apparently carried out by al-Qaeda in Iraq (the forerunner of ISIS), which had earlier said that all Christians in the Middle East were legitimate targets.

One destabilising factor in Egypt has clearly been the Arab spring and its aftermath. Early in 2011 huge demonstrations in Cairo's Tahrir Square, led initially by liberal-minded students but soon supported by the Muslim Brotherhood, forced the resignation of President Hosni Mubarak after almost 30 years in power. Between November 2011 and January 2012 the interim regime of the Supreme Council of the Armed Forces (SCAF) allowed free parliamentary elections, which resulted in the Muslim Brotherhood gaining more than a third of the votes and the Salafists more than a quarter. In the presidential election that followed in May and June the Brotherhood's candidate, Muhammad Morsi, emerged victorious.

But not for long: the Brotherhood-led government proved disastrously ineffective (possibly in part because of a deliberate lack of co-operation by the elites and liberals of the Mubarak era) and demonstrators took to the streets in their thousands to demand that the president step down. In July 2013 General Abdel-Fattah al-Sisi mounted a military coup, sparking violent clashes over the following weeks between the security forces and the Brotherhood that led to hundreds of deaths. By December, following a bomb blast claimed by Ansar Bayt al-Maqdis in the Nile Delta city of Mansoura that killed at least 16, mainly policemen, the Muslim Brotherhood had been declared a terrorist organisation. For his part, Morsi had already spent several months in custody on charges of inciting deadly violence in the nation.

But a second factor, pre-dating the Arab spring, is Egypt's peace treaty with Israel, signed in Washington, DC, in March 1979 between President Anwar Sadat and Israel's prime minister, Menachem Begin. This came about some 16 months after Sadat had become the first Arab leader officially to visit Israel, where he then addressed the Knesset (parliament). The treaty won both men the Nobel peace prize – and led to the assassination of Sadat at a military parade in 1981 by soldiers who turned out to be members of Tanzim al-Jihad (the Organisation of Jihad), the forerunner of al-Jihad al-Islami al-Masri (Egyptian Islamic Jihad) and al-Jama'a al-Islamiyya. One of the leaders of Tanzim al-Jihad was Ayman al-Zawahiri, an Egyptian doctor who succeeded Osama bin Laden as head of al-Qaeda. Ironically, given the anti-Shia stance of Islamist groups such as al-Qaeda, Khalid al-Islambouli, the officer who led the attack on Sadat, was declared a martyr by Iran's Ayatollah Khomeini.

Sadat's assassination, planned by Islamist sympathisers in the intelligence corps, had a symbolic aspect: the military parade marked the eighth anniversary of the Arab–Israeli war of October 1973. Known to Israelis as the Yom Kippur (Day of Atonement) war and to Egyptians as the Ramadan or October war, it ended in a military victory for Israel. But for Egypt it counted as a psychological and diplomatic triumph: not only did its troops cross the Suez Canal into Israeli-occupied Sinai, so erasing the humiliation of defeat in the six-day war of 1967, but their strong performance gave Sadat the impetus he needed to sue for peace with Israel and for the return to Egypt of Sinai.

In the process, Sadat in 1976 cancelled Egypt's five-year-old treaty of friendship with the Soviet Union and chose to ally Egypt with the United States, seeing the Americans both as the only viable Middle East peace-broker and as a source of economic aid. Given the failure of Arab socialism during the Nasser era (from the 1953 coup against King Farouk to Nasser's death in 1970), Sadat's choice seemed sensible: the Nasserite dream of a United Arab Republic with Syria had lasted only from 1958 to 1961; the military adventure in the 1960s in support of the republicans in Yemen, involving up to 70,000 Egyptian troops at the height of the conflict, had ended in costly stalemate; and finally the military, despite all its Soviet-supplied equipment, had been crushed by Israel in the 1967 war.

The choice still holds. The Egyptian military, on paper the most powerful in the Arab world with over 468,000 frontline personnel, receives $1.3 billion a year in aid from the US. President Obama's administration conveniently refused to call the ouster of Muhammad Morsi a coup, since that might have led to Congress cancelling the aid package, which in turn might have curtailed Egypt's co-operation in counter-terrorism efforts and security enforcement along Israel's border with Sinai and Gaza. President Sisi's allies in the Arab world, notably Saudi Arabia and the UAE with their shared loathing of the Muslim Brotherhood, could certainly compensate Egypt for any future loss of US aid – but not for the military equipment that the US supplies.

More than three decades after the peace treaty between Egypt and Israel, the so-called Egyptian street – the mass of ordinary Egyptians – remains instinctively hostile towards Israel and therefore sympathetic to at least some of the Islamists' rhetoric. In an unstable region it is always possible that Egypt's armed forces will find themselves in conflict, but more likely in Libya or Sudan than against Israel. In February 2015, for example, Egyptian jets bombed militants of the Islamic State in Libya who had kidnapped and then beheaded Egyptian Coptic Christians working in Libya. A month later Egypt sent its jets, as part of a Saudi-led coalition, to strike Houthi rebel targets in Yemen and threatened to follow up with ground troops.

Domestically, one threat to the present government in Cairo is from the banned, but popular, Muslim Brotherhood. But the Brotherhood espouses a moderate form of Islam and traditionally avoids violence. The greater threat to any government in Cairo is from extreme Islamist groups using the kind of asymmetric warfare where numbers count for little. In the coming years there will inevitably be more attacks like those by Ansar Bayt al-Maqdis in Sinai, or the bombings by the Abdullah Azzam Brigades in Sharm al-Sheikh. The challenge for the government is to minimise their frequency.

Iran

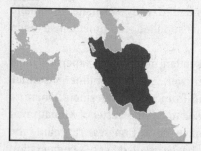

The most militarily powerful country in the Middle East is usually said to be Israel, with its undeclared nuclear weapons and its record of victorious wars against its Arab neighbours. However, it can easily be argued that the power most to be reckoned with in the region is the Islamic Republic of Iran. From a population of 80 million, it has around

425,000 active frontline personnel in its regular armed forces; another 120,000 in the parallel armed forces of the Army of the Guardians of the Islamic Revolution (better known as the Islamic Revolutionary Guards Corps, or IRGC); and military equipment that ranges from fighter aircraft to submarines. To all this must be added a nuclear programme, ostensibly for civilian purposes, that Israel and the United States maintain has been designed to produce nuclear weapons.

The Islamic Republic also has an activist foreign policy that convinced the United States in 1984 to designate Iran a state sponsor of terrorism, which led President George W. Bush in 2002 to denounce Iran – along with North Korea and the Iraq of Saddam Hussein – as part of an axis of evil. This activism is often connected with Iran's Shia identity. In Iraq, for example, Iran has been a virtual kingmaker for the Shia-led governments that followed the dictatorship of the Sunni Saddam Hussein; in the civil war in Syria, which has a Sunni majority, it has given life-saving support to the regime of Bashar al-Assad, a member of the Alawite sect (a heretical branch of Shia Islam); in Bahrain it has given clandestine aid to the Shia majority in their protests against the island's Sunni royal family; and in Yemen it has supported the insurgency of the Houthis, from the Zaydi branch of Shia Islam. Of great concern to Israel, as opposed to Iran's Arab neighbours, is Iran's support for Lebanon's Hizbullah, whose well-armed and effective Shia militia forced Israel in 2000 to end its 18-year occupation of south Lebanon.

The consequence of this Iranian policy is twofold: Saudi Arabia, the traditional standard-bearer of Sunni Islam, fears the creation of a Shia crescent, running from Iran in the east to Lebanon in the west; for its part, Israel fears that Iran poses an existential threat, not least because Mahmoud Ahmadinejad, Iran's president from 2005 to 2013, said in 2005: "This regime that is occupying Quds [Jerusalem] must be eliminated from the pages of history." Adding to Israel's antipathy towards Iran (which before the 1979 Islamic revolution had had good relations with Israel) is Iran's support for the Hamas government in Gaza (even though Hamas is part of the Sunni Muslim Brotherhood) and its alleged involvement in terrorist attacks on Jews abroad, notably the 1994 bombing of a Jewish community centre in Buenos Aires, Argentina, that killed 85 people and injured more than 300.

The mutual antagonism between Iran and Israel (the "little Satan", according to Ayatollah Khomeini) nonetheless has its realpolitik limits: during the destructive Iraq-Iran war of 1980-88 Israel discreetly supplied arms and spare parts to Iran in exchange for Iranian oil, with Israel's prime minister, Ariel Sharon, believing it was important to leave a small window open for friendly relations at some point in the future (ironically, during the Iraq-Iran war the US was helping Saddam Hussein's regime as a counterweight to that of Khomeini). A similar commonality of interests has led to Iran co-operating in the 21st century with the US (the "great Satan"), first in Afghanistan against the Taliban and then against ISIS and its Islamic State.

A defining theme of Iranian politics, long pre-dating the Islamic revolution, is the relationship with the US and, to a lesser extent, the UK. Modern Iran is the successor to the ancient empire of Persia, a country constantly in contention between the UK and Russia in the "Great Game" of the 19th century. The new name, meaning land of the Aryans, from the Sanskrit word for noble, was adopted only in 1935 (with the approval of Nazi Germany), and Iran's support for Germany during the second world war led to its occupation by the UK and Russia in 1941 and the replacement of the pro-Axis Shah Reza Khan by his son Muhammad Reza Pahlavi.

The new shah soon aligned himself with the victors of the second world war. However, Mohammad Mossadeq, installed as prime minister in 1951, did not. An avowed opponent of foreign influence over Iran, Mossadeq proceeded to nationalise Iran's oil industry – which had been under British control since 1913 – and for his pains was deposed two years later in a coup organised by the CIA and the UK's MI6.

The Mossadeq affair ("Operation Ajax" in CIA lore) left Iran with a deep mistrust, even paranoia, of the Americans and the British. This was worsened by the pro-US stance of the shah, who in the 1960s embarked on a breakneck programme of Westernisation and modernisation that he termed the "White Revolution". However well intentioned the shah's programme (which was reminiscent of the Ataturk reforms in Turkey after the first world war), his increasing authoritarianism and megalomania – he declared himself shahanshah (king of kings) in 1967 – alienated even those who sympathised with his secular ideas and recognition of Israel. At the same time the secret police, SAVAK, were extraordinarily brutal in crushing political opposition.

In retrospect, it was no surprise that months of riots should eventually force the shah to flee his country on January 16th 1979. Nor was it a surprise that Iranians of all classes celebrated when Ayatollah Ruhollah Khomeini returned from Paris on February 1st. Before spending 14 years in exile, Khomeini had been imprisoned by the shah in the early 1960s for his denunciation of both the White Revolution and the United States. The real surprise was that even late in 1978 the CIA had failed to recognise the tide of dissent about to sweep away the shah's regime.

What followed was not just the proclamation in April 1979 of the Islamic Republic but the seizure by Iranian students in November of the US embassy in Tehran, complete with 66 American diplomats and staff (though 13 women and African-American hostages were released within a fortnight and a sick hostage was set free in July 1980). The students demanded the shah be returned from the US, where he was having medical treatment. They viewed his presence there as proof of American collusion in the excesses of the shah's rule (the shah left the US in December for asylum in Cairo, where he died in July 1980). American attempts to rescue the hostages failed and it was not until January 1981 that the hostages, after 444 days in detention, were released under an agreement brokered by Algeria. One provision of the Algiers accords was that the US would not intervene in Iran's internal affairs. An added humiliation was that the release of the hostages, occurring on the last day of Jimmy Carter's presidential term, had been delayed long enough to ensure that Carter would lose his bid for re-election.

There was a pragmatic reason for Iran to end the diplomatic distraction of the hostage crisis: in September 1980 Iraq's Saddam Hussein had launched an invasion of Iran that led to a war lasting for almost eight years. Iran's military had been purged of many of its best officers by the new revolutionary regime, but what it now lacked in expertise and materiel (American spare parts were no longer available for Iranian weaponry) was compensated for by an ample supply of human cannon fodder – notably the Basij militia, a volunteer force that is an auxiliary of the Revolutionary Guard and numbers perhaps 90,000 active-duty members and some 300,000 reservists. During the Iraq-Iran war Basij militiamen, some as young as 12, were known to clear minefields by marching across them in human waves. When the war eventually ended with Iran's acceptance of a ceasefire in 1988, there had been precious little gain for either side, and a cost for the two countries of at least half a million dead troops.

Yet even during that war, and certainly in the decades that followed, Iran's relationship with the US commanded the headlines. In 1985 and 1986, despite an official US arms embargo on Iran, the Reagan administration offered to sell anti-tank missiles and other weaponry to Iran via Israel. In return, Iran would use its influence with Hizbullah to secure the release of American hostages held in Lebanon, and the money from the arms sales would be channelled by private means (since the US government could not legally be involved) to the Contra rebels fighting the communist Sandinista regime in Nicaragua.

The so-called Iran–Contra affair did, indeed, lead to the release of some hostages – only for more to be kidnapped later – and to money being supplied to the Contras. It also led to successful prosecutions of Reagan administration officials, though they were subsequently pardoned by Reagan's successor as president, George H.W. Bush (Reagan himself was not prosecuted).

But the Iran–Contra affair was hardly evidence of improving relations between Iran and the US. In April 1988 US warships attacked six Iranian ships and shelled two Iranian oil platforms in the Gulf in retaliation for Iran's mining of Gulf shipping lanes and the damage that had been caused to a US navy vessel. Three months later the USS Vincennes mistakenly shot down an Iran Air airliner, causing the deaths of 290 passengers and crew – a tragedy that leads some to believe that the explosion over Lockerbie, Scotland, of Pan Am 103 in December 1988, leading to 270 deaths, was at the instigation not of Libya (as the courts decided) but of Iran.

US sanctions against Iran were first imposed in 1979 in reaction to the hostage crisis and in 1995, during the presidency of Bill Clinton, they were expanded to target Iran's economically crucial petroleum sector in protest at Iran's alleged sponsorship of terrorism, its attempts to develop nuclear weapons and its hostility to the Middle East peace process that aimed to secure a settlement between Israel and the Palestinians. At first the sanctions applied only to American companies dealing with Iran, but they were quickly tightened to include foreign companies. In 2006, amid evidence that it was secretly developing nuclear weapons and refusing to co-operate with the International Atomic Energy Agency (IAEA), Iran's problems became still worse with the imposition of sanctions by the UN, followed in 2007 by the EU.

The sanctions, designed to cut off Iran almost entirely from the international financial system, have been extremely damaging for the Iranian economy but Israeli sceptics – and their US sympathisers – doubt that sanctions alone will stop Iran from becoming a nuclear power. The Israeli government of Binyamin Netanyahu consistently pressed President Barack Obama after his re-election in 2012 to take a bellicose line with Iran, hinting strongly (albeit unconvincingly, given the military difficulties of destroying underground nuclear sites such as Fordow) that if the US would not bomb Iran's nuclear sites then Israel would.

For Obama (whose stance coincided with that of several members of the Israeli military and intelligence elite) the military option was very much a last and desperate resort. Far better to use not just the stick of sanctions (and the carrot of loosening them) but also the modern weapon of cyber-warfare: hence the clever deployment – possibly as early as 2007 or 2009 and certainly by 2013 – of the Stuxnet virus, in a plan developed by the US and Israel, into the computer system at Iran's Natanz nuclear facility. A careless worker apparently inserted an infected flash drive into his computer and so set back Iran's nuclear programme by months, if not years. Stuxnet was not the only means of delaying the programme; so, too, have been several assassinations – apparently by Israel's secret service, Mossad – of leading Iranian nuclear scientists.

The task of negotiating with Iran to ensure that its nuclear programme is confined to producing energy rather than weapons falls to the so-called P5+1: the US, the UK, France, Russia and China, as the five permanent members of the UN Security Council, plus Germany. The three EU nations began talks with Iran in 2003 and were joined by the US, Russia and China in 2006, and all six have found negotiating with Tehran's envoys extraordinarily frustrating. One reason is that hardliners on the nuclear issue in the US are matched by hardliners in Iran, especially within the Republican Guards. In the end, under the 1979 constitution, decisions in Iran are made not by the nation's president and council of ministers but by the Supreme Leader, namely Ayatollah Ali Khamenei following the death of Ayatollah Khomeini in 1989.

From Iran's point of view, its right to nuclear energy is unquestionable – and is, in fact, accepted by the P5+1. Russia is willing to supply uranium for a reactor at Bushehr, which began operating under Russian control in 2011 and Iranian control in 2013, and Russia plans also to construct more reactors at the Bushehr site. The sticking point is always the level of uranium enrichment that Iran can be permitted to employ: the greater the level, the closer Iran comes to nuclear-weapons capability. Given Iran's history of obfuscation on its nuclear programme, trust between the P5+1 and Iran has been hard to establish (and many Iranians would argue that if Israel can have nuclear weapons, why not Iran?). In 2009 Ayatollah Khamenei declared: "We fundamentally reject nuclear weapons." But two years later the IAEA noted "credible" information of activities "relevant to the development of a nuclear explosive device".

Yet in the political dance between Iran and the international community, and in particular the United States, there have always been reasons to hope for a solution. Back in 2000, the US secretary of state, Madeleine Albright, apologised for the coup against Mossadeq and in 2008 then-president Ahmadinejad congratulated Barack Obama on his election. With the election as president in 2013 of Hassan Rouhani, a reform-minded cleric, and with the need to engage Iran in stabilising Iraq and defeating the Islamic State, the incentive increased for flexibility in the P5+1's negotiating tactics. As Rouhani said in September 2014:

> It is not written in stone that the relationship between Iran and the US must be hostile forever. One day this will change.

One sign of that was a loosening in 2014 of some of the sanctions, as a carrot to encourage Iran to be flexible. But past carrots have not always worked. Back in 1997 the US added to its list of foreign terrorist organisations the Mujahedin-e Khalq (MEK, or the People's Mujahideen of Iran, PMOI), a cult-like body founded in 1965 by Massoud Rajavi and his wife Maryam to oppose the shah. In the 1970s the MEK, or a breakaway faction known as Peykar, with a quasi-Marxist and feminist ideology, attacked American interests in Iran and then took part in the revolution that toppled the shah. But the MEK and the Khomeini regime were soon at odds, and during the Iraq–Iran war the MEK (which had established the National Council of Resistance of Iran, NCRI, as a parliament-in-exile) fought for the Iraqi side. Pursuing their war against the regime, MEK militants in 1992 carried out co-ordinated attacks on ten Iranian diplomatic missions in Europe and North America. By the Iranian government's account, the MEK has been responsible for over 12,000 Iranian deaths in the past three decades.

Clearly, designating the MEK as a terrorist organisation, by the EU as well as the United States, did not stop its activities against the Iranian regime. What did was the fall of Saddam Hussein, which left more than 3,000 MEK followers confined to refugee (or virtual prison) camps in post-Saddam Iraq. The MEK were among the first to alert the world to Iran's nuclear programme, but they have basically been a pawn in the relationship between Iran and the US. Iran may well view the MEK as potentially the biggest threat to its domestic security, so it was surely more stick than carrot when in 2012 the US, following the 2009 lead of the EU, removed the MEK from its list of terrorist organisations.

At least in theory, the nuclear issue is no longer so pressing. On July 14th 2015 Iran and the P5+1 finally announced an accord under which Iran would reduce its capacity to enrich uranium by 66% over the following decade and would lower by 96% over a period of 15 years its stockpile of low- and medium-enriched uranium. In return, sanctions on Iran would be gradually lifted – or reimposed if it were to violate the deal. President Obama argued that if Iran were to break the accord, it would now be at least a year, rather than the previous two months, before it could produce a single nuclear weapon. Critics argued that Iran would now have more economic ability to exert a malign influence in the Middle East. Yet regardless of economic considerations, Iran's position on the map – between Afghanistan to the east, Iraq to the west and Saudi Arabia and the oil-rich Gulf states to the south – gives it an immediate strategic importance that is not about to disappear. The same is true of Iran's importance to Shia Muslims throughout the region. The stability of Lebanon, Syria and Bahrain depends, for better or worse, on the Islamic Republic of Iran.

Iraq

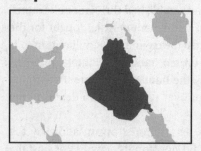

As the country embracing the area that archaeologists call Mesopotamia – the land between the rivers of the Tigris and Euphrates – Iraq can boast that it is the cradle of civilisation. Unfortunately, its modern history has been at times extremely uncivilised and certainly turbulent.

The 2003 invasion by a US-led coalition quickly toppled the brutal dictatorship of Saddam Hussein, but the aftermath has been one of bloody sectarian strife between the Shia majority and the Sunni tribes that had felt secure under the rule of Saddam, a fellow Sunni. This conflict has been made still worse by the establishment in 2014 in large swathes of western Iraq of the Islamic State, a putative and aggressively Sunni caliphate set up by a successor to al-Qaeda in Iraq known variously as ISIS (the Islamic State in Iraq and Sham – Sham being the Arabic for Greater Syria) and ISIL (the Islamic State in Iraq and the Levant). Given the long-thwarted desire for independence on the part of Iraq's Kurds, some 15–20% of Iraq's 32 million people, it is entirely conceivable that Iraq will not survive as a coherent state but will be dismembered into its Shia, Sunni and Kurdish components.

That fate would have seemed most unlikely before the 2003 Iraq war. Granted independence by the UK in 1932, the Kingdom of Iraq (the British had installed King Faisal from the Hashemite clan in what is now Saudi Arabia) had become a republic in 1958 as a result of a military coup led by Brigadier Abdul-Karim Qasim. Five years later he was ousted in the first of a series of coups that in 1968 led to the supremacy of the Arab Socialist Ba'ath Party (*Ba'ath* means renaissance, and the party, which had also in 1963 seized power in neighbouring Syria, split in 1966 into separate Iraqi and Syrian movements).

From its very beginnings in 1947 in the Syrian capital, Damascus, the Ba'ath Party was profoundly secular in its outlook. Its founders were a Christian, Michel Aflaq, a Sunni, Salah al-Din al-Bitar, and followers of Zaki al-Arsuzi, from the Shia-related Alawite sect, and their secularism was shared by Saddam Hussein, who took control of Iraq in 1979 after several years as the strongman of a Ba'athist regime officially headed by Ahmad Hassan al-Bakr.

Saddam's first mistake, after a 1970s decade in which Iraq prospered greatly from the OPEC-inflated value of its oil exports, was to declare war in 1980 on the neighbouring and newly termed Islamic Republic of Iran. One excuse for the war was a border dispute over the Shatt al-Arab waterway between Iraq and Iran at the confluence of the Tigris and Euphrates; another was the possibility of annexing Iran's oil-rich Khuzestan province, which had a large ethnically Arab population. But the real reason was to retaliate against Iran's effort – openly admitted by Ayatollah Khomeini – to spread its Islamic revolution to Iraq by arming Shia and Kurdish rebels and supporting assassination attempts on senior Iraqi officials.

The war ended in a costly stalemate, with at least half a million dead and a similar number disabled on both sides and with huge damage to the two nations' oil facilities. Adding to the barbarity of this war was the use by the Saddam regime of chemical weapons against Iraq's own Kurdish population. In operation Anfal (a Quranic reference to the victory of a small band of the Prophet Muhammad's followers over an army of infidels), Iraqi jets in March 1988 had unleashed poison-gas bombs on the town of Halabja, killing thousands as part of an intentional programme of genocide of the Kurds. An Iraqi gain from the war was Iranian recognition of exclusive

Iraqi sovereignty over the Shatt al-Arab – yet Saddam soon traded that for Iran's neutrality in his preparations for the August 2nd 1990 invasion of neighbouring Kuwait.

That invasion, leading to the first Gulf war, was Saddam's second mistake. Whatever Iraq's historical claim to Kuwaiti territory (it had been part of the Iraqi province of Basra under the Ottomans), the underlying motive for the invasion was at least partly economic: Kuwait had refused to write off its loans to Iraq during the Iraq–Iran war and by producing above its OPEC oil quota it was lowering the price Iraq could get for its oil. Given the discrepancy in military firepower (Iraq, with almost 1 million men under arms, at the time had the world's fourth-largest standing army, compared with a mere 16,000 in Kuwait's armed forces), Iraq's victory in just 12 hours was hardly a surprise, and on August 8th Saddam designated Kuwait as Iraq's 19th province.

Unfortunately for Saddam, a majority of the Arab League condemned the invasion, as did the UN (including the Soviet Union, the traditional superpower ally of Iraq). By January 1991 a US-led coalition of 750,000 troops – 540,000 of them American – had assembled in Saudi Arabia demanding, in vain, that Iraq withdraw from Kuwait by a UN deadline of January 15th. Two days later "Operation Desert Storm" began with a massive air attack on Iraqi air defences and oil installations. The next month, coalition ground troops crossed into Kuwait and southern Iraq and proceeded to crush Iraq's forces. Following the ceasefire of February 28th, with some 8,000–10,000 Iraqi troops killed for the loss of only 300 coalition personnel, Iraq agreed to recognise Kuwaiti sovereignty and to eliminate its weapons of mass destruction: biological, chemical or nuclear.

These weapons, real or pretend, were Saddam's third mistake. Israeli jets had bombed a French-built nuclear reactor at Osirak, near Baghdad, as long ago as June 1981, arguing that the reactor could eventually have produced a nuclear bomb. Part of the agreement to end the first Gulf war was that Saddam would allow UN weapons inspections into Iraq. But the UNSCOM (United Nations Special Commission) inspectors were constantly thwarted in their task, so in December 1998 American and British jets carried out a four-day bombing attack on Iraq's military infrastructure. Meanwhile,

Saddam's dictatorship continued with no real domestic challenge. Because President George H.W. Bush had decided not to go beyond liberating Kuwait, Saddam had stayed in power and been free in the spring of 1991 to suppress a Shia uprising in the south of Iraq and a Kurdish uprising in the north. That quickly, albeit belatedly, led to the imposition of no-fly zones, enforced by the US, the UK and France, across the southern half of Iraq and part of the Kurdish region in the north. With the imposition also of punitive UN sanctions, life for ordinary Iraqis – but not for Saddam and his coterie – was harsh throughout the 1990s.

Whether it has been any better in the 21st century is a matter of political and sectarian bias. It is true, following the dismantling of the Ba'ath Party after the 2003 invasion by a US-led coalition, that there have been genuine elections, and it is also true that the economy has been freed from crippling international sanctions. But by almost any objective measure the 21st century has been disastrous for Iraq and for all its people – with the exception of the Kurds, who now have their own autonomous region in the north, have access to oil revenues and no longer have to fear the ethnic-cleansing brutality of the Saddam regime.

Saddam, committing yet another mistake, played his part in this 21st-century tragedy by his failure to co-operate fully with the UNSCOM inspections. Early in 2003 both the US and the UK, its close ally, said they had evidence from their intelligence agencies that Saddam was continuing to develop or manufacture weapons of mass destruction (WMD), with the British prime minister, Tony Blair, claiming – in what became known as the "dodgy dossier" – that Iraq could launch chemical weapons at targets in Cyprus in just 45 minutes. Despite serious doubts on the legality of any attack on Iraq, and despite pleas by the UNSCOM chief, Hans Blix, for more time, a force of some 192,000 American troops, 45,000 British troops, 2,000 Australian and just under 200 Polish soldiers invaded Iraq on March 20th 2003. On April 9th Baghdad fell to the "coalition of the willing" and Saddam's rule was over (Saddam was captured in December 2003 near his ancestral home of Tikrit and was hanged three years later). On May 1st President George W. Bush stood on the deck of a US aircraft carrier and declared "mission accomplished".

If only this had been true. It turned out that there were no WMD, meaning to the many critics of Bush and Blair that the war had been fought under false pretences – not least to effect regime change (some of Bush's critics claimed he wanted to avenge Saddam's attempt to assassinate his father, George H.W. Bush, during a visit to Kuwait in 1993, some weeks after he left office). One theory held by neoconservative members and advisers of the Bush administration was that once Saddam was gone, Iraq could become a democracy and its democracy would be emulated elsewhere in the Arab world, leading inevitably to a proper peace with Israel, the only true democracy in the Middle East.

Regardless of that particular neo-con illusion, the US-dominated Coalition Provisional Authority – installed in Baghdad to manage Iraq after the invasion – made two decisions that have had lasting and disastrous consequences: it instituted a sweeping programme of de-Ba'athisation, thereby depriving government institutions of their expertise; and it disbanded the Iraqi armed forces, thereby consigning hundreds of thousands of well-armed and doubtless resentful men to unemployment.

In the years that followed until the withdrawal of American troops in December 2011 (British troops had left in May 2011), Iraq was prey to constant attacks on coalition troops, especially through suicide bombs and the use of IEDs, and was subject to extreme sectarian violence between Sunni and Shia Iraqis. The Mahdi Army (Jaish al-Mahdi), formed in 2003, loyal to Muqtada al-Sadr, a Shia cleric, and numbering up to 50,000 fighters, was particularly effective against coalition troops. But so, too, was Asa'ib Ahl al-Haq (League of the Righteous), a Shia group (numbering by 2014 perhaps 50,000 members, though earlier estimates were around 3,000). This group split from the Mahdi Army in 2006 and claims to have carried out over 6,000 attacks on coalition forces and the official Iraqi army. While the estimated numbers of militia fighters vary from year to year and always need to be taken with a large grain of salt, it is clear that they have benefited from Iranian money and training – much of it carried out by the Quds Force, part of the Iranian Revolutionary Guards.

By the time the coalition forces – properly named the Multi-National

Force–Iraq and numbering at their peak in 2007 some 180,000 troops from more than 20 nations – had withdrawn in 2011, at least 100,000 Iraqis had been killed, the majority of them civilian. One academic study estimates the war-related Iraqi death toll at more than 461,000. What is clear is that more than 4,400 American troops were killed and over 32,200 wounded; the UK, the second-largest member of the coalition, lost a relatively modest 179.

But the US (and, to a lesser extent, the UK) lost more than troops and shattered lives; it also suffered damage to its international reputation through revelations of torture and other human-rights abuses, especially at the US-run Abu Ghraib prison. Worse for Iraq's future was the emergence in 2004 of al-Qaeda in Iraq (AQI). Led by the Jordanian-born Abu Musab al-Zarqawi, al-Qaeda launched waves of suicide bombers and IEDs at US and Shia targets. Although al-Zarqawi was killed in a US air strike in 2006, his organisation lives on as the even more brutal ISIS.

Without doubt the real winner of the West's foray into Iraq has been Iran. Elections may have satisfied the neo-cons' demands for democracy, but they have simply led to Shia domination under the direction of Iran and extraordinary levels of sectarian violence (the UN estimated the civilian death toll in 2013 at over 7,000, or more than double the toll in 2012). A more disturbing figure from the independent Iraq Body Count database gives a figure of 9,743 civilian deaths for 2013 and 17,049 for 2014.

The 2014 figure reflects the impact of ISIS and the growth of the Islamic State, and this in turn reflects the corruption and sectarian bias towards Shia interests of the government in Baghdad of the prime minister, Nuri al-Maliki, and the coalition led by his Islamic Dawa Party (*Da'wa* means call in Arabic). Maliki's anti-Sunni bias alienated the Sunni tribes of Anbar province who in 2007 in a so-called "awakening" (*Sahwa*) had co-operated with American troops under the command of General David Petraeus. They jointly managed to turn the tide against AQI.

Yet those same tribes, having been cold-shouldered by the Baghdad government after the departure of the Americans, began in 2012 to side with ISIS. Under extreme pressure from the West, but ultimately because of displeasure on the part of Iran, Maliki resigned in August

2014 and was replaced the following month by Haider al-Abadi, a much less sectarian-inclined Shia politician from the Islamic Dawa Party.

The immediate question for Abadi, who received the backing of Iraq's Grand Ayatollah Ali al-Sistani and also of the Iranian government, was how to deal with the advance of ISIS. This challenge was made urgent by an Iraqi army that had become so corrupt and poorly officered that in 2014 it abandoned the defence of Mosul, Fallujah and other towns in northern and central Iraq and fled in complete disarray.

Reversing ISIS's gains means enlisting the support of Sunni tribes increasingly dismayed by the brutal governance of the Islamic State, where extreme *sharia* punishments such as beheadings and stonings are commonplace, where women must be veiled and where non-Islamic music is banned. It also means improving the performance of the Iraqi army, which has signally failed to benefit from the $25 billion lavished on it by the US for its training and equipment. It depends, too, on the response to the call by Ayatollah al-Sistani on all Iraqis to take up arms against the Islamic State – a call that will inevitably involve more sectarian killings by Shia militias of Sunni Iraqis. Lastly, it depends on the effectiveness of the aerial campaign against ISIS targets in Iraq launched in 2014 by the US, the UK, Australia, Belgium, Canada, Denmark, France and the Netherlands (the British decided that they could attack ISIS targets only in Iraq, leaving ISIS in Syria untouched).

In this context, it needed a sustained aerial campaign in the summer of 2014 and the land efforts of Kurdish Peshmerga ("those who confront death") militiamen to beat back ISIS fighters and free some 40,000 members of the Yazidi sect (an Iraqi minority whose religion stems from Zoroastrianism and who are denounced as devil worshippers by ISIS) from the refuge they had sought on Sinjar mountain, close to Mosul. Many hundreds of Yazidi women and girls had been seized by ISIS fighters and either forcibly converted to Islam or used as sex slaves. Intriguingly, by the end of 2014 there were reports of an undeclared co-operation between the United States and Iran in the war against ISIS, with accounts of Iranian jets making sorties against Islamic State targets. There was evidence, too, that Iran's

Quds Force and Lebanon's Hizbullah were providing training to Iraq's Shia militias and were taking part in battles against ISIS troops, and that in some cases the Quds Force commander, the almost legendary General Qassem Suleimani, had personally directed operations.

However, without an assault by US and other Western troops – almost a political impossibility following the disastrous experience of 2003–11 – the Islamic State will be extremely hard to vanquish. The alternative would be a campaign involving Iran's armed forces, which would surely only worsen Iraq's sectarian divide. So far, the 21st century has brought existential threats to Iraq's many minorities, from Christians and Chaldeans to Yazidis and Assyrians; sectarian savagery between the Shia majority and their Sunni compatriots; the potential dismemberment of the country between Shia, Sunni and Kurd; and massive inroads by the Islamic State, whose fighters in May 2015 had captured the town of Ramadi, a mere 60-odd miles (97 kilometres) from the capital, Baghdad. Even though the country's oil production had recovered by December 2014 to a record 4 million barrels a day, a happy future for Iraq is still one of hope rather than expectation.

Israel and Palestine

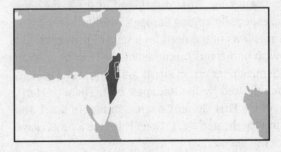

The State of Israel is unique in being the only country in the world with a Jewish majority (some 75% of its 8 million people are Jewish; the rest are mostly Palestinian Arabs – predominantly Sunni Muslim but also Christian and Druze – whose presence pre-dates the 1948 creation of Israel). Israel's other notable characteristic is being in a state of actual or threatened war ever since the proclamation of the country by David Ben-Gurion, head of the Jewish Agency, in May 1948.

In the ensuing decades Israel's military forces, which now have some 187,000 active frontline personnel and an active reserve of 565,000, have won successive victories against Israel's Arab neighbours and have emerged as easily the most effective in the region, armed not just with sophisticated weaponry from fighter jets to submarines but also with nuclear weapons (Israel, thought to have some 80 nuclear warheads, has always refused to confirm or deny its possession of nuclear weapons). Yet Israel's military supremacy, emphasised by defence spending of around 6% of the nation's GDP, has brought it only grudging acceptance: peace treaties with Egypt in 1979 and Jordan in 1994 have failed to lessen Arab resentment over the plight of the Palestinians; and the mutual recognition between Israel and the Palestine Liberation Organisation – signed in 1993 between Yitzhak Rabin and Yasser Arafat, and bringing both men the Nobel peace prize – has not led to a full peace settlement and the creation of a Palestinian state alongside Israel. Instead, the land that is theoretically destined to be that state remains under Israeli occupation or control; and this in the 21st century has created greater international sympathy for the Palestinians and at the same time more anti-Semitism, especially among Europe's Muslim minority, of the kind that convinces Jews of the need for a state of their own.

The idea of a Jewish homeland, prompted by the Dreyfus affair in France and by anti-Semitic pogroms in Russia and central and eastern Europe, was first popularised by the Budapest-born Theodor Herzl, elected as president of the First Zionist Congress in 1897 in Basel. The day before he died in 1904, he declared: "Greet Palestine for me. I gave my heart's blood for my people."

The decisive step in achieving Herzl's dream was made in 1917 when Arthur James Balfour, a British foreign secretary, sent a letter to Baron Walter Rothschild, president of the British Zionist Federation, declaring:

His Majesty's Government view with favour the establishment in Palestine of a national home for the Jewish people, and will use their

*best endeavours to facilitate the achievement of this object, it being
clearly understood that nothing shall be done which may prejudice
the civil and religious rights of existing non-Jewish communities in
Palestine, or the rights and political status enjoyed by Jews in any
other country.*

The context of this Balfour Declaration, and of the talks with
Zionist leaders that preceded it, was the UK's desire to win Jewish
support, not least in the US, for the allied cause in the first world war
against Germany. It also helped gain the UK access to acetone, needed
to propel artillery and bombs. Germany had cornered the market in
the main source of acetone, but Chaim Weizmann, a leading Zionist,
had invented a process to synthesise it. What was conveniently
overlooked at the time was the near-impossibility of reconciling a
national home for the Jewish people (which Zionists saw as their
future state) with the rights of the existing Arab population of what
was then called Palestine.

This basic flaw in the declaration has led to unceasing conflict
for Israelis and a burning sense of injustice for Arabs in general and
Palestinians in particular (the Palestinians refer to the 1948 creation
of Israel as *al-nakba* – the catastrophe). The violence of both Jews
and Arabs was first directed against the UK, which had been granted
a mandate in 1920 by the allied powers after the first world war to
continue its occupation of Palestine – formally part of the now-defeated
Ottoman empire – and prepare it for self-rule. The UK's administration
of Palestine was confirmed two years later by a mandate from the
League of Nations. With Jewish migration to Palestine increasing,
the UK in 1922 separated Transjordan (the territory east of the Jordan
river that accounted for 76% of the original Palestine mandate and
subsequently became the Hashemite Kingdom of Jordan) from
Palestine and banned Jewish settlement there.

This did little to appease disgruntled Arabs, who rioted against
the Jewish inflow in 1920 and 1929. Their anger then erupted in
the Arab revolt of 1936–39 against the British mandate, at the cost
of several thousand Palestinian lives. Nor did British policy appease
Jews fleeing the rise of the Nazis in Germany in the 1930s. In 1920
Vladimir Jabotinsky had founded the Haganah (meaning defence), a

paramilitary force to protect Jews that has become the modern Israel Defence Forces (IDF), and in 1931 Haganah gave birth to the more active and extreme Irgun Zvai Leumi (National Military Organisation), whose aim in pursuit of a Jewish state was to expel the British from Palestine.

When the second world war broke out in 1939, the Irgun suspended their anti-British operations in order to collaborate against "the Hebrew's greatest enemy in the world: German Nazism". Not all Irgun fighters were happy to co-operate with the British, and a faction broke away in 1940 to form Lehi (Lohamei Herut Israel, or Fighters for the Freedom of Israel), better known as the Stern gang, after its founder Avraham Stern. The Stern gang even proposed collaborating with Nazi Germany and fascist Italy against the British if the Axis powers would agree to transfer all Jews from their territories to Palestine.

If proof were ever needed that terrorism is a malleable definition and that victory can make any terrorist a respected politician, Israel provides it. Militants from the Stern gang in 1944 assassinated Lord Moyne in Cairo, where he was the resident minister in charge of the Middle East. In 1946 the Irgun bombed the King David Hotel in Jerusalem, where the British military and government offices were based, killing 92 people, most of them civilian. The Stern gang and the Irgun were jointly responsible for the massacre of more than 100 civilians in the Palestinian village of Deir Yassin in 1948 (the Haganah condemned the killings). But fast-forward to 1977 and Menachem Begin, a leader of the Irgun, became Israel's prime minister (and later a Nobel peace-prize winner with Egypt's Anwar Sadat); fast forward to 1983 and Yitzhak Shamir, a leader of the Stern gang, was Begin's successor as prime minister.

The shortcomings of the Balfour Declaration were starkly revealed by the second world war. In 1939 a British white paper laid down an annual limit of 10,000 for Jewish immigrants to Palestine, but the coming Holocaust and the refusal of many countries to admit Jewish refugees were compelling thousands more to seek refuge in Palestine. By the end of the second world war Jews comprised a third of Palestine's population, compared with 11% in 1922 when the League of Nations granted the UK its mandate.

Perhaps not surprisingly, the UK in 1947 said it would surrender its mandate, leaving the newly created United Nations to devise the partition of Palestine into an independent Jewish state and an independent Arab state, with Jerusalem under an international trusteeship. The Jewish Agency accepted the plan, but the Arab League and the Arab authorities in Palestine did not. On May 14th 1948, with the British mandate ending the next day, David Ben-Gurion announced "the establishment of a Jewish state in Eretz-Israel, to be known as the State of Israel".

This led to the first Arab–Israeli war, as the armies of Egypt, Iraq Jordan and Syria (joined by contingents from Morocco, Saudi Arabia, Sudan and Yemen) crossed into what had been British mandatory Palestine. As the Palestinians, some 700,000 of whom either fled or were driven out to become refugees in the surrounding countries, correctly said, for them it was a catastrophe (*nakba*): ten months of war resulted in victory for Israel and the seizure by the Israelis of more than half of the land the UN had proposed for a Palestinian state. Jordan was left in occupation of east Jerusalem and most of the West Bank of the Jordan river and Egypt in occupation of the Gaza Strip. The war also resulted in the departure for Israel of some 700,000 Jews over a period of three years from Arab countries, such as Iraq, where their families had been resident for centuries.

Subsequent Arab–Israeli wars have all been shorter, and have had the same outcome. In late October 1956 troops from the UK, France and Israel invaded Egypt to secure the Suez Canal, which had just been nationalised by Egypt's Gamal Abdul Nasser. Pressure from the American president, Dwight Eisenhower, who feared intervention on Egypt's behalf by the Soviet Union and who in any case objected to this neo-imperialism, forced the UK and France to withdraw by the end of 1956. Israel, which remained in occupation of Sinai and Gaza until March 1957, was content to have secured access to the Red Sea for its ships through the Straits of Tiran.

When Nasser closed the straits to Israeli shipping in 1967 and ordered UN peacekeepers to leave the Sinai buffer zone Israel assumed he was about to launch an attack, so it launched pre-emptive strikes on June 5th 1967. By June 10th (hence the term the six-day war) Israel had comprehensively defeated not just the armed forces of Egypt but also those of Jordan and Syria. For the Arabs it was humiliation (though described only as *al-naksa* – the setback). For the Israelis it was a triumph that left them in control of the whole of the West Bank, the whole of Jerusalem, the whole of Gaza and also Syria's Golan Heights.

The Arab humiliation was partly assuaged by the October war of 1973, launched by Nasser's successor, Anwar Sadat, in co-ordination with Syria's Hafez al-Assad on October 6th – a date that coincided with the Jewish Yom Kippur, the day of atonement, and was also within the Muslim fasting month of Ramadan (hence alternative descriptions as the Yom Kippur war and the Ramadan war). The initial successes of the Egyptian and Syrian forces (Jordan was also involved, though with less enthusiasm) were such that Israel seemed at one point to be facing defeat. However, its counter-attacks, helped by the provision of intelligence from the United States, soon turned the tide; when a ceasefire was reached on October 25th Israel was the clear victor, still in control of the West Bank, Sinai, Gaza and the Golan Heights.

One lesson of the October war was the supremacy of the IDF when faced by any combination of Arab armies. Yet the strong performance of the Arab armies at the outset of the war removed the shame of the six-day war and enabled Sadat, and later Jordan, to sign peace treaties with Israel.

The second lesson for the Arabs was that conventional warfare would not defeat Israel, but unconventional methods might. The six-day war gave momentum to the fledgling Palestinian guerrilla movement of al-Fatah, founded in 1959 by members of the Palestinian diaspora, and then to the Palestine Liberation Organisation (PLO), founded in 1964 with the express purpose of liberating Palestine and eliminating Zionism through armed struggle.

As an umbrella organisation the PLO has covered an alphabet soup of guerrilla factions, some of which now barely exist. The largest has always been Fatah (the word means opening, or in this case conquest, in Arabic, and is a reverse abbreviation of Harakat al-Tahrir al-Falastini – the Movement for the Liberation of Palestine), with an armed wing called al-Asifa (the storm). Fatah's first operations against Israel took place in the early 1960s, and after the humiliation of the six-day war the Fatah *fedayeen* ("those ready to sacrifice themselves") captured the Arab imagination.

Yet in terms of world opinion it was arguably the smaller Palestinian groups – for example, the Popular Front for the Liberation of Palestine (PFLP), the Popular Democratic Front for the Liberation of Palestine (PDFLP) and the Popular Front for the Liberation of Palestine–General Command (PFLP–GC) – that were more effective in grabbing headlines and discomfiting Israel. The PFLP introduced the tactic of airliner hijacking into the Middle East conflict; the PFLP–GC, headed by Ahmad Jibril and not represented in the PLO, blew up a Swissair airliner en route to Israel in 1970 and attacked the Israeli town of Kiryat Shmona in 1974. Most dramatic of all was the massacre of Israeli athletes at the Munich Olympics in 1972 by members of Black September, a faction of Fatah dissidents named after the month in 1970 when King Hussein of Jordan had crushed a Palestinian attempt to take over his kingdom.

The PLO, founded by Ahmad Shukeiri but headed from 1969 onwards by the Fatah leader, Yasser Arafat, had its greatest impact not so much by its raids on Israel as by gaining the sympathy of much of the world, especially Arab and developing countries. The Arab League Summit of 1974 recognised the PLO as the "sole legitimate representative" of the Palestinian people – meaning that Jordan gave up any claim to the West Bank – and in the same year Arafat addressed the UN General Assembly in New York, famously declaring:

> Today I come bearing an olive branch in one hand, and the freedom fighter's gun in the other. Do not let the olive branch fall from my hand.

Grasping the olive branch has been a tortuous – and torturous – diplomatic experience, only partially achieved and only after years of conflict. The Palestinian groups soon found themselves enmeshed in the Lebanese civil war, which lasted from 1975 to 1990 and prompted Israel to invade Lebanon for the first time in 1978, establishing a security zone manned by its Lebanese Christian allies in the south of the country. In 1982, following the attempted assassination of Israel's ambassador in London by the Abu Nidal Organisation (an extremist faction that split from Fatah in 1974), Israel mounted a full-scale invasion of Lebanon. The IDF stood by as its Lebanese Christian allies massacred hundreds and possibly thousands of Palestinians in the Beirut refugee camps of Sabra and Shatila (Israel's defence minister, Ariel Sharon, was later found by an Israeli commission to bear personal responsibility and was forced to resign).

Despite the international furore over the slaughter in the Sabra and Shatila camps, Israel could congratulate itself that the PLO had been devastated. Arafat and the rest of the leadership had to be evacuated to Tunis and the PLO's military units, bereft of most of their weaponry, were dispersed around the Arab world. Moreover, though by 1985 Israel had withdrawn most of its forces from Lebanon, it remained in control of a security zone in the south in alliance with the Christian-dominated South Lebanon Army (SLA).

Israel's respite was only temporary. In December 1987 Palestinian youths, first in Gaza and then in the West Bank, began a violent, stone-throwing uprising now known as the first *intifada* (the word in Arabic means shaking or tremor). Over a period of almost six years it cost the lives of 160 Israelis – including 47 members of Jewish settlements considered illegal under international law – and 2,162 Palestinians (including hundreds killed as collaborators by Palestinians themselves). But it did lead in 1991 to the US- and Soviet-sponsored Madrid conference that brought together representatives of Israel, Jordan, Lebanon, Syria and the PLO. A year later, Israel's new prime minister, Yitzhak Rabin, opened secret talks with the PLO which led, in September 1993, to the signing by Rabin and Arafat of the Oslo accords, outlining a process in which Israel would gradually hand over territory to the Palestinians in return for peace. Within days Arafat issued a statement: "The PLO recognises the right of the state of Israel to exist in peace and security."

The Oslo process promised much – too much according to some Israeli extremists, one of whom assassinated Rabin in 1995 – and it was followed by a series of other agreements. But ultimately it failed: in 2000 Arafat refused to sign a far-reaching agreement for a Palestinian state with Israel's prime minister, Ehud Barak, at a Camp David summit hosted by President Bill Clinton. The collapse of the talks and a provocative visit to Jerusalem's Temple Mount, the compound containing the al-Aqsa mosque – Islam's third holiest site – by Ariel Sharon as leader of Likud, the main Israeli opposition party, led directly to the second *intifada* (the *Aqsa intifada*, as the Palestinians called it). When the uprising ended almost five years later, more than 1,000 Israelis and 3,000 Palestinians had been killed, and Israel had almost completed an enormously high wall running through the West Bank to guard Israel proper and its illegal West Bank settlements from attack by Palestinians (there were 73 suicide bombings launched from the West Bank between 2000 and July 2003).

In principle, a final peace settlement between Israel and the Palestinians should be attainable under the Clinton parameters – proposals unveiled by the former president in December 2000 under which an independent but essentially demilitarised Palestinian state would comprise more than 90% of the West Bank and all of Gaza; Israel and the Palestinians would make small exchanges of territory to accommodate Jewish settlements; there would be shared sovereignty over sensitive parts of Jerusalem; and the Palestinians would waive an unlimited right of return for Palestinians in the diaspora in exchange for Israel's acknowledgement of the "moral and material suffering caused to the Palestinian people by the 1948 war, and the need to assist the international community in addressing the problem".

Sharon as prime minister withdrew Israel's troops and settlements from Gaza in 2005. Another Likud prime minister, Binyamin Netanyahu, in 2011 accepted (perhaps reluctantly, given his disavowal of the concept in his re-election campaign in 2015) the notion of a two-state solution to the conflict. The Palestine Authority (PA) – properly termed the Palestine National Authority (PNA) and set up in 1994 as a result of the Oslo accords to act as an interim self-government of the areas ceded to Palestinian control in Gaza and the West Bank – has pledged itself to the peace process. Indeed, its security forces co-operate with Israel's against Palestinian terrorism. Yet despite all this, the Oslo accords are widely regarded as dead; UN resolutions criticising Israel are ignored or subject to an American veto; and the road map to peace drawn up in 2003 by the US, the UN, the EU and Russia – the so-called Quartet – has led nowhere. Why?

One reason is obviously mistrust on both sides. After a series of suicide bombings by Palestinian militants in late 2001, Sharon ordered that Arafat be confined to his compound in Ramallah – a form of virtual house arrest that lasted two-and-half years and involved the destruction of the compound around the PA leader (Arafat's death in 2004 in Paris led to Palestinian accusations that Israel had poisoned him). A second reason, despite Sharon's withdrawal from Gaza, is that Likud-led governments are much more committed to creating settlements – a huge obstacle to peace – in the occupied West Bank. A third reason, following the creation of ISIS and in 2014 its brutal Islamic State, is the fear that any future Palestinian state would also be captured by an extremist – and anti-Jewish – ideology.

But at least as important has been the power of Hizbullah in Lebanon and Hamas in Gaza. Hizbullah, backed by Iran and Syria, is a Shia militia that may well be as powerful as the official Lebanese army. It can muster up to 65,000 fighters, according to Iran's Fars News Agency (Hizbullah itself does not disclose any figure), and is equipped with ample supplies of weaponry from assault rifles to anti-aircraft batteries and surface-to-air missiles. Moreover, it has proved itself in combat with the IDF, first in the south Lebanon war of 1982–2000, which ended with Israel's troops leaving their security zone in southern Lebanon, and then in a 34-day conflict in 2006 in which Hizbullah rained thousands of rockets into northern Israel and used effective guerrilla tactics to halt the advance into Lebanon of IDF troops. The 2006 conflict left Lebanon's infrastructure devastated by air strikes and artillery fire and caused more than 1,000 Lebanese deaths, in contrast to just over 40 Israeli civilian deaths; but Hizbullah could still claim a victory by standing up to the region's superpower, and Israel's reputation was undoubtedly harmed by its use of cluster bombs and phosphorus shells.

Its reputation has also suffered because of its successive wars in Gaza: the three-week-long "Operation Cast Lead" at the end of 2008; the week-long "Operation Pillar of Defence" in November 2012; and the seven-week-long "Operation Protective Edge" in July and August 2014. In each case Israel said its goal was to stop rocket attacks from Gaza aimed indiscriminately into Israel; but in each case the damage to Gaza's infrastructure and housing was immense, with a heavy loss of Palestinian lives there (around 1,400 in Operation Cast Lead, compared with 13 Israelis; more than 170 Palestinians and six Israelis in the 2012 conflict; and around 2,200 Palestinians and 71 Israelis in the 2014 war). To those in Europe – and even in the US, Israel's staunchest ally – who accused it of disproportionate violence and of imposing collective punishment on Gaza's 1.8 million population, Israel replied that all violence would stop if only Palestinian groups would stop firing rockets and that Palestinian casualties would be far fewer if Hamas and other groups stopped using Palestinian civilians as human shields.

What is certain is that Hamas – the word means enthusiasm in Arabic and is an acronym of Harakat al-Muqawama al-Islamiyya (Movement of Islamic Resistance) – is an obstacle, perhaps a convenient one, to a final peace settlement. Established in the late 1980s as an offshoot of the Muslim Brotherhood, Hamas enjoys the support of Qatar and Iran (a rare example of Shia Iran favouring a Sunni organisation). In its earliest years it also had the clandestine support of Mossad and other Israeli intelligence agencies, which viewed it as an antidote to Fatah. However, whereas Fatah came to accept Israel's right to exist, the Hamas Charter of 1988 states that it "strives to raise the banner of Allah over every inch of Palestine" and that "Israel will exist and will continue to exist until Islam will obliterate it, just as it obliterated others before it". Instead, the charter proposes a one-state solution:

> Under the wing of Islam, it is possible for the followers of the three religions – Islam, Christianity and Judaism – to coexist in peace and quiet with each other.

In practice, the charter could doubtless be fudged. Hamas's leader in Gaza, Ismail Haniyeh, has on occasion said Hamas would offer a 20-year truce if Israel agreed to return to its 1967 borders and recognise the national rights of the Palestinians. Israel, of course, would prefer that Gaza's impoverished residents oust from power Hamas and its military wing, the Izz al-Din al-Qassam Brigades (created in 1991 with estimates of its numbers now ranging from 20,000 to 40,000). That prospect seems remote. With Palestinian voters tired of the corruption of Fatah within the PA, Hamas won a majority of seats in the parliamentary elections of 2006, setting off a bloody struggle between Fatah and Hamas that forced Fatah out of Gaza but left it still as the main party in the West Bank. There have been several attempts to forge a unity government between Fatah and Hamas but any reconciliation between the two is fragile, thus allowing hardliners and sceptics in Israel to say that Mahmoud Abbas (Abu Mazen), the aged PA president, is too weak to be a real partner in peace.

In short, almost seven decades after Israel's creation, the prospects for an end to the Arab–Israeli conflict look dim. Back in 2002 Saudi Arabia orchestrated an Arab League initiative offering comprehensive Arab recognition of Israel in return for Israel's withdrawal to the 1967 borders and the establishment of a Palestinian state – but the Arab peace initiative was published a day after the Izz al-Din al-Qassam Brigades carried out a suicide bombing inside Israel that killed 30 civilians and injured 140.

In the ensuing years, serious efforts by the US to craft a lasting peace have come to nothing and Islamist groups have gained ground at the expense of the secular Palestinian guerrilla groups (the PFLP and the PDFLP – or DFLP as it was later known – were both led by Christian Palestinians). The Islamists instinctively oppose a two-state solution, and decry the call for the Palestinians of the diaspora to abandon their demand for a right of return while any Jew in the world has the right to make *Aliya* (ascent in Hebrew) by migrating to Israel. But a one-state alternative – the Palestinians in the past called for a democratic secular state to replace Israel – implies an end to the Zionist dream.

In a semantic squabble more serious than it might at first seem, Netanyahu in 2014 called on the PA to recognise Israel as a Jewish state:

> It's time the Palestinians stopped denying history ... Just as Israel is prepared to recognise a Palestinian state, the Palestinians must be prepared to recognise a Jewish state.

But to the Palestinians, backed by the Arab League, such a definition would officially make Israeli Arabs second-class citizens and would compromise any negotiations on a Palestinian right of return.

Meanwhile, Netanyahu is not alone in Israel, or in the United

States, in regarding Iran and its nuclear ambitions as an existential threat to Israel. Yet since Iran is unlikely to go against the wishes of the Palestinian people, a Palestinian state coexisting with Israel is surely the best way to remove that threat. As Israel's former Labour Party prime minister, Ehud Barak, once said:

> If I were a Palestinian at the right age, I would have joined one of the terrorist organisations at a certain stage.

Lebanon

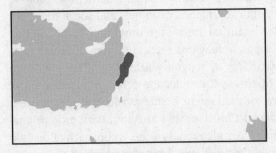

Nestling on the eastern shores of the Mediterranean, with Israel to its south and Syria to the east and north, the Republic of Lebanon – gaining its independence from France in 1943 – has always delighted in its image as the Switzerland of the Middle East, with the capital, Beirut, described as the Paris of the Middle East. Sadly, that image has been tarnished: notably by a vicious sectarian civil war in 1975–90 and in recent years by the repercussions of the civil war in neighbouring Syria, which by 2015 had made the 4.5 million or so Lebanese play host to more than 1 million Syrian refugees.

In the decades following Lebanon's civil war, the Iran-backed Shia political party Hizbullah (Party of Allah), designated a terrorist organisation by the United States and the European Union, has become a component of the otherwise pro-Western government while also fielding a well-armed militia that is at least as powerful as the 74,000-strong Lebanese army. Yet Hizbullah is not the only group to have fighters outside the control of the state. The political families that lead the country's other main religious groups, be they Maronite Christian, Sunni Muslim or Druze, can all call upon what amount to private armies. So, too, can several Palestinian factions, representatives of the 450,000 Palestinians, half of whom live in 12 Palestinian refugee camps established in Lebanon at various points after the creation of Israel in 1948 (three other camps were destroyed during the civil war). When the interventions by foreign powers, notably Syria and Israel, are factored in, it is perhaps not surprising that normal life in Beirut and other cities is frequently disturbed by acts of violence, from air raids to car bombs.

Yet for all its internal tensions, both latent and overt, Lebanon remains an extraordinarily resilient nation, somehow able to surmount its deep political, religious, economic and social divisions. These divisions are manifest in a 1943 unwritten National Pact that recognises 18 separate religious sects, and then allocates roles in government according to religious affiliation. The president, for example, is a Maronite Christian; the prime minister a Sunni Muslim; the speaker of parliament a Shia Muslim; and parliament itself is shared between Christians and Muslims, with proportional representation among the confessional groups within each of the two religious communities. Originally the share of seats in parliament was set at 6:5 in favour of the Christians, but this was adjusted to a 50:50 ratio in the agreement ending the civil war.

The status quo is inherently unstable, but any attempt to change it – as the civil war shows – risks making matters worse. This is why there has been no official census since the one in 1932 that provided the basis for the National Pact. At that time the Christians were a small majority in the country. In the following decades many more Christians than Muslims have emigrated, not least to escape the 1975–90 civil war; the Muslim birth rate has been higher; there has been an influx of Palestinian refugees, most of them Sunni, in 1948 and 1967, and another influx after the Jordanian army defeated the guerrillas of the Palestine Liberation Organisation (PLO) in Jordan's 1970–71 Black September civil war; and now there is the arrival of Syrians, most of them Sunni, in flight from the Syrian civil war.

The result is that Lebanon's confessional proportions have changed. Christians – be they Maronite, Greek Orthodox, Protestant and so on – probably account for at most 40% of the population. Among the Muslims, around 54% of the population and divided more or less equally between Sunni and Shia, it was the Shia, traditionally the poorest section of the Lebanese, who won the most from the civil war – hence the rise of Hizbullah – but their power is now being tempered by the growing numbers of Sunni. Meanwhile the Druze, a secretive offshoot of Shia Islam, comprise only about 6% of the population but delight in a reputation for fierce independence (they emerged as the victors in a civil war against the Maronites in 1860, killing perhaps 20,000 Christians). Their co-religionists in Israel are the only Israeli Arabs in the Israel Defence Forces.

Lebanon's internal complexities are reflected in its relations with its neighbours. "Sister" Syria has always claimed such a special role in Lebanon that until Syria succumbed to foreign diplomatic pressure in 2008 the two countries had felt no need to have an exchange of embassies and normal diplomatic relations with each other. During the Lebanese civil war Syrian troops intervened in 1976 to aid the Christian militias of the Lebanese Front against the increasingly successful Muslim-dominated and leftist-inclined Lebanese National Movement and the Palestinian *fedayeen* guerrilla groups, such as Fatah and the Popular Front for the Liberation of Palestine, which had allied with the Lebanese left. Ironically, this put Syria on the same side as Israel, since Israel had been supplying weapons to the Maronites – many of whom, with a nod to Lebanon's ancient past, consider themselves Phoenician rather than Arab.

But Syria's troops, numbering at their peak 40,000 and operating as an "Arab Deterrent Force" approved by the Arab League, were in Lebanon not to guarantee the victory of one side or the other but to maintain Syria's ability to manipulate Lebanese politics. Soon the Lebanese Front, commanded by the charismatic Bashir Gemayel, found itself fighting against the Syrians. The Gemayel family was (and is) a powerful Maronite clan with its own Phalange party, founded by Bashir's father, Pierre Gemayel, and also known as the Kataeb (phalanx in Arabic, and thus a respectful nod towards General Franco's Phalangists in the Spanish civil war).

Rival Maronite clans were the Chamoun family, whose militia was known as the Tigers (the middle name of their founder, Camille Chamoun, was Nimr, or tiger in Arabic), and the Frangieh family, with its Marada Brigade. It was Camille Chamoun who, as Lebanon's president in the 1950s, successfully appealed for American marines to land in Beirut in 1958 and quash a coup attempt supported by Egypt's President Nasser that aimed to make Lebanon join Egypt and Syria in a United Arab Republic. It was President Suleiman Frangieh who spoke in support of the Palestinian cause at the UN General Assembly in 1974, immediately after the speech there by the PLO chairman, Yasser Arafat.

The internecine rivalry of the Christian clans was horribly demonstrated in the Ehden massacre of 1978, when Phalangist gunmen, apparently in retaliation for the killing of a Kataeb commander, slaughtered around 40 people in the Frangieh fiefdom, including Tony Frangieh, the son of the former president, along with his wife and three-year-old daughter. The Frangieh family was close to Syria's President Hafez al-Assad and his family, and doubtless shed no tears when Bashir Gemayel was assassinated – allegedly with the approval of the Assads – some four years later.

The context of these killings was a civil war that was ignited on April 13th 1975 in Ain al-Rummaneh, a Christian district in Beirut, when Phalangist gunmen ambushed a bus carrying Palestinian *fedayeen* (the Phalangists claimed that a church had previously been attacked by Palestinians). The immediate effect was to bring into the open Lebanon's political and confessional polarisation. In a caricature of ideological differences, the Lebanese left – influenced by Nasserist socialism and representing mainly the Muslims and Druze but also some Greek Orthodox Christians – saw an opportunity to diminish the power of the pro-American Christian right. Arafat tried unavailingly to keep his followers out the fray, but George Habash, a Christian doctor who founded and led the Marxist-inclined Popular Front for the Liberation of Palestine (PFLP), saw the potential for social revolution.

The ideological pretensions quickly gave way to sectarianism and nationalism. The Christians, and indeed many Muslims, resented the Palestinian state within a state, in which Lebanese citizens found themselves held up and questioned at Palestinian checkpoints – at the same time as Palestinian guerrilla operations against Israel invited Israeli air raids on Lebanese territory. Complicating all this were the divisions on both sides: the PFLP and other leftist Palestinian groups, such as Nayef Hawatmeh's Popular Democratic Front for the Liberation of Palestine (PDFLP, later simply DFLP), thought in terms of socialist revolution; so, too, did Lebanese groups such as the Nasserist al-Murabitun (the Sentinels) and the Druze-led Progressive Socialist Party (PSP); by contrast, in the Lebanese Front, the Kataeb, especially under Bashir Gemayel, were close to Israel while the Frangieh clan was an ally of Syria (as was the Ba'athist Palestinian group al-Sa'iqa – the Thunderbolt).

For Lebanon the result was a complex conflict whose repercussions are felt to this day. The Druze warlord and leader of the PSP, Kamal Jumblatt, was assassinated in 1977 and Gemayel (along with a score of other Phalangist politicians) was blown up in 1982. In both cases, suspicion fell on Syria.

The Syrian regime, using agents from Hizbullah, is also the prime suspect in the 2005 assassination of Rafiq al-Hariri, a billionaire former prime minister with strong links to Saudi Arabia and France who had opposed the Syrian role in Lebanon. The car bomb that killed Hariri led to a wave of popular revulsion and the creation of the secular March 14th Alliance, named after a mass demonstration – one month after Hariri's assassination – by the "Cedar revolution" against Syria's occupation of Lebanon. The March 14th Alliance was in stark opposition to the pro-Syrian and Hizbullah-backed March 8th Alliance (named after a demonstration praising Syria's role in Lebanon), which asserted that Israel's Mossad intelligence agency had killed Hariri. International opinion favoured the March 14th Alliance's version, and in April 2005 Syria withdrew its troops from Lebanon, paving the way for the putative normalisation of relations in 2008.

Meanwhile, a Special Tribunal for Lebanon, set up by the UN Security Council in 2007 to investigate the Hariri killing, has indicted several members of Hizbullah, provoking an alarmed Hassan Nasrullah, leader of Hizbullah, to denounce the Netherlands-based court and argue that Israel was responsible for the Hariri assassination.

An Israeli role in Hariri's death seems intrinsically unlikely, but such is Lebanon's history that conspiracy theories are always rife – and it is a fact that Israel has frequently intervened in Lebanon, both clandestinely and overtly. Back in 1973 Israeli commandos commanded by Ehud Barak, a future Israeli prime minister, arrived from the sea to attack PLO targets in Sidon and Beirut. Among the victims of the assault were three senior PLO members, most notably Youssef al-Najjar, a close aide to Arafat and an organiser of the Black September group responsible for the killing of Israeli athletes at the Munich Olympics the previous year.

More Israeli actions were to come. In March 1978, three days after Fatah commandos had arrived from the sea and hijacked two buses in Israel and killed 38 Israeli civilians (including 13 children), Israel launched "Operation Litani", with 25,000 IDF troops invading southern Lebanon up to the Litani river, pushing the PLO to retreat north of the river. Estimates of *fedayeen* and Palestinian and Lebanese civilian deaths range from 1,100 to 2,000, for the loss of 23 Israeli soldiers (Israel was later criticised for its use of US-supplied cluster bombs). As Israel's troops withdrew in June to a narrow security zone just north of its border with Lebanon, the area south of the Litani was occupied by its ally, the 2,500-strong South Lebanon Army, a Christian-dominated renegade faction from the Lebanese army. Given the humanitarian repercussions of Operation Litani, the UN was quick to approve the United Nations Interim Force in Lebanon (UNIFIL), the first of which arrived on March 23rd 1978. The original mandate was to last six months, but such is the febrile nature of the region that UNIFIL, with 10,000 troops in early 2015, is still stationed in southern Lebanon.

One effect of Israel's 1978 invasion was to drive 285,000 southerners, mainly Shia families, from the south to seek refuge in Beirut, where seven years later they helped establish Hizbullah, the most effective force against Israel. In the meantime, Israel launched a second invasion in June 1982, in retaliation for the attempted killing of its ambassador in London by gunmen from the Abu Nidal group, part of the Palestinian rejectionist front opposed to any compromise with Israel and violently at odds with Arafat and Fatah. This time, Israeli troops, some 78,000 at their peak, drove their tanks and armoured vehicles, supported by massive air strikes, all the way to the outskirts of Beirut. Syrian forces in Lebanon – including Syrian military aircraft – were destroyed and the Palestinian *fedayeen* groups were close enough to absolute defeat that at the end of August, under an evacuation plan brokered by the United States and implemented by a multinational force (MNF) from the United States, France and Italy, they agreed that Arafat and the PLO leadership would move to Tunis and Palestinian fighters would go first to Cyprus and then be dispersed to various Arab countries.

For Menachem Begin, Israel's Likud prime minister, the aim of the 1982 invasion was to eliminate the PLO and give Israel "40 years of peace". Yet just two weeks after Arafat's departure for Tunis, Bashir Gemayel, Lebanon's pro-Israeli president-elect, was assassinated, and in the immediate aftermath Israeli troops under Ariel Sharon (a future Israeli prime minister) stood by as their Kataeb militia ally entered the Palestinian refugee camps in Beirut of Sabra and Shatila to massacre as many as 3,000 civilians in retaliation for the death of Gemayel – though it was not the Palestinians who had killed him. (Sharon was later found by an Israeli commission to bear personal responsibility for the massacre.)

For Lebanon, the nightmare of sectarian and political violence still had years to run. Amin Gemayel, brother of Bashir, was installed as president on September 23rd 1982 and immediately invited the MNF to return. Their stabilising mission ended in tragedy: in April 1983 a suicide bomber drove a truck into the US embassy in Beirut killing 63; and in October suicide bombers struck the separate barracks of the MNF's American and French troops, killing 241 American servicemen and 58 French paratroopers. Most intelligence agencies believe Imad Mughniyeh, a Lebanese Shia who had once been a member of Fatah but had become a founder of Islamic Jihad and of Hizbullah, had directed the attacks. (Mughniyeh, who had close links with Iran and Syria, was assassinated in Damascus in 2008; his son, Jihad, along with five other Hizbullah members, was killed by an Israeli air strike in Syria in January 2015.) In reaction to the 1983 Beirut attacks, by the following spring the governments of the US, France and Italy had withdrawn their troops.

Lebanon's civil war finally came to an end in 1990, when Syrian jets strafed the presidential palace in Baabda, just outside Beirut, and forced Michel Aoun, appointed as head of an interim government by the outgoing Amin Gemayel, to flee. General Aoun had opposed a Charter of National Reconciliation forged at Taif in Saudi Arabia the previous year because it had legitimised Syria's occupation of Lebanon.

Yet the end of the civil war, after perhaps 200,000 deaths, brought no lasting stability. The Taif agreement, apart from redressing the Christian–Muslim proportions in parliament, also (at least in theory) ordered the disarming of the country's militias – with the exception of Hizbullah. The Shia militia, whose bargaining power was doubtless increased because of the Western hostages it was holding in the Bekaa valley, retained its weapons as a resistance force against Israel's presence in the south.

That resistance has been tested several times. In April 1996, reacting to Hizbullah rocket attacks, Israel launched "Operation Grapes of Wrath", with an aerial bombardment of Beirut and other towns that destroyed an enormous amount of Lebanon's infrastructure – and also killed 106 civilians who had sought shelter in a UN base at Qana in southern Lebanon. Sixteen days after the start of the bombardment, a US-negotiated truce was reached: Hizbullah recognised Israel's right to defend itself and agreed not to attack Israeli civilians; Israel recognised Hizbullah's right to resist Israel's occupation of southern Lebanon and agreed to withdraw its troops from Lebanon by July 2000 (the Israeli withdrawal was completed six weeks ahead of schedule).

The greatest test of Hizbullah's prowess came a decade after Operation Grapes of Wrath. In July 2006, citing the killing by Hizbullah of three Israeli soldiers and the kidnapping of two others, Israel launched a ground invasion of southern Lebanon and an aerial and artillery bombardment, aiming particularly to destroy Hizbullah's stronghold in the southern suburbs of Beirut. The 2006 Lebanon war lasted for 34 days, with Israel determined to destroy Hizbullah and Hizbullah determined to maintain a missile barrage against Israel, reaching as far south as Haifa, until Israel stopped its incursions into Lebanon. The result, apart from massive damage to Lebanon's infrastructure, was the death of around 1,100 Lebanese, at least half of them civilians, and 165 Israelis, including 44 civilians. Yet, if anything, the outcome was a victory for Hizbullah: it had defied the most powerful army in the Middle East, gaining the admiration even of many Christian Lebanese, and its arsenal of missiles and other weapons was soon replenished by Syria and Iran.

Whether Lebanon, which claims the Sheba'a Farms area in the Israeli-occupied Golan Heights, can ever follow Egypt and Jordan in signing a full peace treaty with Israel will surely depend on Syria, given Syria's continued influence in Lebanon (not least because of its links with Hizbullah). More pressing for Lebanon are the repercussions of the civil war in Syria and the rise of the Islamic State and Islamist extremism. Since early 2013 Hizbullah has been active on behalf of the Assad regime in the Syrian civil war. This has brought Hizbullah into conflict not just with extreme Sunni Islamists such as ISIS and al-Qaeda's Jabhat al-Nusra but also with moderate Sunni and secular groups such as the Western-supported Free Syrian Army. Not surprisingly, some Syrian Sunnis who have sought refuge in Lebanon's Sunni-majority city of Tripoli have joined Lebanese Sunnis in clashing with local Alawites, members of the same heterodox Shia sect as the Assad family. Attempts by the Lebanese army to restore peace tend to be futile: indeed, in August 2014 ISIS and Jabhat al-Nusra fighters took 27 Lebanese soldiers hostage in the Lebanese border town of Arsal.

Traditionally, Lebanon has been a proxy battleground for outside powers: Syria, Israel, France, the United States, Russia, Egypt, Saudi Arabia and Iran have all used the country and its political and confessional factions to advance their own interests. The tradition continues: in November 2013 suicide bombers killed 23 people in an attack outside the Iranian embassy in Beirut, leading Hizbullah to contend that Saudi Arabia had directed the bombers as part of the Saudi struggle with Iran over regional influence (an alternative explanation is that the attack was by the Abdullah Azzam Brigades, an affiliate of al-Qaeda).

Meanwhile, in the Palestinian refugee camps the secular *fedayeen* groups such as Fatah and the PFLP are giving ground to Salafist militias such as Fatah al-Islam, Jund al-Sham (Army of the Levant) and Asbat al-Ansar (League of Partisans). The potential for a renewed Palestinian conflict with the state is clear: back in 2007 Fatah al-Islam fighters who had mounted a bank robbery south of Tripoli were besieged by the Lebanese army for three months in the Nahr al-Bared refugee camp (under a 1969 agreement the army is not supposed to enter the refugee camps). By the time the army had finally won control of the camp, dozens of soldiers and Fatah al-Islam fighters had been killed.

The question is whether the rise of the Islamist Sunnis, the power of Hizbullah and the poverty of the Palestinians (the refugees and their descendants have virtually no right to work in Lebanon) mean a new Lebanese civil war is inevitable. The optimists think not, if only because the horrifying memories of the last one have yet to fade from the collective memory. Nonetheless, the optimists will concede that the nation, just as at any moment since its independence, will still be dancing close to the precipice. In short, there is a lot riding on Lebanon's reputation for resilience.

Libya

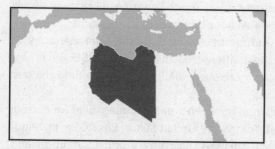

In October 2011, after an increasingly eccentric and dictatorial rule lasting 42 years, Muammar al-Qaddafi, leader of the grandiosely named Socialist People's Libyan Arab Jamahiriya, was captured and killed by exultant Libyan rebels. In the ensuing years, the State of Libya – as the country is now simply named – has endured a continuing civil war and disintegrated into a failed state divided by regional and tribal loyalties: elections in 2014 led to two rival parliaments and two rival governments, with neither able to control well-armed militias, both secular and Islamist.

None of this conforms to the optimists' forecast that the Arab spring that blossomed in Tunisia in December 2010 would lead to a stable, pluralistic democracy in neighbouring Libya. The effort to remove Qaddafi began with an uprising in February 2011 in Benghazi, the main city in the eastern region of Cyrenaica, and within days the unrest had spread west to Tripolitania and the capital, Tripoli. However, in early March the regime's armed forces – roughly 76,000 at their height – struck back, threatening a humanitarian disaster for the rebels and the population of Benghazi. That prospect led to a UN Security Council resolution on March 17th by a vote of 10–0 (Russia, China and Germany were among five abstentions) to authorise a no-fly zone and aerial strikes to protect civilians. This was followed two days later by an air campaign and naval blockade, initially featuring France, the UK and the US (where one official declared it was "leading from behind"). Soon, though, outside powers were acting under a NATO umbrella and expanding into a coalition with almost a score of nations, including Jordan, Qatar and the United Arab Emirates.

Qaddafi enlisted Tuareg tribesmen from Mali and several hundred mercenaries from Europe and South Africa, and also pressed migrant workers from sub-Saharan Africa into his forces, but to no avail. By July 2011 the International Contact Group on Libya, representing governments from both the West and the Arab world, had recognised the National Transitional Council (NTC) as the legitimate government of Libya. By August Qaddafi had fled Tripoli, and by September the African Union, which had originally opposed regime change, also recognised the NTC. On October 20th 2011 Qaddafi was dragged out of a drainage pipe near the coastal town of Sirte and summarily shot (according to some rumours by a French spy who had infiltrated the rebel side and wanted to stop any subsequent revelations of Qaddafi's dealings with the French president, Nicolas Sarkozy). The following month, Qaddafi's favourite son and presumed heir, Saif al-Islam, was captured, marking the complete demise of the Qaddafi clan.

Yet with clashes breaking out in Benghazi in January 2012 between rival groups of the former rebels, the NTC quickly proved inadequate to the challenge of stabilising post-Qaddafi Libya. One reason is the enduring imprint of the Qaddafi years. The "Brother Colonel" seized power at the age of just 27 on September 1st 1969 in a bloodless coup against King Idris, leader of the important Senussi tribe and monarch since Libya (a former Italian colony) attained its independence in 1951.

At first the Qaddafi regime was popular: Italian properties were nationalised and the UK was ordered to evacuate its military base in Tobruk and the US its Wheelus airbase in Tripoli. The growing oil revenues from a vast country with a small population (today numbering around 6.2 million, almost all of them Sunni Muslims) were distributed to allow housing, health and education for all.

In retrospect one mistake was Qaddafi's version of popular democracy, explained in his 1975 *Green Book* (an obvious allusion to Mao Zedong's *Little Red Book*). This "third universal theory" of political and social organisation, first outlined by Qaddafi in 1973, involved the creation of around 2,000 people's committees, whose decisions would be passed upwards to a General People's Congress. In practice, this local democracy was strictly controlled by the establishment in 1977 of revolutionary committees. In other words, within less than a decade revolutionary Libya had become more or less a dictatorship, with the population monitored by an extraordinary number of secret police. In such conditions, dissent was bound to build under the surface – not least because, much to the chagrin of a potentially prosperous middle class, Libyans were forbidden to own more than one house in the Jamahiriya, a neologism coined by Qaddafi to mean state of the masses (the usual *jumhuriyya* means simply republic).

A second mistake was Qaddafi's foreign-policy adventurism. This included abortive efforts in the early 1970s to create an Arab federation with Egypt and Syria; the military occupation of part of Chad in 1973; an impractical Arab Maghreb Union with Morocco, Mauritania, Algeria and Tunisia in 1989; and, with his pan-Arabism having failed, an attempt at the end of the 20th century to make Libya the leader of pan-Africanism (Libya was a founder in 2001 of the African Union). Meanwhile, Libya had become an enthusiastic supporter, often with both money and arms, of dissident movements around the world, from the IRA in the UK's Northern Ireland to Muslim separatists in the Philippines and Thailand.

The result was that by the 1980s Qaddafi had become an international pariah. In the view of the US president, Ronald Reagan, in 1986, the Libyan leader was "the mad dog of the Middle East" seeking "world revolution, Moslem fundamentalist revolution, which is targeted on many of his own Arab compatriots" (though, in fact, Qaddafi was never a religious zealot and opposed Islamic extremism). The tensions with the US were reflected in 1981 by the shooting down by American fighter jets of two Libyan aircraft over the Gulf of Sirte, which Libya claimed as its territorial waters, and by the bombing – allegedly by Libyan agents – of a Berlin discotheque in 1986 frequented by American servicemen. The discotheque bombing precipitated US air strikes on Libyan military targets in Tripoli and Benghazi, and also on Qaddafi's own home. The bombardment killed 101 people, including an adopted daughter of Qaddafi (in the wake of the bombing, Qaddafi decided to add the prefix "Great" to the Socialist People's Libyan Arab Jamahiriya).

Relations with the UK were equally sour. In 1984 the UK cut diplomatic ties with Libya after a shot fired from the Libyan embassy in London during an anti-Qaddafi demonstration killed a young policewoman, Yvonne Fletcher. Then in December 1988 a Pan Am flight en route from Germany to the United States was blown up over the Scottish town of Lockerbie. The UK and the US blamed Libya for the 270 deaths (though a credible alternative theory blames Iran, seeking to retaliate for the US shooting down of an Iranian airliner in July 1988).

The Lockerbie disaster led to economic sanctions by the UN to force Libya to hand two suspects to a Netherlands court for trial under Scottish law. Libya complied in 1999, leading to the suspension of the sanctions, the restoration of diplomatic ties with the UK and the beginning of Qaddafi's rehabilitation. By 2003 Libya had agreed to accept responsibility and pay $2.7 billion in compensation for the Lockerbie bombing, and in January 2004 Libya also agreed compensation for the 1989 bombing of a French airliner over the Sahara. Most important, to regain international respectability, was Qaddafi's decision in December 2003 to stop Libya's production, real or planned, of chemical and biological weapons and abandon its quest for nuclear weapons. The welcome back into the international fold was sealed in March 2004 with a visit to Libya and a public hug for Qaddafi by the British prime minister, Tony Blair.

The Qaddafi era lasted for four decades because the regime – helped by ample oil revenues – was able to suppress Libya's underlying regional and tribal identities. The country has more than 130 tribes, representing the indigenous Berbers, the Arabs who arrived by conquest in the 7th century and black Africans in the south. Of the 30 or so important tribes, Qaddafi himself was from the relatively less powerful Qaddafda tribe; Abdul-Salam Jalloud, his second-in-command for two decades, was from the much more powerful Magarha tribe, which joined the Warfalla, the country's largest tribe, in a failed uprising against the regime in 1993. Once the Arab spring reached Libya, with popular protests first in Benghazi, tribal differences – often sparked by arguments over the regime's power of patronage to allocate jobs and military positions – were bound to assert themselves.

In a country awash with arms wielded by hundreds of militia groups, the result has been continuing internecine chaos. In August 2012 the NTC handed power to the newly elected General National Congress, charged with drawing up a new constitution and preparing for the 2014 elections for a Council of Deputies. But almost immediately the country was scarred by sectarianism, with Islamist groups destroying Sufi shrines. Then, in September 2012, Islamist militants – apparently from Ansar al-Sharia (Supporters of Islamic Law), a Salafist group linked with al-Qaeda – attacked the US consulate in Benghazi, killing the ambassador and three other Americans. Political turmoil was such that in 2014 Abdullah al-Thani, serving briefly as prime minister, toyed with the idea of inviting the monarchy back. When secular and liberal parties did well in the 2014 elections, Islamists in the General National Congress refused to recognise the Council of Deputies and instead announced the New General National Congress, establishing its headquarters in Tripoli and forcing the new parliament and government (which retained their international recognition) to take refuge in the eastern city of Tobruk.

Will the chaos eventually give way to stability and unity? In the summer of 2015 the country was being fought over by four main groups. In Tobruk, the Council of Deputies, internationally accepted as the legitimate government, had the support of the Libyan Army (now renamed the Libyan National Army) under the secular General Khalifa Haftar, who had taken part in the coup that brought Qaddafi to power but had later conspired against him (and had been given asylum in the United States). In Tripoli, the New General National Congress is an Islamist coalition, ranging from the moderate Muslim Brotherhood (backed by Qatar and Turkey) to the extremist Libya Dawn (Fajr Libya), an umbrella organisation for many more extreme groups (Libya Dawn denounces terrorism but maintains links with Ansar al-Sharia). Benghazi is the stronghold of Ansar al-Sharia, as part of the Shura Council of Benghazi Revolutionaries. The port of Derna, near Benghazi, was captured in late 2014 by militants who declared their allegiance to the Islamic State and its self-proclaimed caliph (and founder of ISIS), Abu Bakr al-Baghdadi. In February 2015 this "Islamic State in Libya" beheaded 20 Coptic Christians from Egypt, provoking an immediate strike on Derna by Egypt's air force.

But these groups only have partial sway. Virtually every town has its militia, operating sometimes independently and sometimes under the umbrella of coalitions such as Libya Dawn. The prize for all is to profit from Libya's oil exports, which have plummeted from the Qaddafi-era level of 1.6 million barrels a day. Conceivably the Libyan National Army, with support from Egypt, will be able to dominate Cyrenaica and then move west along the coast. But the odds are long. Meanwhile, there are much shorter odds on the ability of Islamic State militants to create havoc, not just in Libya but – as was shown by the murderous attacks on foreign tourists at a Tunis museum in March 2015 and on a Tunisian beach in June 2015 – beyond its borders.

Syria

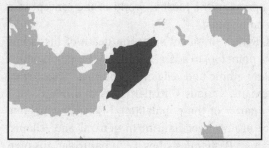

In the Arab world Damascus, Syria's capital, has always been – with Cairo and Baghdad – one of the three great centres of power, culture and influence. But the glories of the Umayyad caliphate, centred on Damascus in the 7th century, are long gone. In the 21st century, following the political upheavals across the Arab world of the Arab spring, the inhabitants of today's Syrian Arab Republic have become embroiled in a sectarian and geopolitical conflict of sustained and terrifying violence.

The statistics are damning. In a civil war spawned by demonstrations against the regime of Bashar al-Assad in the southern city of Dera'a in 2011, some 11 million of the country's pre-war population of 22 million have been displaced, with more than 3 million of them fleeing to sanctuary in Lebanon (where Syrians now make up a fifth of the population), Jordan, Turkey and even turbulent Iraq. By the spring of 2015 the death toll had reached at least 210,000 and ancient cities such as Aleppo and Homs had been devastated.

As the regime and a plethora of rival militias (there are said to be as many as 1,000 armed opposition groups) struggle for advantage, the very borders of the modern country risk being erased. Those frontiers are based on the lines drawn in 1916 by the UK's Sir Mark Sykes and France's François Georges-Picot in a secret Asia-Minor agreement to carve up the Ottoman empire once the first world war was concluded – yet to the Islamic State (IS), announced in June 2014 by the self-proclaimed caliph, Abu Bakr al-Baghdadi, the frontiers are a colonial irrelevance and there is no need to retain the acronyms of ISIS and ISIL (the Islamic State in Iraq and Sham/the Levant). Given the control ISIS had attained over large sections of Syria and Iraq and the emotional appeal in the Muslim world of the concept of a caliphate, Baghdadi had a point.

Bashar al-Assad, Syria's president since the death of his father, Hafez, in 2000, has a point too. In a largely Sunni Arab nation which nonetheless has many ethnic and religious minorities (Shia Arabs, Kurds, Druze, Armenians, various Christian sects and other small groups make up a quarter of the population), his Ba'athist regime is a secular defence against sectarianism in general and Islamist extremism – terrorism, as Bashar describes it – in particular. His own family is from the Alawite community, a sect that is connected with Shia Islam but has beliefs that mainstream Sunni and Shia Muslims often consider heretical. Though the Alawites, whose stronghold is the coastal region around Latakia, number only 12% of Syrians, they have a disproportionately large share of the economy and the higher echelons of politics and the military.

It is the Assad family's Shia links that over the decades have made Syria the only Arab country to be allied with Iran, a Shia nation intensely proud of its Persian, non-Arab identity. In the post-2011 civil war Iran's support, not least in supplying Hizbullah fighters from neighbouring Lebanon to reinforce Syrian government troops, has helped stave off what in 2012 appeared to be imminent defeat. Indeed, Bashar's only other significant ally has been Russia, which uses the Syrian port of Tartus for its navy and which opposes the idea of regime change that the United States and the West have favoured (and seen achieved in Iraq and Libya). In a telling sign of the regime's isolation the Arab League in November 2011, just eight months after the Dera'a demonstrations, suspended Syria's membership.

Yet whatever the present importance of Syria's links with Shia Iran, the characteristic of Syrian governments ever since independence from the French mandate in 1946 has been secularism. A period of coups and counter-coups and an ineffectual union from 1958 to 1961 with Nasser's Egypt as the United Arab Republic (UAR) were followed in 1963 by a military coup in favour of the Ba'ath Party, founded by a Christian, Michel Aflaq, a Sunni, Salah al-Din al-Bitar, and followers of the Alawite Zaki al-Arsuzi to advocate socialism and pan-Arab nationalism.

Ba'ath in Arabic means renaissance or resurrection, and Ba'athism had not only played a part in establishing the UAR but also gained power in Iraq. However, in 1966 ideological infighting between the Ba'ath Party's civilian and military factions led to the arrest of Aflaq and Bitar, a split with the Ba'ath in Iraq and the assumption of power by General Salah Jadid, with Hafez al-Assad as his defence minister. Just over a year later the government was reeling from the shock of Israel's comprehensive victory against Egypt, Jordan and Syria in the six-day war of June 1967, in which Israel destroyed much of the Syrian air force and seized the strategically important Golan Heights.

One consequence of the six-day war was growing tension between Jadid, who controlled the party, and Hafez al-Assad, who controlled the military. This power struggle was made worse in September 1970 when Syrian troops, dispatched by Jadid to Jordan to help the Palestine Liberation Organisation in its Black September war with the Jordanian army, were forced to retreat (Hafez refused to provide air cover, lest his air force be destroyed by Israel). Two months later, in November 1970, a bloodless coup by the "corrective movement" removed Jadid (who spent the rest of his life in prison) and installed

Hafez as prime minister (he took the title of president the following March).

Hafez was an extraordinarily ruthless leader, but also subtle and pragmatic. He installed fellow Alawites to control the ubiquitous security and intelligence agencies (the *mukhabarat*), but appointed Sunni Muslims to lead institutions, had himself verified as a genuine Muslim by the Sunni religious authority in Damascus and made the *hajj* pilgrimage to Mecca. Yet in practice he maintained the non-sectarian Ba'athist approach to politics, intervening in the Lebanese civil war in 1976 to save the Maronite Christian Phalangist forces (thus beginning a 29-year Syrian occupation of "sister" Lebanon) but also crushing a Muslim Brotherhood uprising in 1982 in the Syrian city of Hama with extreme brutality. Three weeks of relentless shelling by troops commanded by Hafez's brother, Rifaat al-Assad, killed anywhere between 10,000 and 40,000 of Hama's residents (Rifaat has denied any role, blaming Hafez for the bombardment).

Hafez's policy towards Israel after the Arab defeat in the October war of 1973 kept Syria – unlike Egypt, Jordan and, as the years went by, the PLO – firmly in the rejectionist camp. His formula for a settlement with Israel was full peace for full withdrawal. Yet he also made sure that there were no Palestinian attacks on Israel from Syrian territory, and with the same pragmatism joined the US-led coalition in 1990 to drive Saddam Hussein's Iraq from its occupation of Kuwait.

The civil war has shown that Bashar, doubtless egged on by others in the Assad family such as his brother Maher (commander of the Republican Guard), has inherited the ability to be ruthless. To many, this was a surprise. Bashar, who trained as an ophthalmologist in London, is an accidental leader, promoted to be Hafez's heir by the exile of his uncle Rifaat to Paris in the 1990s and by the death of his brother Basil in a 1994 car crash. Certainly, when Bashar assumed power in 2000, he raised hopes of a more liberal approach by freeing several hundred political prisoners. But in Syria's relations with Lebanon little changed: the assassination in 2005 of Rafiq al-Hariri, a former Lebanese prime minister, and the killings – threatened or implemented – of other Lebanese politicians were all believed to involve Syria. Similarly, after the Dera'a protests in March 2011, Bashar raised hopes in the following month by releasing dissidents and ending a state of emergency that had lasted for 48 years (in a sop to conservative Muslims he also closed the country's only casino and reversed a 2010 ban on the wearing of the face veil by women teachers).

But promises of institutional and political reform were accompanied by the increasingly brutal repression of increasingly frequent popular protests, and by the end of 2011 the country was falling into full-scale civil war. The years since have seen a shift of power among the opposition groups, and a softening of the West's implacability towards Bashar. Initially, the fight against the regime was spearheaded by the Free Syrian Army (FSA), formed by defecting officers from the Syrian armed forces. The FSA's political equivalent was the Syrian National Council (SNC), formed in the summer of 2011 in Istanbul and beset from the start by ideological and ethnic frictions in a membership that included not just Sunnis and Christians but also Kurds, Muslim Brothers and even representatives of the tiny Assyrian minority. Those frictions were hardly smoothed over when the SNC joined with other opposition groups in November 2012 to form the National Coalition of Syrian Revolutionary and Opposition Forces – also known as the Syrian National Coalition and recognised in December by the US, the UK, France and the Gulf Arab states as the legitimate representative of the Syrian people.

The brutal truth, however, is that the moderate opposition, promoting a vision of a pluralistic and democratic Syria, has been long on words but short on effective action. Arguably, much of the blame lies with the shifting interests of the outside world. At the UN, for example, Russia and China in March 2012 endorsed a peace plan drafted by Kofi Annan only after it had been watered down (Annan abandoned his mission in August, handing the poisoned chalice over to a distinguished former Algerian diplomat and UN luminary, Lakhdar Brahimi, who finally gave up in May 2014).

Equally important was the refusal of several Islamist groups, notably Jabhat al-Nusra (more precisely Jabhat al-Nusra li-Ahli al-Sham – the Support Front for the People of Sham/the Levant), to join the coalition. As the West dithered on whether or not to create no-fly zones to provide safe havens alongside the frontier with Turkey for the growing number of displaced Syria families, the FSA began to be supplanted by Islamist groups that were more motivated and inspired support, official or private, from sympathisers in the Gulf states. The FSA could still field 40,000 or more fighters in 2013, but so could the Islamic Front, supported by Saudi Arabia and consisting of Harakat Ahrar al-Sham al-Islamiyya (the Islamic Movement of the Free Men of Sham/the Levant), Jaysh al-Islam (the Army of Islam), Suqour al-Sham (Falcons of Sham), Liwa al-Tawhid (the Brigade of Belief in One God), Liwa al-Haqq (Brigade of Justice), Ansar al-Sham (Supporters of Sham) and the Kurdish Islamic Front (a Salafist movement among the Kurds). Meanwhile, there were many jihadist groups that remained independent of the Islamic Front, notably Jabhat al-Nusra, which has 5,000–8,000 fighters and has declared its allegiance to al-Qaeda.

In theory, the Syrian armed forces, with 178,000 active frontline personnel and active reserves of over 500,000, should have had no problem in crushing the opposition, especially since they are equipped with reasonably modern Russian armaments, ranging from some 4,500 tanks to more than 460 aircraft and helicopters. In practice, the armed forces have been weakened by many defections and by the asymmetric tactics of guerrilla warfare. In response, the regime has employed extreme brutality, from chemical attacks on civilians to the use of barrel bombs, dropped from helicopters without discrimination on civilian populations supposedly hostile to the government.

The use of chemical weapons was a red line that President Barack Obama in August 2012 said Bashar would cross at his peril. The following April he repeated the warning, with the clear implication that the US would take military action if Bashar were proved to be using chemical weapons. That proof came with a report by UN weapons inspectors in September 2013 into an attack on part of Damascus the previous month in which hundreds died (the United States reckoned the toll was just over 1,400; the FSA reckoned more than 1,700). The inspectors did not identify who had launched the sarin gas attack, but the UK said that there was no remaining doubt of the Assad regime's responsibility.

The red line had been crossed, but, to the dismay of the FSA and other rebels, there was no retaliatory strike on regime assets by US or allied jets. Instead, on August 30th 2013 the British Parliament voted against any military action against Syria. Bereft of his most faithful ally, Obama on September 10th announced that the US would endorse a Russian proposal, quickly accepted by Syria, that the Assad regime would allow the verified elimination of its stockpiles of chemical weapons and would sign up to the Chemical Weapons Convention (the UN and the Organisation for the Prohibition of Chemical Weapons declared the elimination complete in June 2014). Clearly, an international escalation of the Syrian conflict had been avoided – but at the cost of at least some of the US's credibility.

Red lines or not, the reality was that after the prolonged and painful morass of Afghanistan and Iraq and the ultimately disastrous intervention in Libya, the West had lost its appetite for war in the Muslim world. At the same time, diplomatic efforts at the UN and in two rounds of talks in Geneva had failed to find a political solution to the continuing horrors in Syria: the rebels and most outside powers insisted that Bashar would have to go into exile; Bashar's position, made clear to *Russia Today* in November 2012, was simple: "I was made in Syria. I have to live and die in Syria." In June 2014 Bashar pointedly defied his critics by holding an election in which he claimed to have won 88.7% of the vote (from a turnout alleged to be 73.42%) for a third term as president.

If the 15-year civil war in neighbouring Lebanon is a precedent, there can be no military solution to Syria's agony – and the agony could continue for many years to come. In the great game of regional politics, it will be hard for Iran to abandon Bashar, which is why in the spring of 2013 Hizbullah fighters from Lebanon, presumably at Iran's behest, entered Syria to help recapture the town of Qusayr from the FSA and Jabhat al-Nusra. Yet it will be equally hard for Saudi Arabia, with its obsessive fear of Iran's influence, to abandon the rebel groups.

One complicating factor is that while some groups, notably the FSA, are the kind of secular-inclined moderates that win the favour of the West, others, notably in the Islamic Front, espouse an Islamist zeal that appeals to the Sunni countries of the Arabian peninsula but definitely not to the West. A second complication is the growing strength of Jabhat al-Nusra and ISIS, both of them shunned not just by the West but also – except for private donations – by the Gulf states.

A third is that the rebel groups in recent years have been fighting not just the Syrian regime but each other, with the momentum in mid-2014 favouring ISIS, hence the announcement of the Islamic State by the self-appointed caliph, Abu Bakr al-Baghdadi.

It was the slickly publicised brutality of ISIS, including the beheading of American and British hostages, that in August 2014 led the United States to launch air strikes on Islamic State targets in Iraq and, from September, in Syria. The UK, conscious of legal implications, was willing to bomb in Iraq but not in Syria. From the Arab world, however, the US was joined in the strikes on targets in Syria by Saudi Arabia, the United Arab Emirates, Jordan, Qatar and Bahrain (and later by Morocco). The targets were not just the Islamic State but also Jabhat al-Nusra and its offshoot, the Khorasan Group.

Yet air strikes can have only a limited impact: to reverse ISIS gains takes boots on the ground, which the US and others are unwilling to supply. The Syrian town of Kobane (also known as Ayn al-Arab), near the Turkish border, was captured by the Kurdish People's Protection Units (YPG) in July 2012, but from September 2014 was besieged by Islamic State forces, who managed to enter part of the town. With the Islamic State regarding Kobane as symbolically important, it took four months of heavy fighting for the YPG, the FSA and Kurdish Pershmerga fighters finally to repel the Islamic State forces.

The realpolitik consequence of a conflict that is both fluid and stalemated has been some cynical marriages of convenience: the Assad regime has benefited from ISIS's attacks on other rebels; Iran and the US have acknowledged unofficially co-ordinating aerial attacks on ISIS; and Russia, which started bombing ISIS in late 2015, was careful to keep the US informed. Meanwhile, Israel, which in 2007 sent its jets to destroy an unfinished Syrian nuclear reactor, has mainly watched from the sidelines, grabbing headlines by giving medical aid inside Israel to hundreds of wounded Syrian civilians and rebels, but also launching occasional air strikes – as in January 2013, when the Assad regime accused Israel of bombing a military research facility near Damascus (a convincing alternative explanation was that the target was a convoy of advanced weaponry on its way to Hizbullah in Lebanon).

As with the Lebanese civil war, it may be the sheer exhaustion of the warring parties that ends the Syrian conflict, and it is hard to predict the eventual victors and vanquished. In March 2015 Jabhat al-Nusra and several other Islamist groups joined in a new coalition, the Jaysh al-Fatah (Army of Conquest), and were able to capture the important town of Idlib. To the alarm of Western governments, Jaysh al-Fatah had the active support of Saudi Arabia, Qatar and Turkey. Two months after the regime's loss of Idlib, Islamic State forces seized the ancient town of Palmyra and the last border crossing into Iraq. Faced with these setbacks, the Syrian regime retaliated with its own harsh tactics, launching barrel bombs laced with chlorine on rebel-held areas. However the Syrian tragedy finally ends, it will clearly take many more years for the Syrian people to recover from its horrors.

Yemen

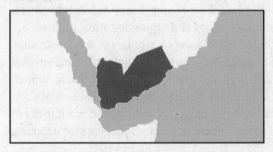

Strategically placed at the south-west corner of the Arabian peninsula, where much of the world's oil is transported through the Bab al-Mandab strait at the mouth of the Red Sea, Yemen was known to ancient Rome as Arabia Felix – happy or fortunate – as opposed to the Arabia Deserta of what is now Saudi Arabia. In recent years the Roman epithet has proved singularly inappropriate for the 26 million inhabitants of the Republic of Yemen: their country is bedevilled by perpetual tribal and increasingly sectarian conflict; by the meddling of outside powers, notably Saudi Arabia, Iran and the US; and by the powerful presence of al-Qaeda. Vying with Somalia to be the poorest in the Arab world, the country is also so environmentally vulnerable that Sana'a is likely soon to be the world's first capital city to run out of water. In short, Yemen deserves its place on the list of the world's failed states.

Yemen's most recent turmoil began in tandem with the Arab spring: demonstrations in Sana'a in early 2011 against President Ali Abdullah Saleh led to an increasing cycle of violence, with several ministers and military figures, most notably the powerful Major-General Ali Mohsen al-Ahmar, joining a growing tribal movement against a regime that had been in place for 33 years. In April the beleaguered Saleh seemed ready to sign a peace plan negotiated by the Gulf Cooperation Council (GCC – an alliance of Saudi Arabia, Kuwait, Bahrain, the United Arab Emirates, Qatar and Oman) and accepted by the Yemeni opposition. Under this agreement Saleh and his family would be granted immunity from prosecution and would go into exile. However, in May he insisted on some modifications and then, at the last minute, refused to sign, prompting the GCC to suspend its peace efforts and provoking heavy fighting in Sana'a between loyal government troops and opposition tribal militias.

The fighting included the placing of a bomb in the presidential palace on June 3rd that left Saleh severely injured. Transported to Saudi Arabia the next day for medical treatment, Saleh handed operational power over to his vice-president, Abd Rabbuh Mansur Hadi. Saleh's enforced absence did not, however, lead to a transfer of power, or to an end to the violent gun battles that erupted in Sana'a in September.

As the situation worsened, Saleh returned to Yemen on September 23rd 2011 and two months later formally handed power to Hadi, with a GCC-brokered agreement that Hadi would be the sole candidate in an election in February 2012 that would make him president charged with the drafting of a new constitution. Following the subsequent National Dialogue Conference, President Hadi announced plans in February 2014 for the country to be a federation of six regions – an idea immediately denounced by Houthi insurgents from the northern area next to Saudi Arabia on the grounds that they would then be disadvantaged.

The Houthis, otherwise known as Ansar Allah (Helpers of God), are Zaydi Muslims, a Shia sect close to Sunni Islam and revering five imams in their history (other Shias are "seveners" and "twelvers").

They take their name from Hussein Badreddin al-Houthi, a former member of the Yemeni parliament who launched a rebellion against President Saleh in June 2004 and was killed in combat in September 2004. So far their rebellion against the central government – and also pro-government tribes – has involved them in several rounds of warfare, culminating in their seizure of Sana'a in September 2014. The UN then proposed a peace plan under which the Houthis would withdraw from the cities they held after the formation of a new unity government.

Within weeks, however, the Houthis, demanding further concessions in the drafting of a new constitution, put President Hadi and his ministers under virtual house arrest. In January 2015 the Houthis seized the national TV network and in February announced they were appointing a five-member presidential council to replace Hadi, who sensibly fled from Sana'a to the southern port of Aden, which his supporters said would now be the de facto capital of Yemen. Even so, the Houthi advance continued: by March 26th Hadi had sought refuge in Saudi Arabia, just as Saudi aircraft began airstrikes on Houthi targets as head of a coalition with the UAE, Bahrain, Kuwait, Qatar, Jordan, Morocco, Sudan and Egypt (with an invitation – declined by the Islamabad government – extended also to Pakistan). The US was a member of the coalition by proxy, having agreed to supply intelligence and logistics.

The Houthis may be Shia and the Saudi-led coalition Sunni, but the Yemen conflict is not so much sectarian as an inter-tribal friction that has become a struggle for regional influence between Saudi Arabia and Iran, which is accused of supplying arms to the Houthis. The conflict is also seen by many as a Machiavellian plot by Ali Abdullah Saleh, a Zaydi Shia supported in the past by Saudi Arabia, to regain power by secretly lending his loyalists to the Houthi cause in order to topple President Hadi.

Historically, there has been little confessional tension in Yemen – where some 35% of the almost entirely Muslim population are Shia – but there have been countless episodes of conflict between tribes and between north and south, which for much of the 20th century were two separate countries. The north gained its independence from Ottoman rule in 1918 under Yahya Muhammad Hamid ed-Din, a Zaydi imam, who in 1926 declared himself monarch of the Mutawakkilite Kingdom of Yemen. By contrast, the south was under the control of the British, who occupied the port of Aden in 1839 and went on to establish a protectorate ended only by the withdrawal of the UK from east of Suez in 1967.

Yet neither north nor south enjoyed stability. In the north, army officers mounted a coup in 1962 that sparked a tribal war between royalists, supported by Saudi Arabia, and republicans, who were joined by thousands of Egyptian troops sent by Gamal Abdul Nasser to support the new Yemen Arab Republic (YAR). Egypt's troops eventually numbered some 70,000 (they were withdrawn in 1967, partly because of the economic drain on Egypt from its venture in Yemen) but a republican victory was not finally achieved until early 1968 and was not accepted by Saudi Arabia until 1970. One feature of this North Yemen civil war was the use of poison gas, allegedly by the Egyptians. Another was its cold-war aspect: the pro-American Saudis feared the encroachment into the Arabian peninsula of pro-Soviet, pan-Arab Nasserism.

The cold war and the example of the YAR also inspired an armed struggle from 1963 onwards against British rule in the south by the Front for the Liberation of Occupied South Yemen (FLOSY) and the National Liberation Front (NLF). FLOSY had the backing of Nasser, but it was the NLF that emerged triumphant in fighting between the two groups and formed the government of the People's Republic of South Yemen in 1967; and it was a Marxist faction of the NLF that in 1970 changed the name to the People's Democratic Republic of Yemen (PDRY) – proof, as cynics delight in noting, that "democratic" in a title in reality signals the opposite.

The PDRY had brief border clashes with North Yemen in the 1970s and also a brief but vicious civil war in January 1986. But, with the promise of oil and gas having been discovered in both countries and with the Soviet Union collapsing, the PDRY agreed in 1990 to unite with the north and become today's Republic of Yemen. Ali Abdullah Saleh, president of North Yemen since 1978, became the first president of the new nation.

Unity, however, has not been a comfortable experience. Yemen's refusal to join the American coalition in the first Gulf war against

Iraq's occupation of Kuwait led to the expulsion from Saudi Arabia of thousands of Yemeni workers and the loss of their economically crucial remittances. Economic strains and factional disputes led to clashes between north and south in April 1994 and a full-scale civil war in May, with the south officially declaring secession as the Democratic Republic of Yemen on May 21st 1994. However, it was President Saleh who triumphed; the vice-president, Ali Salim al-Bayd, and his fellow secessionists in the Yemen Socialist Party fled to neighbouring Oman.

The tensions between north and south are so entrenched that they may well be permanent. But the question that preoccupies the outside world is whether the same will be true of the presence of al-Qaeda in Yemen. The organisation's origins in Yemen go back to President Saleh's embrace of Yemeni *mujahideen* returning to the country in the 1980s after their successful war against the Soviet occupation of Afghanistan. Saleh then used these *mujahideen* to help defeat the southern Marxist secessionists in the 1994 civil war.

But in a classic case of unintended consequences, after the welcome given to the jihadists some formed Islamic Jihad in Yemen in the early 1990s, soon followed by the Aden-Abyan Islamic Army (notorious for the 1998 kidnapping of 16 foreign tourists in the south) and al-Qaeda in Yemen (AQY). It was a speedboat manned by AQY militants that was responsible in October 2000 for a suicide attack on the USS *Cole*, moored in Aden, killing 17 American servicemen. Two years later the Aden port suffered another AQY suicide attack, with the bombing of a French oil tanker, M/V *Limburg*, resulting in the death of one crewman and increasing the level of Western alarm over Yemen's instability. In subsequent years, following the escape of al-Qaeda members from prison, President Saleh was rumoured to have allowed the jihadist movement to grow as a ploy to retain Western support for his regime, which regarded southern secessionists and northern tribal dissent as greater threats to its survival than the presence of al-Qaeda.

US efforts to punish those responsible for the attack on the USS *Cole* and then the 9/11 attacks on New York and Washington involved the immediate dispatch to Yemen of special forces and intelligence agents. In 2002 a missile fired by an American Predator drone – the first such

strike in the Arabian peninsula – killed Abu Ali al-Harithi, the leader of AQY and the man thought to have planned the attack on the USS Cole. But US retaliation did not deter the jihadists: in September 2008 Islamic Jihad in Yemen, now part of al-Qaeda, mounted an assault on the US embassy in Sana'a – killing 19, including six of the attackers – in an operation apparently directly ordered by Osama bin Laden. In the following January the al-Qaeda branches in Yemen and Saudi Arabia formally united as al-Qaeda in the Arabian peninsula (AQAP), based principally in Yemen to escape an increasing crackdown by the Saudi authorities and led by a Yemeni, Nasir al-Wuhayshi (who was killed in Yemen by a US drone strike in June 2015).

Despite the joint counter-terrorism efforts of the US, with its drones and special forces, and the Yemeni regime with around 67,000 frontline servicemen, AQAP, thought to comprise between 1,000 and 3,000 fighters, continues to profit from the country's constant turmoil, its tribal conflicts and the divided loyalties within the government's forces. Occasionally, AQAP has suffered damaging blows, such as the drone strike that in September 2011 killed Anwar al-Awlaki, an American-born preacher whose sermons via YouTube and the internet attracted followers from the English-speaking world. Al-Awlaki was the first American citizen to be targeted and killed by the United States (his son was killed by another drone strike two weeks later).

But the setbacks have been temporary. AQAP has launched several attacks on Western embassies in Sana'a and it was thanks to Saudi intelligence that bombs disguised as printer cartridges were found in 2010 before they could be loaded on cargo planes flying to Chicago. In May 2010 an AQAP suicide bomber attacked a military parade rehearsing for Unity Day, killing over 120 and wounding some 200. In December 2013 an attack on the defence ministry left at least 52 dead. Meanwhile, AQAP's bombmaker, Saudi-born Ibrahim Hassan Tali al-Asiri, has won the grudging respect of Western intelligence agencies for his expertise – hence a $5 million bounty offered by the US for his capture (Wuhayshi had a $10 million price on his head). There is perhaps less Western respect for Ali Abdullah Saleh. His policy has frequently seemed ambiguous, not least because of his good relations with the *mujahideen* in the 1980s and 1990s: in 2010

he offered to talk to AQAP as long as it renounced violence, yet in the same year he also promised total war.

AQAP can hardly be ignored, and not just in Yemen and Saudi Arabia. In January 2015 AQAP claimed responsibility for the attack by two Frenchmen of Algerian descent on the offices in Paris of a satirical magazine, *Charlie Hebdo*, killing 11 French citizens. Within Yemen its mission to spread a fundamentalist reading of Islam includes the *takfiri* view that non-Sunnis are heretics or apostates, which automatically puts AQAP at odds with the Houthis but which may well bring marriages of convenience with anti-Houthi tribes in the south.

The question is whether AQAP will find itself playing second fiddle to the Islamic State. In April 2011, Shaykh Abu Zubayr Adil bin Abdullah al-Abab, AQAP's chief religious figure, defined an Islamist group, Ansar al-Sharia (Supporters of Islamic Law), as part of AQAP:

> *The name Ansar al-Sharia is what we use to introduce ourselves in areas where we work to tell people about our work and goals.*

The US State Department agreed: in October 2012 it defined the organisation on its list of foreign terrorist organisations as an alias for AQAP. But in February 2015 at least some members of Ansar al-Sharia pledged allegiance to the Islamic State and the following month the Islamic State claimed responsibility for co-ordinated suicide attacks on four Zaydi mosques in Sana'a, leaving at least 142 dead and 345 injured.

President Hadi condemned the attacks as heinous, but he can hardly have been surprised. For decades Yemen has been anarchic and horribly violent – and it is likely to remain so for many years to come. Rather like Afghanistan, it is a country permanently at war with itself, and one that invariably humbles interfering outsiders.

3   Africa: rich in resources, poor in governance

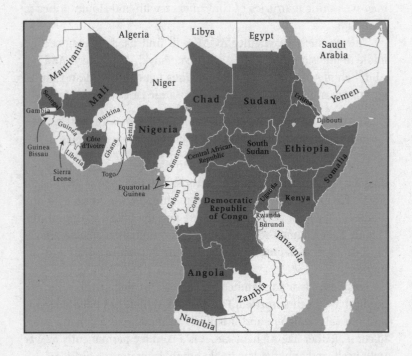

WITH OVER 50 COUNTRIES, a population of more than 800 million and myriad languages and tribes, Africa can never be a continent as homogeneous as Europe – despite frequent attempts by outsiders to fit its differences into a single mould. There is, after all, precious little similarity topographically between vast Nigeria and mountainous Ethiopia, and none at all ethnically between, say, the Ashanti of Ghana and the Hutus of Rwanda. "Black Africa" is convenient shorthand for non-Africans but means nothing other than an approximation of skin colour.

Nonetheless, there are some features depressingly common to most of the continent's countries: glaring social inequalities, young populations (usually with high rates of unemployment) and inefficient, corrupt governments. Each year a foundation created by Mo Ibrahim, a Sudanese-born British telecoms tycoon, offers a prize of $5 million – plus $200,000 a year for life – to any African head of state who has been democratically elected and who has retired after demonstrating good governance of his or her country. The prize was first offered in 2007; significantly, the foundation could find no worthy winner in 2009, 2010, 2012 and 2013.

In a continent south of the Sahara in which far too many of its nations are scarred by current conflicts, bad governance and corruption are clearly important factors. But other factors come into play, too: conflict over natural resources, from oil (as in Nigeria) to diamonds (as in the Central African Republic and the Democratic Republic of the Congo); conflict between tribes, as in Kenya or Rwanda; and conflict between religions, as in Mali and Nigeria.

Inevitably, the various factors tend to overlap. The result has been wars across frontiers – drawn by colonial powers with scant concern for ethnic or religious identities – and within frontiers. The Sierra Leone civil war of 1991–2002, for example, was encouraged by President Charles Taylor of Liberia, trading arms to the rebels in exchange for diamonds. Taylor, now serving a 50-year prison sentence imposed by the International Criminal Court (ICC) for war crimes and crimes against humanity in Sierra Leone, had himself come to power – with the help of Libya – in 1997 after a civil war in Liberia that began in 1989, and which was followed by a second civil war in 1999 that ended only in 2003 when Taylor sought refuge in Nigeria.

Without doubt, the worst of these conflicts took place in the 1990s in Rwanda, which has the distinction of being host to the only fully fledged genocide of the 21st century. The country had been scarred by ethnic conflict between the Tutsi minority and Hutu majority even before gaining independence from Belgium in 1962, with some 150,000 Tutsis seeking refuge over the years in neighbouring countries. In 1990 the Rwandan Patriotic Front (RPF), a Tutsi rebel group, launched a civil war. When an aircraft carrying President Juvénal Habyarimana of Rwanda and President Cyprien Ntaryamira (a fellow Hutu) of neighbouring Burundi was shot down in April 1994, the scene was set for a campaign to kill all Tutsis. Within 100 days some 800,000 Tutsis and moderate Hutus had been massacred by the Rwandan military and the Hutu Interahamwe militia before the RPF emerged victorious in July 1994 and established a government of national unity.

Today, Rwanda, with 12 million people, is often hailed as an example to others in Africa of modernisation and stable, effective government, with convincing efforts to bring reconciliation between Hutus and Tutsis under the policies of Paul Kagame, a former head of the RPF who has been president since 2000. But critics point to the reluctance of many Hutu refugees to return and to accusations that the Rwanda regime is assassinating political opponents – mainly Hutu – based abroad. The FDLR (Forces Démocratiques de Libération du Rwanda), the main Hutu militia in exile, declared as long ago as 2005 that it was abandoning its armed struggle, but instead it is accused of committing acts of terror and pillage in the Democratic Republic of Congo. In short, the Rwanda genocide still has consequences for much of central Africa.

It is striking, meanwhile, to see the inroads made by Islamist extremists such as Boko Haram in Nigeria. The effort to confront them – let alone defeat them – has involved US surveillance technology to hunt down Boko Haram, and European and African troops to fight in Mali. Even where Islamist extremists are not active, there can still be religiously influenced conflicts, as in the Central African Republic.

It is tempting, but in practice futile, to ascribe the blame for Africa's conflicts to the continent's colonial past, from national frontiers bearing no relationship to ethnic or religious loyalties to the desire by former colonisers to retain political and economic influence – hence, for example, the *Françafrique* policy of successive French presidents (though President François Hollande in 2012 said, unconvincingly, that it was time to bid farewell to a term that implied secret economic and political ties in France's favour). The conceit of France and the UK is that – unlike, say, Belgium – they were "good" imperialists, providing efficient civil services and spreading the benefits of education. Unfortunately, those purported benefits have not spared many of their former colonies from violence and civil war. Though Western development specialists often praise Rwanda – and, for that matter, Ethiopia – for their economic progress, Western human rights activists say it has been at the expense of civil liberties.

Yet if ill-advised national boundaries help provoke conflict, redrawing them risks creating more harm than good, which is why the African Union has traditionally insisted on the inviolability of its members' frontiers. Only Eritrea and South Sudan have succeeded in separating from a post-colonial African state.

Optimists see Africa, with its youthful population and natural resources, supplanting Asia as the continent of the 21st century. Progress towards this will doubtless be troubled, but for all the obstacles on the way it is worth noting the gains already made: since 1991 more than 30 African leaders or government have been peacefully ejected at the ballot box – a far better record than the Arab world can boast.

Angola

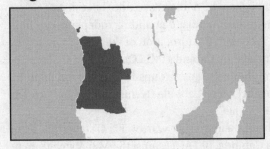

The Republic of Angola has an unenviable reputation for corruption and economic disparity. Even though the country is rich in oil (Angola joined the Organisation of Petroleum Exporting Countries, or OPEC, in 2007) and diamonds, some 40% of its 22 million people live beneath the poverty line.

Added to this dubious reputation is a history of conflict. Independence in 1975 from Portugal was achieved only after 14 years of armed struggle by the People's Movement for the Liberation of Angola (Movimento Popular de Libertação de Angola, or MPLA), the National Front for the Liberation of Angola (Frente Nacional de Libertação de Angola, or FNLA) and the National Union for the Total Independence of Angola (União Nacional para a Independência Total de Angola, or UNITA).

Independence, however, was followed by a 27-year civil war – much of it fuelled by the trade in "blood diamonds" – between the dominant MPLA, supported by the Soviet Union and Cuba, and UNITA, supported at times by the US, South Africa and Zaire (which is now the Democratic Republic of Congo). By the time the war ended in 2002 with the death in battle of UNITA's leader, Joseph Savimbi, some 1.5 million lives had been lost and 4 million people had been displaced.

Regrettably, the end of the civil war has not meant the end of conflict. The oil industry accounts for around half of Angola's GDP, and most of the oil comes from the fields offshore from the province of Cabinda, farther north on the Atlantic coast but separated from the rest of the country by the sliver of the Democratic Republic of Congo that reaches the sea. Historically, the people of Cabinda (the population now is thought to be perhaps 690,000) have distinguished themselves from the rest of Angola, demanding independence from Portugal as early as 1960 with the formation of the Movement for the Liberation of the Enclave of Cabinda (MLEC). Three years later the MLEC merged with other separatist groups to become the Front for the Liberation of the Enclave of Cabinda (Frente para a Libertação do Enclave de Cabinda, or FLEC).

The result has been a simmering war by FLEC's guerrilla army (Forças Armadas de Cabinda, or FAC) against the MPLA government, especially in the 1970s and 1980s. As is common with insurgent groups, FLEC has experienced several splits in its ranks. In August 2006 a ceasefire was declared between the Angolan government and

FLEC-Renovada, but most Cabindan groups denounced it and the main group, FLEC-FAC (that is, FLEC with the FAC), has continued its struggle.

The Angolan government has spoken of a referendum on Cabinda's status, but only with all in Angola voting. FLEC, of course, will accept a referendum voted on only by Cabindans. Angola maintains that FLEC is no longer operational as a guerrilla group, but that may be wishful thinking. In January 2010 an offshoot of FLEC calling itself the Front for the Liberation of the Enclave of Cabinda–Military Position (FLEC-PM) opened fire on a bus carrying members of the Togo football team to a match in Cabinda as part of the Africa Cup of Nations. The assistant coach, the team's spokesman and the bus driver were all killed. FLEC-PM's secretary-general, Rodrigues Mingas, said the attack had been aimed at the Angolans escorting the bus, and added: "Weapons will continue to talk." Claiming, surely unrealistically, that the self-declared Federal State of Cabinda had 50,000 armed security forces, he declared: "This is our home, and it's time Angola understood that."

The reality is that separatist movements are extraordinarily durable. In 2006 the Angolan government and the leader of the Cabinda Forum for Dialogue (FCD), António Bento Bembe (who is also the secretary-general of FLEC-FAC), signed a Memorandum of Understanding for Peace and National Reconciliation, envisaging an amnesty, the integration of guerrillas into the Angolan armed forces and a special status for Cabinda. Eight years later a meeting of FLEC leaders in the sanctuary of Lisbon declared that "the objective conditions for the resumption of a political process for Cabinda" had still not been satisfied.

Central African Republic

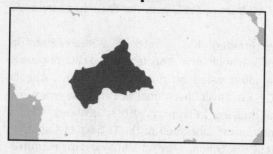

Ever since the French colony of Ubangi-Shari attained its independence in 1960 as the Central African Republic (CAR), the nation has been chronically unstable, prone to coups and stained by extraordinary levels of corruption. By all the usual economic and social measurements, the CAR is one of the world's most desperate countries – and, as a result of continuing internal conflict, one of the modern world's failed states.

Ironically, the CAR's most sustained period of political continuity came under the rule of a megalomaniac, Colonel Jean-Bédel Bokassa, who seized power at the end of 1965 and in 1976 renamed the country the Central African Empire (declaring himself Emperor Bokassa I). Bokassa was overthrown with the help of French troops in 1979, but his departure and the return of the "empire" to a mere "republic" brought only decades of coups and failed democratic endeavours, culminating in a civil war in 2004 between the government of François Bozizé (who had seized power in a 2003 coup) and a plethora of rebel groups led by the Union des Forces Démocratiques pour le Rassemblement (UFDR).

A peace accord was signed between the government and the UFDR in 2007 but was never fully implemented. In late 2012 a coalition of rebel groups, known as Séléka CPSK-CPJP-UFDR (conventionally shortened to Séléka, which means coalition in the local Sango language), seized control of several northern towns and then marched southwards to capture the capital, Bangui, in March 2013 and install their leader, Michel Djotodia, as president. The mainly Muslim Séléka followed their victory with a rampage against the country's Christians, who they said had been favoured by the

Bozizé government. In reaction, Christians formed *anti-balaka* (anti-machete in the Sango language) groups that took savage reprisals on Muslim villages. Djotodia, the country's first Muslim leader, was not accepted as president by other African governments and was forced to appoint a National Transitional Council. When he resigned in January 2014 and sought exile in Benin, Catherine Samba-Panza was elected as the republic's interim president. Born in neighbouring Chad to a Cameroonian father and a Central African mother, she was immediately mocked on the front page of one newspaper as "Samba-Panza: the president who thinks in Chadian, speaks in Cameroonian and acts in Central African".

Whether the country can manage its transition to stability seems doubtful, at least in the short term. The loyalty of the 4,500-strong armed forces – who mutinied several times in the 1990s over unpaid wages – is questionable. And the fighting between Séléka and *anti-balaka* forces is creating a partitioned country in which the Muslims – perhaps 15% of the country's 5 million people, compared with 50% for Christians and 35% for indigenous beliefs – have fled from the south. Meanwhile, the human cost has been heavy: around 1 million people have had to flee their homes and, though credible statistics are hard to find, the death toll since the 2004 civil war is in the scores of thousands.

There is a cost, too, to the outside world. Ever since its independence there have been French troops (2,400 to protect French citizens during the Séléka attacks on Bangui) in the CAR. But fellow African countries have also contributed peacekeeping troops, with the ten-nation Economic Community of Central African States providing an ineffective force of 380 troops as early as 2002. This initiative was succeeded in 2013 by an African Union-led mission of troops from Gabon, Chad, Congo-Brazzaville and Cameroon. In September 2014 the African Union force, eventually amounting to 5,000 troops, was subsumed into a UN force, MINUSCA (United Nations Multidimensional Integrated Stabilisation Mission in the Central African Republic), which boasts 10,000 soldiers and 1,820 police.

With luck, MINUSCA will safeguard the implementation of a peace agreement signed on May 10th 2015 in Bangui between the government and ten rival armed groups. The accord, under which some militiamen will be incorporated into the government's armed forces, commits the groups "to disposing their arms and renouncing armed fighting as a means of making political claims and to enter into the process of Disarmament, Demobilisation, Reinsertion and Repatriation (DDRR)". A week earlier the groups had agreed to free children they had used as soldiers, sex slaves or menial workers.

Yet the presence of so many international troops (their reputation tarnished in 2015 by accusations of child sex abuse by French soldiers) is no guarantee that the CAR will achieve a reasonable degree of stability. One reason, of course, is that memories of the ethnic and religious bloodshed will take time to fade. Another is that the country is part of a larger area of instability. In April 2014 Chad withdrew all its 800 troops from the African Union peacekeeping force after well-founded accusations that they had sided with their fellow Muslims in the Séléka forces and had killed dozens of civilians in a Bangui market. A third reason is that so many warlords and armed groups – including the small but murderous Lord's Resistance Army, fleeing from Uganda – profit from poaching ivory and trading in the country's diamonds. The sale of these diamonds, because they are the product of violent conflict, is meant to be impossible because of the ban imposed by the 2003 Kimberley Process Certification Scheme. Sadly, blood diamonds still find eager buyers and so prolong the CAR's political, social and economic tragedy.

Chad

For the 12 million population of Chad, a landlocked republic that is

Africa's fifth-largest country, life is not easy: poverty is ubiquitous; infrastructure – from roads to schools – is lacking; and life expectancy for women is 51 and for men an even less impressive 48. Whether life will get easier remains doubtful, despite the presence of uranium and recently discovered oil (now being pumped to market via a pipeline to Cameroon). Ever since gaining its independence from French Equatorial Africa in 1960, the country has been racked by civil wars, ethnic rivalries and sporadic rebellions, usually fomented by the animosity between the Arab and Muslim north of the country (Muslims account for roughly half of the population) and the mainly Christian, animist and black African south.

The sectarian tension was there from the beginning, with civil war erupting in the mid-1960s as the Muslim north, led by the Chadian National Liberation Front (Front de Libération Nationale de Tchad, or Frolinat), rejected the policies – for example the banning of political parties in 1963 – of the Christian first president, François (N'Garta) Tombalbaye. In 1973 French troops helped to quieten the revolt, but Frolinat continued its guerrilla operations, helped by military aid from Libya, throughout the 1970s and 1980s.

Libyan intervention in Chad was a constant factor for decades. Indeed, in 1977 Libya annexed the Aouzou strip in the north of the country, though its claim to the area was rejected by the International Court of Justice in 1994 (in the meantime, in 1987 a combination of French troops, Frolinat and the Chadian army had forced Libya out of most of the north). After Tombalbaye was assassinated in a 1975 coup by a fellow Christian, Félix Malloum, Libya threw its support behind a Muslim northerner, Goukouni Oueddei, who seized power in 1979. But due to Frolinat's internecine politics, Oueddei was ousted (he found exile in Libya) in 1982 by a former prime minister, Hissène Habré (who is now in exile in Senegal, where before a special court he is facing charges of crimes against humanity during his despotic rule).

Habré's rule was ended by a 1990 coup mounted by Idriss Déby, a Muslim northerner who had once been close to Habré but who in the late 1980s formed the Patriotic Salvation Movement against him with support from Libya and Sudan. But President Déby's tenure (which, following a 2005 referendum, is no longer subject to term limits) has been marked by several rebel insurgencies and frequent coup attempts. Much of this was because of support for the rebel groups from neighbouring Sudan, making a mockery of peace agreements such as the Libya-brokered – and temporary – accord in 2002 between the government and the Movement for Democracy and Justice in Chad (MDJT) or the 2003 agreement with the National Resistance Army (ANR). In 2008 a coalition of rebel groups besieged Déby in the capital N'Djamena, and were repelled only through the intervention of French troops.

Will such threats to the regime be quashed? A UN peacekeeping mission withdrew from the country at the end of 2010, with Déby's government saying it could now protect all its citizens, including along the border with Sudan. Superficially at least, Chad's argument seemed plausible, since the governments of Chad and Sudan had agreed in 2010 not to wage proxy wars in each other's country. However, the Darfur conflict in Sudan, which has led to thousands seeking refuge in Chad, remains unresolved and so is always a complicating factor. Moreover, in 2013, the Union of Forces of Resistance (UFR), a coalition of rebel groups in Chad that had put down its weapons after the 2010 agreement between Chad and Sudan, declared that it would again take up arms against Déby, since his government had refused to talk to the rebel groups.

The size of the threat is hard to assess. The UFR leader, Timane Erdimi, who is a nephew and former aide of Déby, said in 2013 from exile in Doha:

> The UFR had about 6,000 men in July 2010 and 300 vehicles. Even if we have only 50% of that now, it's a good number.

The Chadian armed forces number about 30,000, some 2,400 of them fighting alongside French troops against Islamist insurgents in Mali. But if history is any guide, their loyalty is hardly absolute. And, of course, the country is awash with weapons after the fall of Qaddafi and the disintegration of Libya. In short, stability for Chad is something to hope for rather than expect.

Côte d'Ivoire

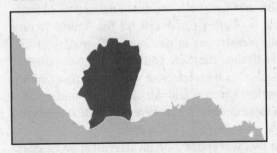

The Republic of Côte d'Ivoire – also known as Ivory Coast and the world's leading cocoa exporter – was once an enviably prosperous and stable Atlantic-coast neighbour to Liberia to the west and Ghana to the east. That stability may now be returning, but for a population of 23 million there are no guarantees given the continuing tensions, often violent, between the supporters of President Alassane Ouattara and those of the man he replaced, Laurent Gbagbo (who in November 2011 was spirited off to The Hague to face charges before the ICC of crimes against humanity). Another factor is that President Ouattara, a former senior economist at the International Monetary Fund (IMF), is in his 70s and may not be in good health (in 2014 he spent a month in France for medical treatment).

The halcyon period for Ivorians, after independence from France in 1960, were the three decades – until his death in 1993 – under the rule of President Félix Houphouët-Boigny. While Houphouët-Boigny had taken care to avoid ethnic conflict, his successor, Henri Konan Bédié, introduced the concept of *ivoirité*, a dangerous idea in a nation hosting many immigrants but deliberately used to exclude from any presidential campaign Ouattara, who had served as Houphouët-Boigny's prime minister but whose parents were apparently from Burkina Faso.

President Bédié was overthrown in 1999 and replaced by Houphouët-Boigny's former chief of the army, Robert Guéi, who after elections in 2000 lost power to Gbagbo. What soon followed were an army rebellion and civil war, from late 2002 (the year in which Guéi was killed) to the spring of 2007. In the complex mix of tribal loyalties and religious differences – the north of the country is essentially Muslim and the south, including the capital Abidjan, is mainly Christian – Gbagbo could call on the Young Patriots (Congrès Panafricain des Jeunes et des Patriotes, or COJEP) and various mercenaries against the New Forces (Forces Nouvelles, or FN) supporting Ouattara. In between were several thousand French troops under Opération Unicorn and African troops under a UN mandate (the UN Operation in Côte d'Ivoire, or UNOCI) protecting foreign residents and managing their evacuation.

This first Ivorian civil war ended with an agreement by President Gbagbo that Guillaume Soro, the leader of the FN, should be his prime minister and that the rebels would disarm. But the sectarian and tribal divisions were not to be healed. In the much delayed presidential election of 2010, Ouattara emerged as the winner – at least according to the Independent Election Commission and international observers, but not according to Gbagbo. What followed was the second Ivorian civil war, with the FN – now renamed the Republican Forces of Côte d'Ivoire (RFCI) – marching south and in April 2011, with the help of French troops and helicopters, storming Gbagbo's residence in Abidjan and installing Ouattara as president.

It would be naive, however, to imagine that the wounds of the war to topple Gbagbo will heal quickly. Some 3,000 Ivorians are said to have been killed, and although it is Gbagbo who was sent for trial in The Hague, it is clear that both sides in the conflict committed atrocities and abuses of human rights. Moreover, the desire for revenge continues. Indeed, in December 2013 Ghana accused the Côte d'Ivoire government of sending agents to kidnap or assassinate Gbagbo supporters who had taken refuge in Ghana. Significantly, Gbagbo's Ivorian Popular Front in September 2014 withdrew from the electoral commission preparing for the presidential election scheduled for October 2015 – an indication that the country remains on the brink of violence.

Democratic Republic of Congo

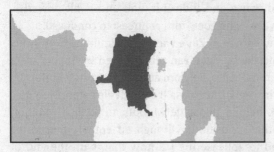

Despite their nation's vast natural resources, from diamonds, gold and rare minerals to coffee and oil, the majority of the 77 million people of the Democratic Republic of Congo (DRC) exist in poverty, their lives all too often cut short by disease or war. In 2013 the UN Development Programme ranked the DRC at the bottom of its Human Development Index; in 2014 it was beaten to that dubious distinction only by Niger. In decades of conflict, beginning in the late 1990s and involving outside forces from Rwanda and Uganda to Burundi and Angola, more than 5 million people have died – the worst death toll in conflict since the second world war.

Gaining its independence from Belgium in 1960, the Republic of Congo – as it was then termed – was immersed in conflict almost from the start, with the mineral-rich south-eastern province of Katanga, under the leadership of Moise Tshombe, seeking to secede. Early in 1961 Katangan troops, helped by Belgian forces and with CIA encouragement, kidnapped and later killed the founder of the Mouvement National Congolais, Patrice Lumumba, who had earlier been removed as the country's first prime minister by President Joseph Kasavubu.

The Katangan war ended in 1963 with an accord in which Kasavubu appointed Tshombe as his prime minister. However, their rule was short-lived: in 1965 they were ousted by the chief of the army, Joseph-Désiré Mobutu, backed by the US and Belgium. Mobutu then began a dictatorial reign of three decades marked by staggering corruption and an extraordinary personality cult. In 1971, for example, he renamed both the country, as Zaire, and himself as Mobutu Sese

Seko Kuku Ngbendu Wa Za Banga (the warrior who knows no defeat because of his endurance and inflexible will and is all powerful, leaving fire in his wake as he goes from conquest to conquest).

The country now known as Zaire was hardly immune from strife. In 1977 and 1978 attacks by Katangan rebels based in Angola were repulsed by troops from France, Belgium and Morocco. In 1991 riots by unpaid soldiers in the capital, Kinshasa (Leopoldville before Mobutu's renaming exercise), helped persuade Mobutu to form a coalition government with the opposition – though an equally persuasive factor was the need to appease the US now that, with the end of the cold war, his professed anti-communism was no longer such a valuable political asset.

The demise of the Mobutu regime came as a consequence of the civil war in neighbouring Rwanda and the victory there of a Tutsi-led government. The defeated Hutus had sought refuge in eastern Zaire, and in 1996 Mobutu ordered Tutsi residents to leave. This then provoked Tutsi rebels (the Banyamulenge), aided by troops from Rwanda and Uganda, to seize the eastern part of the country in the first Congo war. With Mobutu abroad for medical treatment, the rebels went on to occupy Kinshasa in 1997, appoint Laurent-Désiré Kabila, from the Luba tribe (the country's largest), as president and rename the country as the Democratic Republic of Congo.

Sadly, this did not mean stability. Kabila's decision to expel the Rwandan and Ugandan forces led, within a year, to the second Congo war, involving directly or indirectly some nine African nations and at least 20 armed groups. In 1999 a ceasefire agreement was signed in the Zambian capital of Lusaka by six combatant nations (the DRC, Angola, Namibia, Rwanda, Zimbabwe and Uganda), but in practice, and despite the presence of a 5,500-strong UN monitoring force, the fighting continued. In 2001 Kabila was assassinated by a bodyguard, perhaps at the behest of Rwanda, and was succeeded by his son, Joseph, who agreed to a peace accord signed in Pretoria in 2002 by all the warring parties, followed by a transitional government of national unity in July 2003 and elections in 2006.

Despite the elections, characterised by violence but with Joseph Kabila emerging as victor, coup attempts continued, as did conflict in the east, with government forces clashing with Rwandan Hutus, who ironically had once been their allies. In 2009, after yet more turmoil in the eastern part of the country, the government signed a peace deal with the National Congress for the Defence of the People (CNDP, its French abbreviation), a mostly Tutsi rebel group. However, attempts to integrate CNDP troops into the government's forces failed, provoking CNDP defectors in 2012 to set up the M23 armed movement, named after an abortive March 23rd 2009 peace accord.

The M23 movement signed a peace agreement with the government in December 2013, but it is hard to see this as a precursor to genuine stability in the DRC – despite the efforts of some 22,000 peacekeepers from more than 50 countries in a UN mission set up after the 1999 Lusaka accord. Meanwhile, there are community-based militias known as Mai-Mai; armed groups led by local warlords; and the Lord's Resistance Army (in flight from neighbouring Uganda): all continue to terrorise the population, burning villages, raping women and forcibly recruiting children as soldiers.

There have been a few examples of the perpetrators being held to account. In the first Congo war Thomas Lubanga was a commander of the pro-Uganda Congolese Rally for Democracy–Liberation (RCD–ML, its French abbreviation). He then founded the Union of Congolese Patriots (UPC) and led its military wing, the Patriotic Force for the Liberation of the Congo (FPLC). But in 2006 he became the first person to be hauled off to the ICC in The Hague for war crimes (he was found guilty in 2012).

Another to appear in The Hague is Bosco Ntaganda, a Rwandan-born Tutsi who in 2009 was a general in President Kabila's Congolese army, even though the ICC had already indicted him in 2006 on charges of conscripting child soldiers during his previous stints as a rebel commander. Ntaganda, nicknamed "the Terminator", defected with 600 soldiers from the government's side in 2012 and formed the M23 group; but it was a dispute with another M23 commander, Sultani Makenga, that led to his appearance in The Hague. Apparently fearing for his life, Ntaganda sought refuge in the US embassy in the Rwandan capital, Kigali, from where he was whisked away to face the court.

Whatever the occasional success of the ICC or of the UN peacekeepers, the underlying truth is that the DRC is close to being a failed state, prone to constant conflict, especially in the five eastern provinces of Orientale, North Kivu, South Kivu, Maniema and Katanga. Insurgents from neighbouring countries, such as Uganda's Allied Democratic Forces (ADF), Rwanda's Forces Démocratiques de Libération du Rwanda (FDLR) and Burundi's Forces Nationales de Libération (FNL), use the DRC territory as a haven and prey on the local population. At the same time Rwanda aids Congolese Tutsi groups rebelling against Kinshasa and confronting the DRC army. Most depressing of all, perhaps, is the simple fact that so many warlords – Ntanganda was a good example – profit so handsomely from illegal logging, "conflict diamonds" and other aspects of the war economy. As Peace Direct, a non-governmental organisation, has pointed out, peace agreements in the DRC have often been flawed, allowing rebel commanders to join the national army and yet keep their illegal moneymaking networks intact.

Eritrea

The 6 million inhabitants of the State of Eritrea have the misfortune to live in the African equivalent of North Korea, condemned to poverty and frequent famine and to the dictatorial rule of President Isaias Afewerki – in office since independence in 1993 – and his People's Front for Democracy and Justice (PFDJ). As a result the UN High Commissioner for Refugees estimates that despite the government's ban on free departure from the country, over 357,000 Eritreans, around 6% of the population, have managed to flee since 2003.

A constitution was ratified in 1997, but by 2015 it had still not gone into effect, leaving the PFDJ as the only political party recognised by the government. The PFDJ has strong roots in the independence movement, as the heir to the Eritrean People's Liberation Front (EPLF), a Marxist-Leninist group, led by Afewerki, which broke away in 1970 from the Eritrean Liberation Front (ELF), the guerrillas who had been fighting for independence from Ethiopia since 1961. The ELF was itself the child of the Eritrean Liberation Movement, formed in 1958.

The legacy of the EPLF's long years of warfare is doubtless one factor in Eritrea's bellicose attitude to the world and its occasionally violent tensions with its neighbours. But the greater factor is the relationship with Ethiopia. Both countries (though Ethiopia only briefly) were colonies of Italy until British and Commonwealth troops ousted the Italians in 1941. The British then administered Eritrea, from 1949 as a UN trust territory, until in 1952 the UN made Eritrea an autonomous region of the Ethiopian federation. Ten years later Ethiopia's Emperor Haile Selassie formally annexed Eritrea, making it a province of Ethiopia and condemning both countries to three decades of war.

The incentives for both sides to gain victory were clear enough: Eritrea shared few ethnic or linguistic links with Ethiopia, while landlocked Ethiopia coveted access to the Red Sea through Eritrean territory. In 1991 the EPLF finally defeated the Ethiopian army and then, in 1993, after an overwhelming referendum vote for independence, Eritrea joined the UN.

Tragically for the people of Eritrea, where men are expected to perform national military service until the age of 40, independence did not bring tranquillity. In 1995 Eritrean troops invaded the Yemeni-held Red Sea islands of Hanish (three years later international arbitration gave the biggest island to Yemen and the others to Eritrea). Between 1998 and 2001 a border war with Ethiopia claimed some 70,000 lives, and left Ethiopia in charge of the town of Badme, which it still controls, despite an international boundary commission ruling in 2007 that the town belonged to Eritrea.

Eritrea's fraught relationship with Ethiopia has not been an isolated example of tensions with the neighbours. Sudan in 2002 accused Eritrea of aiding rebels in eastern Sudan, and the UN in 2006 charged Eritrea with supplying weapons to Islamist fighters in Somalia (Eritrea denied the charge and accused Ethiopia of aiding the Islamists). In 2008 Eritrean troops clashed with Djibouti's in a disputed border area, and in 2011 the UN accused Eritrea of plotting to attack an African Union summit in the Ethiopian capital, Addis Ababa.

Given President Afewerki's despotic rule and the turbulent politics of the Horn of Africa region, it seems extremely unlikely that Eritrea will achieve peace at home or abroad in the short or even the medium term. The UN Security Council voted unanimously in 2008 to end the UN peacekeeping mission monitoring the border with Ethiopia, and the UN has imposed several military and economic sanctions on Eritrea for its support of armed insurgencies in the region. For Eritrea's opposition groups, such as the Eritrean National Salvation Front (ENSF), Ethiopia provides a safe haven: in September 2013 two of these groups, the Red Sea Afar Democratic Organisation (RSADO) and the Saho People's Democratic Movement (SPDM), agreed, in the words of a spokesman:

> *To jointly carry out military attacks to topple the oppressive regime and to eventually place a new democratic rule that respects the rights of the Eritrean people.*

In March 2015 a unit of the ENSF destroyed government vehicles at a garage south-east of Asmara, later issuing a statement saying that the organisation "doesn't target the helpless Eritrean army but the regime and anyone who supports it".

Ethiopia

Living in the largest nation in the Horn of Africa, Ethiopia's 97 million people, just over 60% of them Christians (around 30% are Muslim), endure not just grinding poverty and occasional devastating famines but also tense – and at times violent – relations with almost all their neighbours.

Apart from the five years from 1936 to 1941 of occupation by Mussolini's Italy, Ethiopia's ancient monarchy was able to keep the country free from colonial rule – a unique achievement in the African continent. But the monarchy is no more, with Emperor Haile Selassie toppled in 1974 by a Marxist junta known as the Derg, led by Mengistu Haile Mariam (though General Teferi Benti was the official head of state until he was killed in 1977). The Derg was in turn overthrown in 1991 by a rebel coalition led by the Ethiopian People's Revolutionary Democratic Front (EPRDF), hence a change in the country's official name: no longer the People's Democratic Republic of Ethiopia, but now the Federal Democratic Republic of Ethiopia.

The overthrow of the monarchy brought Ethiopia's citizens decades of violence. The Derg (properly known as the Provisional Military Administrative Council, or PMAC) introduced collectivised agriculture and enforced its extreme Marxism with a regime of "red terror" between 1976 and 1978 in which thousands (estimates range from 30,000 to 500,000) died, often from hunger. Meanwhile, the late 1970s brought threats to the Derg's authority: the Tigrayan People's Liberation Front began an armed struggle for the autonomy of the Tigray region in the north of the country; and in 1977 troops from neighbouring Somalia invaded the Ogaden region in the southeast (they were repulsed the following year with the help of 15,000 combat troops from Cuba and aid from the Soviet Union).

The Derg's red terror was opposed by the "white terror" of the EPRDF, a geographically and ethnically diverse coalition of the Oromo People's Democratic Organisation (OPDO), the Amhara National Democratic Movement (ANDM), the South Ethiopia People's Democratic Front (SEPDF) and the Tigrayan People's Liberation Front (TPLF). With the Derg's authority weakened by the famines of the 1980s and then by the collapse of the Soviet Union, the EPRDF seized the capital, Addis Ababa, in 1991 and established a transitional government that led to multi-party elections in 1995 and the appointment as prime minister – and, in effect, the nation's leader

– of Meles Zenawi (the Derg's leader, Mengistu Haile Mariam, fled in exile to Zimbabwe). Zenawi died in office in 2012 and was succeeded by his deputy, Hailemariam Desalegn. Remarkably, this has been the first peaceful transfer of power in Ethiopia's post-monarchic history.

Just as remarkable, perhaps, was Ethiopia's defeat in 1991 in a war with Eritrean separatists dating back to Haile Selassie's annexation of Eritrea in 1962. Given the disparity in population between the two sides, the victory by the Eritreans is a tribute to their resilience and determination, and the imbalance of their armed forces: Ethiopia today has 182,500 active personnel in its military, far fewer than the 320,000 pressed into service in Eritrea.

The relationship with Eritrea remains the most sensitive issue of Ethiopian foreign policy. Frequent border clashes with Eritrea, which formally gained its independence in 1993, led to a full-scale war in 1999 that was ended, at least on paper, by a peace deal signed in Algiers at the end of 2000. However, Ethiopia has maintained control of the disputed border town of Badme, despite it having been ruled by international arbiters to be part of Eritrea.

Another source of tension with Eritrea is both countries' relationship with neighbouring Somalia. Ethiopia, which accuses Eritrea of supporting Somalia's Islamists, sent troops into Somalia in late 2006 to confront the Islamists and in January 2007 routed the so-called Islamic Courts Union in the Somali capital, Mogadishu. In 2009 Ethiopia announced the withdrawal of its troops from Somalia, but that has not stopped Ethiopian reconnaissance missions on Somali soil and frequent clashes with the Somali Islamists known as al-Shabab (the Young Men in Arabic). Nor has it stopped efforts by the Ogaden National Liberation Front (ONLF) to gain independence for their ethnically Somali region of Ethiopia.

One bright spot for landlocked Ethiopia in its relations with the neighbours is that the self-proclaimed state of Somaliland, which declared its independence from the rest of Somalia in 1991, gives Ethiopia access to the Gulf of Aden and so the Indian Ocean through the port of Berbera (it was the denial of access to the sea that underlined Ethiopia's opposition to Eritrean secession). Less comforting, however, is Ethiopia's relationship with Egypt, which worries that Ethiopian construction of the Grand Renaissance Dam on the Nile will jeopardise the supply of sufficient water to Egypt.

Given the instability throughout the Horn of Africa and also in neighbouring South Sudan, Ethiopia – if only because of its geographical position, size and military assets – can hardly be immune from the region's conflicts (in August 2014 the UN declared that Ethiopia has supplanted Kenya as the continent's leading host of refugees). Ogaden separatism is not about to disappear; nor will boundary disputes with Eritrea and South Sudan. Most likely of all is continuing Ethiopian involvement, directly or indirectly, in Somalia, with Ethiopia – which gets substantial annual aid from the US – acting, along with Kenya, as the regional power best able to confront Islamic extremism there.

Kenya

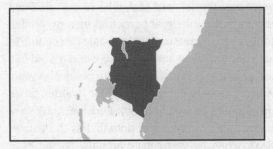

The Republic of Kenya boasts the largest economy in east Africa, but its position in the perennially troubled Horn of Africa and its own recent history of ethnic conflict threaten the health of its tourism sector – the country's largest source of foreign exchange. For Kenya's 45 million people political and regional stability has long been more wished for than realised.

The disputed presidential election of December 2007, for example, led to two months of violence, principally between the Kikuyu community and members of the Luo and Kalenjin ethnic groups, with the defeated candidate, Raila Odinga, a Luo, protesting that the voting had been rigged. The conflict, which caused the ICC to accuse prominent politicians of crimes against humanity, led to around 1,500 deaths and displaced tens of thousands. In September 2013 al-Shabab militants from neighbouring Somalia, demanding the withdrawal of

Kenyan troops from Somalia, occupied a shopping mall in the Kenyan capital, Nairobi, and killed more than 60. In April 2015 al-Shabab gunmen attacked a university in eastern Kenya, killing 148, mainly students. In short, Kenya is experiencing troubled times.

This is not a new experience. Independence from the UK in 1963 came after a decade of warfare, with atrocities on both sides, pitting British troops against a mainly Kikuyu guerrilla group known as the Mau Mau and involving (according to the British colonial courts) Jomo Kenyatta and the Kenya African National Union party (KANU). Kenyatta became the independent nation's first president, remaining in office until his death in 1978. Kenyatta was praised, not least by the British, as a great African statesman – proof, as so often, of the clichéd truism that "one man's terrorist is another's freedom fighter", and that gaining power is the best form of rehabilitation.

Kenyatta's successor was Daniel arap Moi, who in 1982 declared that KANU was henceforth the sole legal party and then proceeded to dismay foreign donors with increasing levels of state corruption. In late 1991 Moi bowed to domestic and foreign pressure (foreign aid had been suspended) and agreed to accept a multi-party political system. However, the opposition parties, weakened by ethnic rivalries, failed to dislodge KANU in elections in 1992 and 1997. Both elections were marred by violence and fraud, but Moi was nonetheless the winner and served until 2002, when he was constitutionally barred from standing again. In a fair and peaceful election Mwai Kibaki, leader of the multi-ethnic National Rainbow Coalition (NARC), defeated KANU's Uhuru Kenyatta (son of Jomo), marking the first defeat for KANU in what appeared to be a turning point in Kenyan democracy.

This turned out to be an illusion. Defectors from NARC joined KANU and formed the Orange Democratic Movement (ODM). Kibaki was re-elected president in 2007 amid accusations of massive fraud by Odinga, the ODM candidate, and the country quickly plunged into the politically motivated ethnic carnage that still commands the attention of the ICC. African Union-sponsored mediation by Kofi Annan, a Ghanaian former UN secretary-general, in 2008 resulted in a power-sharing agreement under which Odinga became prime minister. However, according to a new constitution approved by a national referendum in 2010, this post was to be abolished following the next presidential election. This took place in March 2013. With Kibaki barred from running for a third term, Uhuru Kenyatta defeated Odinga by some 830,000 votes. As his running mate, Kenyatta chose William Ruto from the rival Kalenjin group in the so-called Jubilee alliance. This gesture of reconciliation, however, did not stop the ICC from pursuing cases against both men for their alleged role in the violence of 2007 – though the prosecutor in December 2014 dropped her case against President Kenyatta, citing a lack of co-operation by Kenya and her failure to gather sufficient evidence.

Although tribal tensions are endemic to Kenya's politics, the country is bound also to suffer repercussions from external strife – notably in the need to play host to well over 500,000 refugees and displaced persons, from Ugandans fleeing the Lord's Resistance Army to asylum seekers from the Democratic Republic of Congo. The greatest number, however, are the 426,000 Somalis, their presence reflecting the continuing turmoil in neighbouring Somalia.

Kenya's relationship with Somalia is historically fraught, not least because of attitudes towards Kenya's own Somali inhabitants (the newly independent Kenya in 1963 fought the four-year long *Shifta*, or "bandit", war to prevent their joining Somalia). In 1984 Kenyan troops massacred as many as 3,000 or more ethnic Somalis at the Wagalla airstrip in the north-east of the country (a truth and reconciliation commission was eventually set up in 2011 to investigate the Wagalla massacre).

Where Kenya and Somalia do agree is on the need to combat the extreme Islamist al-Shabab group. In 2011 Kenyan troops (the Kenyan military numbers 24,000 frontline personnel) supported Somali troops in "Operation Linda Nchi" against al-Shabab and later became part of the 22,000-strong African Union force in the country. In response al-Shabab, which has plenty of Kenyan Somali members, has vowed to take revenge – and has on several occasions carried out its pledge.

Al-Shabab's attack on Nairobi's Westgate shopping mall in September 2013 drew television coverage and headlines around the world, but perhaps even more damaging to Kenya's tourism industry was a June 2014 attack, killing 65 people who could not identify themselves as ethnically Somali and Muslim, in and around the coastal town of Mpeketoni, uncomfortably close to Kenya's Lamu island and other resorts. Al-Shabab issued a chilling statement:

> *We hereby warn the Kenyan government and its public that as long as you continue to invade our lands and oppress innocent Muslims, such attacks will continue and the prospect of peace and stability in Kenya will be but a distant mirage. Do not ever dream of living peacefully in your lands while your forces kill the innocent in our lands.*

This threat doubtless reminded Kenya's security forces that al-Shabab is part of the al-Qaeda franchise, and it was al-Qaeda operatives who in 1998 bombed the US embassy in Nairobi, killing 224 people and injuring thousands.

In the short term it seems unlikely that Kenyans can look forward to a tranquil future. In domestic politics tribal and ethnic differences remain too sharp to fade quickly (ethnic Somalis are particularly at risk of violent discrimination). At the same time, Kenya will find Somalia's internal wars dangerously contagious. There is, too, the risk that Somali criminality, notably piracy and the kidnapping of foreigners for ransom, will on occasion spill over into Kenya and affect its tourism industry (in a raid on a Kenyan beach resort in December 2011 Somali pirates shot a British holidaymaker and then held his wife hostage in Somalia for the following six months). Yet the gloom should not be overdone: with its vibrant and fast-growing economy, Kenya is a nation that many in the region, from the Great Lakes to the Horn of Africa, will justly admire – and envy.

Mali

The Republic of Mali was once a proud (if rare) example of democracy in Africa, even though its people, now numbering over 16 million,

were among the poorest in the world. Today, the country remains nearly destitute and struggles to end an internal conflict that pits the Berber and Arab north against the black African south and involves not just Tuareg separatists and al-Qaeda incomers but also the French military and an array of troops from other African countries.

Just how Mali reached this point is a lesson in the politics of race, geopolitics and the rise of Islamist extremism. In the 14th century the empire of Mali covered an area twice the size of France and controlled much of the trade across the Sahara. Conquered by France in the 19th century, Mali became known as French Sudan and then in 1959 entered a union – the Mali Federation – with Senegal. A year later Senegal left the federation and Mali attained its independence as a one-party, socialist state under Modibo Keïta. After eight years of Keïta's rule, in 1968 Lieutenant Moussa Traoré mounted a successful (and bloodless) coup.

The Traoré regime dealt harshly with dissent – much of it arising from the austerity measures imposed on Mali by the IMF – but did eventually allow limited political freedom. In part this was a reaction to ethnic violence in the north, exacerbated by the return to Mali of large numbers of the nomadic Tuareg, who had earlier escaped a prolonged drought by migrating to Libya and Algeria and who now clashed with the sedentary population. The Traoré government, however, was powerless to resist the popular demonstrations that may have taken their inspiration from the collapse of communism in faraway Europe. In March 1991, after the military had been ordered to fire on the demonstrators (around 100 were killed), the troops joined the protesters and, led by Amadou Toumani Touré, arrested Traoré, overthrew his regime and established a transitional government. This led to multi-party democracy, the election as president in 1992 of Alpha Oumar Konaré and a period of political stability (Konaré served two terms as president, the maximum under the constitution, before being succeeded in 2002 by Touré).

The stability was not to last, even though President Touré had included in his government members of the country's various political parties. In January 2012 Tuareg militias – many of them returning from their pro-Qaddafi involvement in the Libyan civil war – began an insurrection in their quest for an independent homeland for the

Tuareg people in northern Mali to be known as Azawad. In March President Touré, criticised for his inability to end the insurrection, was ousted in a coup by mutinous troops led by Amadou Sanogo, who proclaimed himself the leader of the National Committee for Recovering Democracy and Restoring the State (CNRDRE, its French abbreviation). Mediation by the Economic Community of West African States (ECOWAS) succeeded in restoring a civilian administration in April under Dioncounda Traoré as Mali's interim president, but in the same month the National Movement for the Liberation of Azawad (MNLA, its French abbreviation) was able to proclaim Azawad's independence.

The difficulty for the MNLA was that its Islamist allies then turned against it: Ansar al-Dine (helpers of the religion – led by a Tuareg, Iyad ag Ghaly), al-Qaeda in the Islamic Maghreb (AQIM) and an AQIM offshoot, the Movement for Belief in One God and Jihad in West Africa (MUJAO, its French abbreviation), collaborated to impose stern *sharia* law on a region hitherto characterised by tolerance (music, for which Mali is famous, was banned and Muslim shrines were destroyed as idolatrous). By July 2012 the MNLA had lost control of northern cities such as Timbuktu to the Islamists.

With government troops proving to be ill disciplined and ineffective, the Islamist forces seized the central town of Konna in January 2013 and seemed intent on marching south to seize the capital, Bamako, at which point a desperate President Traoré asked France's President François Hollande to intervene. Belying his reputation for indecision, Hollande dispatched 2,500 troops in "Opération Serval" (Operation Wildcat) to repel the Islamists' advance – which they did in quick order, driving them from Timbuktu and other major towns. By April, French troops, which by then numbered around 4,000, began a partial withdrawal as other African forces arrived to support the Malian military under a UN-sanctioned African-led International Support Mission in Mali, AFISMA (which subsequently became the 9,000-strong United Nations Multidimensional Integrated Stabilisation Mission in Mali, or MINUSMA).

The French success brought relative calm. In June 2013 the MNLA signed a peace accord with the government, so paving the way for presidential elections in the summer, won by Ibrahim Boubacer Keïta, and for France formally to hand over peacekeeping responsibility to MINUSMA.

The calm did not last. Clashes between government forces and Tuareg separatists resumed in late 2013; in May 2014 the separatists seized control of the north-eastern city of Kidal and several other towns; in September the MNLA opened an Azawad "embassy" in the Netherlands; and in October nine UN peacekeepers from Niger were killed in an ambush, a month after ten Chadian peacekeepers had been killed. Six months later, in April 2015, the Coordination of Azawad Movements (CMA, its French abbreviation) representing five rebel groups, including the MNLA, clashed with UN peacekeepers in Timbuktu and captured the nearby town of Léré.

One apparent reason for the continuing violence is the departure of so many of the French forces in Mali to join France's "Opération Barkhane", a counter-terrorism force headquartered in the Chad capital, N'Djamena, which aims to defeat Islamic extremism across the whole of the Sahel region. This task will be neither easy nor quick – which means that Mali's travails are far from over.

Nigeria

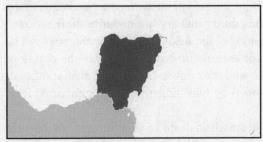

With a population of around 180 million, the Federal Republic of Nigeria is Africa's most populous country, and, with its petroleum reserves, potentially its richest. Yet ever since gaining independence from the UK in 1960, Nigeria, with more than 350 different ethnic groups and languages, has been cursed by tribal conflicts and by tensions between the largely Christian south and the mainly Muslim north.

In the 21st century the most notorious threat to the state's stability has been – and remains – the violence meted out by the Jama'atu Ahlis Sunna Lidda'Awati Wal-Jihad (Assembly of People Committed to the Propagation of the Prophet's Teachings and Jihad), better known as Boko Haram (loosely translated from the Hausa language as "Western education is forbidden"). At its most basic, the country is divided between a Muslim north, increasingly prone to Boko Haram attacks and dominated by the Hausa and Fulani people, and a mainly Christian south, where the Yoruba and Igbo are dominant.

But that division is not the only one. In 1967 three of Nigeria's south-eastern states, dominated by the Igbo tribe, attempted to break away as the republic of Biafra, plunging the nation into a savage civil war that lasted for three years. The Biafrans, led by Colonel Odumegwu Ojukwu, were supported behind the scenes by France, but were defeated by the military regime of General Yakubu Gowon, a Christian from a minority tribe in the centre of the country who enjoyed the backing of both the UK and the Soviet Union.

The defeat of separatism did not, however, bring stability to a country where military juntas held sway between 1966 and 1979 and between 1983 and 1998. General Gowon, for example, was ousted in a coup in 1975 and his immediate successor was assassinated the following year. Whether during military rule or during the democratic interlude at the beginning of the 1980s, Nigeria was characterised by extraordinary levels of corruption, especially during the tenure of General Sani Abacha, who took power in 1993 and died in office in 1998 – possibly poisoned by two Indian prostitutes imported from Dubai.

In the aftermath of Abacha's death Nigeria turned to democracy, first in 1999 with the election of Olusegun Obasanjo, a Yoruba former head of the military who had been the country's military dictator in 1976–79. Obasanjo was re-elected in 2003 in a poll flawed by serious irregularities, according to European Union observers. The presidential election in 2007 was won by Umaru Yar'Adua, an aristocratic Fulani from the north of the country. After his death in 2010, vice-president Goodluck Jonathan, a Christian from the Ijaw ethnic group in the coastal state of Bayelsa, assumed the leadership role before himself winning the presidential election of March 2011.

Given that Jonathan was then defeated in the presidential election of March 2015 by Muhammadu Buhari, it could be that Nigeria's democracy is here to stay, since Buhari was the first opposition candidate in Nigerian history to defeat an incumbent. Sceptics will note that President Buhari, a Muslim from the northern state of Katsina, has been head of state before, as the country's military ruler in 1984–85 after the December 31st 1983 coup against the civilian president, Shehu Shagari. But Buhari's appeal to many – Christian as well as Muslim – will be his reputation for incorruptibility and discipline.

The defeated President Jonathan's given name was perhaps unfortunate. One reason is the failure of his government – as with all its predecessors – to bring peace to the petroleum-rich Niger Delta region in the south. Local ethnic groups, particularly the Ogoni and Ijaw, protest that they have been deprived of the benefits of the region's oil. They object, too, to the environmental degradation of their land, accusing Royal Dutch Shell in particular of being responsible. At the beginning of the 1990s the Movement for the Survival of the Ogoni People (MOSOP) was formed to bring the Ogoni cause to the world's attention; but the Abacha regime reacted in 1995 by executing nine MOSOP activists, including its leader, Ken Saro-Wiwa, an internationally renowned playwright.

Although MOSOP advocates non-violence, the Delta has suffered decades of armed unrest: government troops have opened fire on civilians; employees of Shell and other oil companies have been kidnapped; and various ethnic groups have clashed with each other over compensation paid by the oil companies. In addition, local organisations indulge in "oil bunkering", siphoning off oil from the pipelines for their own profit – a practice fraught with both danger and the threat of violence from rivals or from the military.

Perhaps not surprisingly, several militant organisations emerged and resorted to armed conflict in the early years of the 21st century. The Movement for the Emancipation of the Niger Delta (MEND), which launched its first kidnapping operation in January 2006, has acted as an umbrella for several militant organisations that threaten multinational corporations with kidnapping and sabotage. Operating beyond the MEND umbrella are other groups, such as the Niger Delta

People's Volunteer Force (NDPVF), which was formed in late 2003 and has threatened outright war against the oil industry.

Given the importance of the oil industry to the Nigerian economy, it is obviously in the government's interest to resolve the region's dissent – hence an amnesty declared in 2009 for any militant willing to lay down his weapons. The amnesty has been broadly successful, but not completely. Many militant commanders have laid down their arms, but others have refused, not least in order to take advantage of the opportunities for personal gain. The result is continuing insecurity in the Niger Delta: nine people were kidnapped and three policemen were killed in just a few days in October 2014.

The conflict in the Niger Delta is a chronic problem for the government in the capital, Abuja. But a more serious one, in terms of the loss of Nigerian lives and the stain on Nigeria's international reputation is the struggle with Boko Haram – especially given that Boko Haram's fighters number around 9,000 while the Nigerian armed forces have some 130,000 active frontline personnel.

Boko Haram gained worldwide attention in April 2014 when its fighters abducted more than 200 schoolgirls from Chibok, a town in the northern region of Borno. This act, coupled with the threat that the girls would be sold into slavery or be raped by Boko Haram fighters, provoked an international campaign, "Bring Back Our Girls", backed by the US.

Yet if Boko Haram was little known outside Africa, it was depressingly familiar to Nigerians themselves. Founded in 2002 in Maiduguri, the capital of the north-eastern state of Borno, by Muhammad Yusuf, a cleric following the fundamentalist Salafist strain of Islam, its declared aim is to establish an Islamic state in Nigeria, complete with *sharia* law. Though Boko Haram did not at first advocate violence, there were frequent deadly clashes over the years between Christians and Muslims (for example, at least 216 deaths occurred in November 2002 during riots after a newspaper had commented that the Prophet Muhammad, if still alive, would have married a beauty queen at the Miss World pageant – abruptly cancelled – in Abuja).

The turning point for Boko Haram came in 2009 when its members refused to follow a motorcycle-helmet law and then suffered a violent police crackdown. In the armed uprising that followed across the north of Nigeria at least 800 died, and Yusuf died – or was executed – in police custody. His successor, Abubakar Shekau, has been reported killed several times; but he was certainly alive during the Chibok abductions, by which time Boko Haram had killed some 5,000 civilians, some 2,000 of them in the first half of 2014.

Most worrying perhaps for the Nigerian authorities are the apparent links between Boko Haram (designated a terrorist organisation by the United States only in November 2013) and al-Qaeda in the Islamic Maghreb (AQIM), Somalia's al-Shabab and al-Qaeda in the Arabian peninsula. AQIM is said to have supplied Boko Haram fighters with training and weapons, and it is certainly true that Boko Haram has begun to use such al-Qaeda tactics as suicide bombers (for example, the 2011 attack on the UN headquarters in Abuja). Another example was an attack, resulting in more than 30 deaths, by two suicide bombers on the marketplace in Yola in north-eastern Nigeria in June 2015 – three months after Shekau pledged allegiance to the Islamic State. Given that President Buhari had declared at his inauguration in May that his command centre would be moved from Abuja to Maiduguri, this latest in a virtually daily sequence of attacks smacked of a deliberate challenge to the new regime.

An additional headache for the government is that Boko Haram is not the only Islamist organisation threatening the state. Jama'atu Ansarul Muslimina Fi Biladis-Sudan (Vanguards for the Protection of Muslims in Black Lands), better known as Ansaru, was an offshoot of Boko Haram formed in the northern city of Kano in January 2012 by Abu Usama al-Ansari, who denounced Boko Haram as "inhuman to the Muslim *umma* [community]".

Ansari, whose original identity is thought to be Mamman Nur or perhaps Khalid al-Barnawi, both former Boko Haram commanders, has a point, given the number of Muslim civilian deaths caused by Boko Haram. Whereas Boko Haram concentrates on Nigerian targets, Ansaru focuses its attacks on Western interests, not least by kidnapping – and sometimes executing – Western expatriates. Furthermore, Ansaru's ambitions for an Islamic caliphate spreading into Niger and Cameroon go well beyond Nigeria's borders and so link up with those of AQIM.

None of this augurs well for a Nigeria free from conflict. Whereas offers of an amnesty and economic aid may well bring stability to the Niger Delta, the government seems at a loss when confronted by the Islamist insurgents, whose cause is perversely helped by the brutality of the Nigerian military. Describing Boko Haram as "better armed and better motivated than our own troops", the Borno state governor concluded in February 2014: "Given the present state of affairs, it is absolutely impossible for us to defeat Boko Haram."

Senegal

Since gaining its independence from France in 1960, the Republic of Senegal has maintained an enviable reputation for stable, democratic government. With more than 90% of its 13.6 million people adhering to Sunni Islam, there are none of the religious divisions that cause conflict elsewhere in sub-Saharan Africa. Léopold Sédar Senghor, who as the country's first president was in office from 1960 to the end of 1980, was both a distinguished poet and the first African to be elected to the Académie française. The second president, Abdou Diouf, was in office until 2000, and the third, Abdoulaye Wade, until 2012, when he gracefully accepted defeat by Macky Sall in a controversial attempt to win a third term in office.

Yet it would be naive to conclude that Senegal, for all its achievements, is a democratic paradise. The Casamance region in the south, separated from most of the rest of Senegal by the intrusion of the Gambia from the Atlantic coastline, feels that it is not properly rewarded for its agricultural richness. It also feels ethnically separate: about two-fifths of the Senegalese are from the Wolof ethnic group;

by contrast the majority in Casamance are Jola (Diola in the French transliteration), who comprise a mere 4% of the nation and are mainly Christian – hence a long-running demand for secession by the Movement of Democratic Forces of Casamance (Mouvement des Forces Démocratiques de la Casamance, or MFDC).

The Casamance rebellion began in December 1982 when hundreds of demonstrators in the regional capital, Ziguinchor, replaced the national flag flying over public buildings with the white flag of Casamance. But the armed wing of the MFDC did not mount its attacks in earnest until the end of the 1980s. In the ensuing years of government repression and MFDC assaults, more than 10,000 of the Casamance population have sought refuge in the Gambia or Guinea-Bissau, and the death toll may have been as many as 5,000 (hundreds have been killed by landmines). Unsurprisingly, the conflict has at times involved the armed forces of both the Gambia and, especially, Guinea-Bissau in their attempts to halt cross-border raids by Senegalese forces and arms smuggling by the separatists. The attitude of Guinea-Bissau was initially supportive of the MFDC, but by early in the 21st century Guinea-Bissau had allied itself to the Senegal government.

A ceasefire was signed in 2004, but it had little effect – not least because the MFDC had already split into rival factions, notably a Front Nord, which had abandoned violence, and a hardline Front Sud. Conceivably, true peace will also elude the unilateral ceasefire announced in April 2014 by Salif Sadio, leader of the MFDC's hardliners. Given that the MFDC probably has no more than a few hundred fighters, secession or even an enhanced autonomy for Casamance are surely unwinnable. Moreover, the presence of the thousands of refugees in neighbouring countries, the displacement of many more thousands within Casamance, the complex international politics of west Africa, and the fact that guerrilla fighters may well have a vested financial interest in a continuing conflict mean that although violence may have lessened, a durable settlement will demand political imagination.

Somalia

The Federal Republic of Somalia is perhaps the poster child (along with Yemen and more recently Libya) of the 21st century's failed states. Ever since Muhammad Siad Barre, a military strongman from the Marehan Darod clan who had himself attained power in a coup, was ousted in 1991 after almost 22 years in power, this nation in the Horn of Africa has been beset by the internecine violence of its various clans and by frequent conflict with neighbouring Ethiopia, Kenya and Djibouti. These problems have been exacerbated by famine and economic failure (the most profitable Somali business for much of this century has been piracy, undertaken initially to deter foreign fishing boats illegally exploiting Somali waters but soon simply to extract large ransoms from the seizure of oil tankers and other foreign-owned vessels, big and small). The statistics of political and economic failure include some 1.1 million refugees, a similar number of internally displaced persons, and a death toll from civil war and famine estimated at 350,000–500,000.

Making this dismal picture even more dispiriting is the presence of Islamist extremism in the form of al-Shabab (the Young Men in Arabic), a group affiliated with al-Qaeda and responsible for deadly terrorist attacks not just within Somalia but also in neighbouring Kenya. Meanwhile, the notion of Somalia as a federation stretches credulity: the northern part of the country, which was in colonial times a British protectorate and which had rebelled against the Siad Barre regime during the 1980s, declared unilateral independence in 1991 as Somaliland after Siad Barre's overthrow. In a similar disaffection with central authority, the Puntland region in the north-east declared its autonomy as the Puntland State of Somalia – in practice, quasi-independence – in 1998.

Somaliland, with about 3.5 million people, and Puntland, with some 4 million, occasionally clash with each other over border claims. Without doubt both are more stable than Somalia as a whole (Somaliland has held a series of free elections), but foreign governments advise that no part is safe, as illustrated in an October 2014 note from the US State Department that remains relevant:

> *Terrorist operatives and armed groups in Somalia have demonstrated their intent to attack Somali authorities, the African Union Mission in Somalia (AMISOM), and other non-military targets. Kidnapping, bombings, murder, illegal roadblocks, banditry, and other violent incidents and threats to US citizens and other foreign nationals can occur in any region of Somalia. In addition, there is a particular threat to foreigners in places where large crowds gather and Westerners frequent, including airports, government buildings, and shopping areas. Inter-clan and inter-factional fighting can flare up with little or no warning. This type of violence has resulted in the deaths of Somali nationals and the displacement of more than one million people.*

Almost all the 12 million people of Somalia (according to a government estimate in 2015) are Sunni Muslim, but their religious uniformity does not imply national coherence. When Somalis in the surrounding countries are included, the total Somali population is perhaps 14 million, but a common ethnicity and culture come second to clan loyalties. There are four main "noble" clans in Somalia: Darod, Dir, Hawiye and Isaaq. But there are lesser clans and myriad sub-clans, giving enormous scope for politics to be conducted by warlords rather than ideologues.

Foreign states enter at their peril into Somalia's internal strife. After the dictatorial Siad Barre was ousted by clans supported by Libya and by Ethiopia's leftist Derg government, the country fell into a chaotic civil war between two rival clan warlords, Mohamed Farah Aideed and Ali Mahdi Mohamed. This led to the arrival of American marines in December 1992 ahead of a 35,000-strong UN peacekeeping force from a dozen countries. Their mission was to restore order after a year in which some 300,000 Somalis had been killed and international donations of food had constantly been siphoned off by looters and gangsters.

So much for good intentions. In October 1993, after American marines had tried to arrest two of Aideed's officers, Somali militiamen shot down two US Black Hawk helicopters (hence the 2001 Hollywood film *Black Hawk Down*). The attempt to rescue the helicopter crews led to 18 American deaths, one Pakistani death, one Malaysian death and 300 or more Somali deaths. Two years later the UN accepted failure, withdrew its peacekeepers and left Somalia's warlords to their own devices (the Americans had already ended their mission in March 1994).

In 2000 clan leaders meeting in Djibouti agreed to select Abdulkassim Salat Hassan as Somalia's president, but within a year he and the Transitional National Government (TNG) had proved unacceptable to several warlords backed by Ethiopia. In late 2004, in what was the 14th attempt since the Siad Barre era to restore Somalia's central authority, a new Transitional Federal Government (TFG) was formed in neighbouring Kenya with Abdullahi Yusuf chosen as its president. There were immediate quarrels over where in Somalia the new 275-member Transitional Federal Parliament should be sited, and it was not until February 2006 that it finally met in the central town of Baidoa.

Any hopes that this could lead to stability had already been long discounted, not least by the emergence in 2003 of an extreme faction of al-Ittihad al-Islami (Islamic Union), a Salafist group originating in the 1980s to preach fundamentalist Islam to what was otherwise a moderate Sufi population. Many of the group had been educated in Arab countries of the Middle East and had fought in Afghanistan in the late 1990s. Hardliners from al-Ittihad al-Islami pledged their support for an alliance of *sharia* courts known as the Islamic Courts Union (ICU) and became its militia, al-Shabab, which seized control of the capital Mogadishu in June 2006. This in turn led to an appeal by the TFG for outside intervention and to an invasion by troops from neighbouring Ethiopia, a Christian country that feared Muslim jihadism would cross the border.

Though Ethiopian troops were able to capture Mogadishu and pave the way for the TFG to enter the capital for the first time in January 2007, the perverse effect was to rally recruits for al-Shabab, whose numbers quickly rose from around 400 to several thousand (recent estimates range up to 9,000), fighting not just the Ethiopians but also a UN-approved African Union Mission in Somalia (AMISOM) set up in January 2007. Ethiopia's troops withdrew in January 2009 following the establishment, as a result of UN-sponsored talks in Djibouti, of a government uniting the TFG with the Alliance for the Re-Liberation of Somalia (ARS), an opposition movement based on the more moderate elements of the ICU.

In legal terms, Somalia's transition was complete by September 2012, when clan elders appointed 275 members to a new parliament, which then elected Hassan Sheikh Mohamud as president. But although the government, helped by AMISOM's 22,000 men in uniform (mainly from Burundi, Djibouti, Ethiopia, Kenya, Sierra Leone and Uganda), has control of Mogadishu and Somalia's main cities (Kenyan troops drove al-Shabab out of the port of Kismayo, the group's last major stronghold, in October 2012), the transition has hardly brought peace and stability for the hard-pressed population. In March 2015, for example, AMISOM was unable to stop an al-Shabab attack on an elite hotel in Mogadishu that lasted for 17 hours and left at least 20 dead, including Somalia's representative at the UN in Geneva.

The reality is that al-Shabab, designated as a foreign terrorist organisation by the United States as long ago as February 2008, has proved both resilient and dangerous, not just to other Somalis but also to other countries. In July 2010, for example, al-Shabab, having vowed to "connect the Horn of Africa *jihad* to the one led by al-Qaeda and its leader Sheikh Osama bin Laden", launched co-ordinated suicide-bomb attacks in the Ugandan capital, Kampala, against crowds that had gathered to watch the football World Cup. Some 76 died and another 70 were injured. Chillingly, in March 2015 gunmen killed Joan Kagezi, a Ugandan and lead prosecutor in the trial of 13 men accused of complicity in the attacks.

At the time of the Kampala bombings, an al-Shabab spokesman had commented:

We are sending a message to every country who is willing to send troops to Somalia that they will face attacks on their territory.

This message has certainly been delivered in Kenya. In September 2013 al-Shabab militants stormed a shopping mall in Nairobi and the three-day siege ended in the death of 67 people, including the four attackers, and the wounding of over 170. Worse was to come: at the beginning of April 2015 al-Shabab gunmen stormed a university in north-eastern Kenya and – having apparently spared many Muslim undergraduates – proceeded to kill at least 148 students.

Conceivably, al-Shabab will be weakened by a combination of factional infighting and economic pressure – and by US drone attacks. In June 2013 Sheikh Hassan Dahir Aweys, who had been a leader of the ICU and was a founding force of al-Shabab, surrendered himself to the federal government in Mogadishu after falling out with al-Shabab's ruthless leader, Ahmed Abdi Godane, who was later killed by a US air strike in September 2014, an event described by the US government as "a major symbolic and operational loss to the largest al-Qaeda affiliate in Africa". The economic pressure on al-Shabab stems essentially from their loss of Kismayo, but their control of the profitable and illegal trade in charcoal (used to heat the *shisha* pipes smoked in Gulf states such as Qatar and the United Arab Emirates) continues, as does the supply of funds from sympathisers in the Arab world and the Somali diaspora.

Yet even a weakened al-Shabab would be a threat to Somalia's stability. The Siad Barre era was hardly a paradise, but older Somalis can be forgiven a sense of nostalgia. For younger Somalis, vicious clan rivalry and the importation of al-Qaeda extremism promise continued uncertainty. Even though a multinational maritime force has sharply reduced Somali piracy in the Indian Ocean, it will be a long time before Somalia shakes off the tag of failed state.

South Sudan

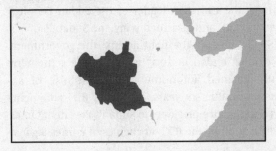

On July 9th 2011 the Republic of South Sudan became the world's newest country, separating from Sudan after decades of war that claimed perhaps 1.5 million lives and displaced more than 4 million people. Independence, however, has brought neither peace and stability nor wealth to the new nation's 11.5 million or so citizens.

Instead, they must endure a civil war, pitting the president, Salva Kiir Mayardit, against his former vice-president, Riek Machar. This conflict, which has driven from their homes over 1.6 million people, involves ethnic warfare, especially between the Dinka (who comprise around 36% of the population and include President Kiir) and the Nuer (who make up about 16% of the population and include Machar). At the same time, tensions – at times violent – continue with Sudan, and there are frequent attacks by guerrillas of the Lord's Resistance Army, driven out of their original bases in Uganda. By some reckonings, South Sudan is at war with at least seven armed groups in nine of its ten states. All that is missing is religious conflict, the Christian, black African and animist South Sudan having seceded from Arab and Muslim Sudan (ironically, Sudan in Arabic means blacks, *bilad al-sudan* meaning country of the blacks).

The secession was a long time in the making. Some six years after Sudan gained its independence from British and Egyptian rule in 1956, the Anyanya guerrilla group began an armed struggle for southern separation. This first civil war lasted for a decade until in 1972 Sudan's socialist president, Ja'afar Numeiri, granted the south a degree of autonomy after a peace accord signed in Addis Ababa.

A decade of relative calm followed until 1983 when, after Numeiri had revoked the autonomy agreement, a second civil war broke out, with John Garang, the Christian leader of the Sudan People's Liberation Movement (SPLM) and its armed wing, the Sudan People's Liberation Army (SPLA), leading the fight against the government in Khartoum. The conflict ended in 2005 with a peace settlement in which the south regained autonomy with a promise of an independence referendum after six years. As part of the settlement, Garang in July 2005 became vice-president to Sudan's President Omar al-Bashir (wanted since 2008 by the ICC on charges of crimes against humanity).

The settlement frayed almost from the beginning, not least because in August 2005 Garang was killed in an air crash. He was succeeded by Salva Kiir, but the scene was set for clashes in Khartoum and elsewhere between southerners and northern Arabs. In the ensuing years fierce conflict broke out between the SPLA and the Sudan government over what has remained the disputed oil-rich area of Abyei. Even so, the referendum took place as scheduled in January 2011, with some 98% of voters choosing independence.

What has gone wrong since is partly economic wrangling between the new country and its old parent. South Sudan contains most of the region's oil (which provides virtually all of the state's budget), but Sudan has the only pipeline access to the Red Sea (disputes over fees led Sudan in 2012 to close down the pipelines for over a year, forcing South Sudan into a budget crisis).

But a large part of South Sudan's plight stems from its own bad governance, corruption and inter-ethnic conflicts – some of them, it seems, stoked by Sudan. The most obvious conflict is between the Dinka and Nuer tribes, a proxy war between Kiir and Machar. But jockeying for wealth or power has led several former SPLA members to form their own armed groups, such as the mainly Nuer South Sudan Liberation Army of Peter Gadet, accused of leading a massacre of some 400 people – targeted according to their ethnic group – in the town of Bentiu in April 2014, or the South Sudan Democratic Army, composed mainly of people from the Murle ethnic group and fighting the Lou Nuer over livestock and grazing grounds.

The SPLA in its role as the armed forces of the state could supposedly muster 210,000 troops in 2013, but the figure seems extraordinarily high and the government is in any case committed to streamlining the military to 120,000 by 2017. One reason for the high figure is genuinely the number of men under arms during the civil wars before independence; but another is that corrupt officers have a vested interest in taking the pay of "ghost" soldiers. Whatever the truth, the South Sudan reality is one of conflict involving many groups, with the SPLA unable to impose peace and with all and sundry committing atrocities and abuses of human rights.

Optimists will point to the frequent peace deals signed between the rebel groups and the government, and to the 2014 negotiations in Addis Ababa between Kiir and Machar. Others will point to the ephemeral nature of many of the settlements and to the huge task ahead if the government in the capital, Juba, is to bring stability to the nation. So far, realism does not favour the optimists.

Sudan

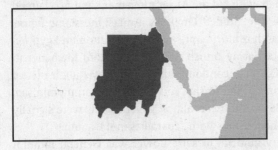

The Republic of Sudan, situated between the Red Sea to the east, Chad to the west and Egypt to the north, is the third-largest country in Africa after Algeria and the Democratic Republic of Congo – but it is smaller than it was. Decades of turmoil between the Arab and Muslim north and the mainly Christian, animist and black African south led in 2011 to the creation of South Sudan, with Sudan's government in Khartoum the first to recognise the new country.

Yet the resolution of one conflict – albeit imperfect, given continuing clashes over the transit of oil from South Sudan to the Red Sea – has failed to bring prosperity and stability for a population of over 34 million. Instead, Sudan remains embroiled in a conflict of an almost genocidal nature in the western region of Darfur and in clashes with rebels in states such as South Kordofan and Blue Nile. Adding to the country's woes are border disputes with Egypt and Ethiopia and an extraordinary roster of civilians displaced by conflict: by 2015 it was reckoned that some 600,000 Sudanese had sought refuge in the Central African Republic, Chad, Egypt, Ethiopia, Israel and South Sudan; and that Sudan, in its turn, was host to 115,000 Eritreans, 32,000 Chadians and many thousands from the CAR and Ethiopia. According to the extraordinarily precise counting of the UN High Commissioner for Refugees, at the start of 2015 Sudan was host to a "population of concern" amounting to 2,479,885 unfortunate individuals.

Since the end in 1956 of the Anglo-Egyptian condominium which had ruled Sudan – in practice, as a British colony – since 1899, Sudan has been dominated by military strongmen. The notable exception was Sadiq al-Mahdi, the great-grandson of the Sufi leader Muhammad Ahmad bin Abdullah, who led the Ansar movement and proclaimed himself the Mahdi (the Guided One). As a quasi-messianic figure, the Mahdi led a 19th-century uprising against Ottoman-Egyptian rule, only for his defeat by British troops under Lord Kitchener to lead to the Anglo-Egyptian condominium. Sadiq al-Mahdi, leader of the Umma Party (and of the Ansar), served twice as prime minister, in 1966–67 and 1986–89, but his coalition governments were signally unable to resolve the tensions with separatists in the south.

The first military autocrat to seize power was General Ibrahim Abboud, with a 1958 coup against the civilian government elected the previous year. But Abboud was overthrown in 1964, leading to a return to civilian rule until the military coup of Colonel Ja'afar al-Numeiri and his Free Officers' Movement in 1969 against the government of Ismail al-Azhari. Numeiri, briefly ousted by a Marxist coup in 1971 (the ringleaders were later executed), began as a pan-Arab socialist but then took the US side in the cold war. In 1972 Numeiri, as leader of the Revolutionary Command Council (RCC), negotiated an end – though it turned out to be only a ten-year interruption – to the long-running war in the south with the Anyanya, a separatist movement of Sudan's black African tribes such as the Nuer and Dinka.

What followed was more than a decade in which President

Numeiri attempted to cope with the threat of both Sadiq al-Mahdi, whose forces were backed by Libya, and of an Islamist opposition. A measure of reconciliation with Mahdi was achieved in the late 1970s, and Hassan al-Turabi, leader of the National Islamic Front and Mahdi's brother-in-law, was invited to return from exile in 1979 and was made justice minister. In 1983, as the separatist war in the south resumed, Numeiri also wooed the Islamists by introducing *sharia* law. Even so, two years later the Numeiri era came to an end with a bloodless military coup mounted while he was on a trip to Washington, DC. After the transitional military government gave way to subsequent elections in 1986, Mahdi became head of a coalition government combining his Umma Party, the National Islamic Front, the Democratic Unionist Party and four small southern parties.

The coalition turned out to be merely an ineffectual, faction-ridden interregnum between Sudan's periods of military rule. In 1989 Colonel (later Lieutenant-General) Omar al-Bashir led a bloodless military coup and as chairman of the Revolutionary Command Council for National Salvation dissolved parliament and banned political parties. In this he was supported by Turabi, who joined him in further Islamising the country – with the obvious result of further alienating the Christian south.

The Bashir era has been at least as dictatorial as the Numeiri one. In 1993 the Revolutionary Council was disbanded and Bashir, while retaining military rule, was appointed president – a post he has maintained through successive elections of dubious credibility and with an impressive degree of political and military ruthlessness (when Bashir suspected that Turabi, unanimously elected president of the National Assembly in 1996, was plotting against him, he dissolved the assembly in 1999 and declared a state of emergency).

The degree of ruthlessness deployed in the effort to forestall the secessionist ambition of rebels in the south led to Sudan becoming subject to international sanctions. The conflict in the south between the Bashir regime and the Sudan People's Liberation Army (SPLA), led by John Garang, involved in part a struggle over resources (oil reserves were in the south) and the north's desire to retain control over the south's superior access to water and fertile land. But it was also very much an ethnic and religious conflict. Though the name

Sudan comes from the Arabic *bilad al-sudan* (land of the blacks), the Arabic-speaking and Muslim northerners consider themselves superior to the Christian southerners from such black African tribes as the Nuer, Dinka and Murle.

The human cost of two decades of the second war with the south was huge, with abuses on both sides but especially by government forces. Estimates of the death toll, from war, famine, drought and disease, range as high as 2 million, and around 4 million southerners were driven from their homes. With international pressure increasing, the Bashir government and the SPLA finally signed a North/South Comprehensive Peace Agreement (CPA) in 2005 under which the south would be given autonomy for six years followed by a referendum on independence. This referendum duly took place in January 2011, with an overwhelming vote for secession. On July 9th 2011 South Sudan, with the acquiescence of the Sudan government in Khartoum, became the 21st century's most recent country, following Kosovo, Serbia, Montenegro and East Timor.

But the formal end of war with the south has not brought peace to Sudan. Instead, the western region of Darfur remains the focus of a conflict characterised in 2004 by Colin Powell, then the US secretary of state, as genocide and the worst humanitarian crisis of the new century (he clearly had not reckoned with many subsequent events in the Middle East).

At its simplest, the Darfur rebellion, beginning in 2003, is a conflict between local pro-government Arab militias, collectively known as *janjaweed*, and African rebel groups such as the Sudan Liberation Movement/Army (SLM or SLA) and the Justice and Equality Movement (JEM). The rebels accuse the government in faraway Khartoum of economic neglect; the government fears the involvement of other countries and the secession of Darfur and its 7 million people.

Inevitably, there is truth on both sides. The formation of the *janjaweed* (a name which may originate from the Arabic *jinni*, meaning spirit, and *jawad* or horse) can be traced back to the turmoil in neighbouring Chad in the 1980s in which Libya under Colonel Qaddafi supplied weapons to Arab Bedouin in eastern Chad. For its part the government in Sudan armed camel-herding, Arabic-speaking Abbala nomads to stop the Chadian conflict spilling over into Sudan.

These two Arab groups were the foundation of today's *janjaweed*, and during the 1990s they clashed frequently with Darfur's farmers and livestock owners over land and access to water, all the time receiving the tacit support of the government, not least so that they could help it combat the SPLA in the war in the south.

What is certain is that after the SLA and the JEM in 2003 launched a joint attack on a military airbase at al-Fashir, the capital of North Darfur, destroying several aircraft and seizing dozens of prisoners, the Bashir government unleashed the *janjaweed* to seek revenge. The result was a horrifying campaign of ethnic cleansing against Darfur's African peoples, notably the Fur and Masalit, who make up most of the SLA, and the Zaghawa, who dominate the JEM. In a typical clash, Sudanese helicopters or fixed-wing aircraft would strafe civilian settlements, paving the way for the *janjaweed* to ride in by horse or camel to slaughter the men, rape the women, kill or kidnap the children (who, if spared, could be sold as slaves), poison the wells and burn the houses.

The human cost has been immense. Though the Sudan government plays down the death toll, the UN reckons that as many as 300,000 may have died, and more than 2 million Darfuris have been driven from their homes (the ICC has said that 2.5 million people in refugee camps were subject to a campaign of rape, hunger and fear).

Tragically, successive attempts to resolve the conflict have failed: in 2006 a peace accord, brokered by the African Union, was reached in the Nigerian capital, Abuja, but on the rebel side only one faction of the SLA (led by Minni Minnawi of the Zaghawa) was prepared to sign – and it later rejoined the rebellion. In 2011 the so-called Doha Document for Peace in Darfur (DDPD) was published in Qatar but was signed on the rebel side only by the Liberation and Justice Movement (LJM), a coalition formed a year earlier from ten minor Darfuri groups.

Meanwhile, the Darfur crisis has provoked international concern and, indeed, rage – due, in part, to publicity about the war given by George Clooney, an American film star. By 2005 the African Union had dispatched some 7,000 peacekeepers to Darfur, and in 2007 the UN authorised UNAMID (the Africa–United Nations Mission in Darfur), a joint force with the African Union that in the spring of 2015 was deploying over 12,000 troops and 3,000 police in Darfur.

Sadly, foreign intervention has yet to succeed, and President Bashir mocked international opinion in 2009 by expelling 13 foreign aid organisations from Sudan.

The spur for the president's action was a decision by the ICC (of which Sudan is not a signatory) on March 4th 2009 to issue an arrest warrant for him, following his indictment in July 2008 for crimes against humanity, war crimes and genocide in Darfur. The ICC's decision meant that Bashir was the first sitting head of state to be subject to an arrest warrant, but its chances of being exercised have always looked slim. Proof of that came in December 2014 when Fatou Bensouda, a Gambian and the chief ICC prosecutor, citing a lack of support from the UN Security Council, halted her investigations into the president's alleged crimes:

> I am left with no choice but to hibernate investigative activities in Darfur as I shift resources to other urgent cases.

Bashir had already ignored the arrest warrant, travelling without hindrance in previous months to Egypt, Ethiopia, Qatar and Saudi Arabia. In June 2015 Bashir attended an African Union summit in South Africa, whose government – in defiance of an order by the Pretoria high court – then allowed him to return home. The political reality is that Sudan remains a member of the Arab League – always reluctant to criticise one of its members – and at the UN Sudan enjoys the backing of China, the country's leading foreign investor. By contrast, the United States in 1993 designated Sudan as a state sponsor of terrorism, not least because it had given sanctuary in 1991 to Osama bin Laden (the al-Qaeda leader was finally asked to leave Sudan in 1996).

During the Numeiri era, which coincided with the cold war, Sudan's relationship with the US gradually warmed to such an extent that by the mid-1980s Sudan was enjoying massive economic and military assistance. Although the US acknowledges both the successful secession, in line with the CPA, of South Sudan and Sudan's co-operation in some aspects of counter-terrorism, the Islamist stance of the Bashir era and the horrors of the Darfur war mean that relations between the two countries have always been extremely sensitive.

Whether Sudan's relations with the US and the West would improve in a post-Bashir era depends not just on the country's policy on Islam but on the situation in the Horn of Africa – always potentially or actually unstable – and beyond. This means relations with countries on the African continent such as Chad and the Central African Republic, but also the wider politics of the Arab world across the Red Sea: in the spring of 2015 Sudan joined a Saudi Arabian-led coalition against the Houthi insurgency in Yemen, sending its aircraft (acquired from Belarus in 2013) to bomb targets in Yemen. Given that the Saudis, protectors of Sunni Islam, view the Houthis, part of the Zaydi faction of Shia Islam, as proxies for Shia and non-Arab Iran, Sudan – for better or for worse – has made itself a combatant in a struggle within Islam that began 14 centuries ago and that now pits Saudi Arabia against Iran for influence in the modern Middle East.

Uganda

Blessed with agricultural riches, minerals and – recently discovered – oil reserves, the Republic of Uganda has the potential to offer a bright future to its citizens. Indeed, President Yoweri Museveni, first elected in 1986, can reasonably claim to have brought the country stability and economic growth after the years of civil war and repression under Milton Obote and then Idi Amin (Museveni's National Resistance Army had helped topple both).

However, when the UK granted independence to Uganda in 1962, the legacy was far from ideal: among the ten main ethnic groups the largest is the Baganda, but it makes up only 17% of a population that is overwhelmingly Christian and, as a result of one of the world's highest birth rates, has grown to almost 40 million from a mere 5 million in 1950. With such a demographic make-up stability is hardly a given. As the CIA notes:

> Uganda is subject to armed fighting among hostile ethnic groups, rebels, armed gangs, militias, and various government forces that extend across its borders; Ugandan refugees as well as members of the Lord's Resistance Army (LRA) seek shelter in southern Sudan and the Democratic Republic of the Congo's Garamba National Park; LRA forces have also attacked Kenyan villages across the border.

The origins of the Lord's Resistance Army (LRA) lie in the resistance of the Acholi ethnic group (5% of the population) in northern Uganda in the late 1980s to Museveni's National Resistance Army, which was seeking a bloody revenge against tribes that had opposed its successful coup against Tito Okello, the temporary successor to the second term in power of Obote. But its defining characteristic is its cult-like following of Joseph Kony, who declares himself a prophet sent to purify Uganda. The cult actually pre-dates Kony, since it began with his aunt, Alice Lakwena (also known as Alice Auma, her birth name), who founded the Holy Spirit Movement to redeem the Acholi from violence by conquering the capital, Kampala, and so creating a paradise on earth.

That, of course, was not to be. Kony had been a member of the rebel Uganda People's Democratic Army (UPDA), but he rejected a UPDA peace accord with the government in 1988 and set up the Uganda Christian Democratic Army, renamed in 1991 the Lord's Resistance Army (LRA). Since then the LRA has become a byword for extreme violence, rape and the forced recruitment of child soldiers (a UNICEF study reported in 2006 that some 66,000 children were abducted by the LRA between 1986 and 2005, though most were held for only a brief time).

In one sense the LRA is no longer much of a problem for Uganda, since pressure by the 45,000-strong Ugandan armed forces had by 2006 more or less driven Kony's forces out of the country and by 2012 some 12,000 LRA fighters had taken advantage of a government amnesty.

Today, according to the US State Department, there are perhaps 200 core LRA guerrillas, but they spread their sadistic mayhem mainly in the Democratic Republic of Congo, the Central African Republic and South Sudan. None of this pleases the surrounding countries (and the DRC also accuses Uganda of aiding the M23 rebels).

A lesser-known guerrilla group troubling both Uganda and the DRC is the Allied Democratic Forces–National Army for the Liberation of Uganda (ADF–NALU), more usually termed the ADF, and formed in 1989 by Jamil Mukulu, a Christian convert to an extremist form of Islam (Uganda's Muslims make up about 12% of the population) preached by the Tabligh, an evangelical sect. Mukulu was arrested in Tanzania in April 2015, and both Uganda and the DRC immediately demanded his extradition for the various atrocities committed by the ADF over the previous two decades.

In their aim to topple the Museveni government and bring in Islamist rule, the ADF fighters were supported both by the late President Mobutu of what was then Zaire and by Sudan's Hassan al-Turabi, angered by Uganda's support for the Sudan People's Liberation Army. Launching its first attacks in 1996, the ADF at that time may have numbered 4,000–5,000 fighters; today there are around 1,300 who seemingly pose a greater threat within the DRC than inside Uganda, from which ADF guerrillas were forced out in 2002. Even so, in a regional context they cannot be ignored, especially with their well-attested links to al-Shabab in Somalia.

It is true that Uganda's mass killings (some 300,000 of the president's opponents) in the era of Amin in the 1970s have faded from the memory, as has his expulsion of the country's Indian business community. With luck, the two decades of conflict with the LRA, which by 2006 had displaced about 2 million people in northern Uganda, will follow a similar course. Yet Uganda, for all its relative stability, can hardly afford to relax – and not just because it lives in a dangerous neighbourhood. In July 2014 some 90 people in western Uganda were killed by armed men (possibly ADF) attacking police and army installations, and late in the same year the British Foreign Office issued a travel alert to British citizens, with a warning of a "high threat of terrorism".

4 The UK and Europe: bloodied past, complacent present, uncertain future

THE EUROPEAN UNION, with a population of over 500 million, is the world's biggest economic bloc, and NATO, 26 of whose 28 members are European nations, remains the world's biggest – and most successful – military alliance in history. At first glance, therefore, Europe's citizens, at least those within the EU, should feel secure. Indeed, in 2012 the EU was awarded the Nobel peace prize because it had "for over six decades contributed to the advancement of peace and reconciliation, democracy and human rights in Europe".

That contribution was sorely needed. In 2009 Mark Mazower, a British historian, wrote a book with an arresting title: *Dark Continent: Europe's Twentieth Century*. This was hardly an exaggeration, given the horrendous death toll of two world wars and the various wars of independence fought by the colonies of the European powers. Even as the 20th century neared its end, Europe was scarred by war: this time because of the violent disintegration of Yugoslavia in the 1990s.

But a Nobel prize for the EU should not induce complacency. Europe's peace and security are hardly absolute. One threat comes from secessionist movements – as in Spain and Northern Ireland – with a proven propensity for violent conflict. A second comes from extreme Islamism, with European jihadists, particularly French and British Muslims, returning from conflict in the Middle East and prepared to commit acts of terrorism in their home countries. A third threat is that some European nations will find themselves drawn into wars beyond Europe, as in Iraq and Afghanistan or in Mali and the Central African Republic.

There is, too, a fourth threat that until recently seemed inconceivable, namely that the cold war between the West and Russia will revive and could even, at least at times, become hot. The evidence for this is the conflict that began in 2014 in Ukraine, with Crimea seceding and becoming part of Russia and then with Russian-speakers in eastern Ukraine defying the Ukrainian armed forces in a bloody attempt to break away and join Russia. Given the sympathy that Russia's president, Vladimir Putin, has for ethnic Russians outside Russia, former satellite states of the Soviet Union that are now part of the EU and of NATO are feeling nervous, and are emphasising to their fellow members the importance of article 5 of NATO's founding treaty: an attack on one member is an attack on all – and will provoke a collective response. So far, article 5 has been invoked only once, in response to the 9/11 attack on the United States.

In short, Europe's 21st century is not (so far, at least) as dark as the 20th, but it still has plenty of nasty shadows. Many of them stem from the collapse of the Soviet Union (which President Putin in 2005 famously described as "the greatest geopolitical catastrophe of the [20th] century"). Russia and Georgia, for example, clashed militarily in 2008 over the status of the pro-Russian breakaway republics of Abkhazia and South Ossetia. Chechnya's desire to secede from the Russian Federation means sporadic conflict and the constant threat of terrorism. Indeed, the whole Caucasus region is prone to violent strains of ethnic and religious nationalism, for example the dispute between Armenia and Azerbaijan over Nagorno-Karabakh, an Armenian enclave in Azerbaijan whose secession led to a war between 1988 and 1994 that involved combatants from Turkey as well as Armenia, Nagorno-Karabakh and Azerbaijan.

Even the Balkans have yet to banish all the shadows of their wars of the 1990s, which cost at least 130,000 lives and displaced more than 2 million people. Though the nations that have emerged from the dismemberment of communist Yugoslavia now seem peaceful enough, ethnic and religious tensions between Bosniak Muslims, Croats and Serbs remain high in Bosnia and Herzegovina and are similarly high between Muslim Kosovo and Christian Orthodox Serbia. Only Montenegro, seceding from its union with Serbia after a referendum in 2006, achieved independence without bloodshed.

Sadly, therefore, for all the stability in Europe since the end of the second world war, the actuality of conflict remains – and so does the threat of more – in far too much of the continent.

The UK

For a relatively small nation of just over 63 million, the United Kingdom of Great Britain and Northern Ireland (to give the country its full title) likes to punch above its weight in military and diplomatic affairs. Its status as one of the five recognised nuclear powers gives it a permanent seat on the UN Security Council; its armed forces – the British army, the Royal Navy and the Royal Air Force – have a deserved reputation for professionalism; and its special forces, notably the SAS (Special Air Service) and the Special Boat Service, are equal with the best in the world.

To this must be added the legacy of the British Empire, the couple of centuries in which the UK ruled not just the waves but huge tracts of Africa and Asia. Such a history is one reason for its familiarity with war and willingness to go to war. A second reason is the conflict between European powers that culminated in the first and second world wars: for all the economic damage they did to the UK, the eventual presence on the winning side confirmed the nation's pride in its armed forces.

A third reason stems from the UK's partnership with the US, which in turn is influenced by a less glorious episode in British history: the UK invasion in 1956, along with France and Israel, of Egypt to seize the Suez Canal after its nationalisation by Gamal Abdul Nasser. The Suez affair ended when pressure from the United States (and the threat of intervention by the Soviet Union) forced the UK, France and Israel to withdraw their troops. The lesson that France took from the Suez debacle was the need for Europe to build itself up as a counterweight to the US – an ambition that led to the European Union. The lesson that the UK learned was that since it could not defy the power of the US, it would be well to side with it at almost any cost. With the notable exception of the Vietnam war, to which Harold Wilson, the UK's Labour prime minister, refused to commit British troops, the UK has been a faithful ally (the critics say "poodle") of the US ever since – hence the decision by Tony Blair, another Labour prime minister, to send British troops to the invasions of Iraq and Afghanistan.

Just how well and for how long the UK can continue to punch above its weight is a tricky question. It remains one of just four NATO members (the others are the United States, Greece and Estonia) to spend over 2% of their GDP on defence, but this budget is under constant threat and the 2% threshold is not necessarily sacrosanct. (It should also be noted that the Greek percentage is paradoxically increased when shrinking defence purchases are measured against an economy shrinking even faster.)

In April 2014 the UK's armed forces ranked fifth in the world in terms of manpower, with a total of 159,630 active personnel. However, by 2020 the government plans to cut the total to 147,000; most of the surgery would be performed on the army, reducing its manpower from 91,000 to just 82,000. The other services would not suffer so much in manpower, but they have already felt constraints on their equipment (many of the navy's ships have been decommissioned and the RAF's lack of heavy-lift aircraft means that the armed forces must frequently turn to the US for help). The UK maintains the capacity for small-scale and limited operations, such as its decisive intervention in 2000 in Sierra Leone's civil war or its 2,000 airstrikes in Libya in 2011 to help oust Muammar Qaddafi, but whether it could repeat its dramatic victory over Argentina in the Falklands war of 1982 is open to question.

Does this matter? Robert Gates, a former American defence secretary under both George W. Bush and Barack Obama, declared in 2014:

> With the fairly substantial reductions in defence spending in Great Britain, what we're finding is that it won't have full spectrum capabilities and the ability to be a full partner as they have been in the past.

The implication, therefore, is that the UK's role as the lead ally in US military adventures abroad will be under pressure.

But those adventures are unlikely to demand British manpower of the level demanded in the Iraq and Afghanistan wars. Assuming that tensions with Russia do not lead, by accident rather than design, to a larger war in Europe, the UK's military and intelligence efforts will be devoted mostly to counter-terrorism and counter-insurgency – or perhaps, as in Sierra Leone, to humanitarian intervention, a concept expounded by Tony Blair in a speech in Chicago in 1999 justifying NATO's role in the war in Kosovo as the "doctrine of the international community".

Domestically, the UK faces two threats: Islamist-inspired attacks on its citizens and institutions and violence by extreme Northern Irish republican groups seeking to secede from the UK and unite with the Irish Republic.

The threat from Northern Irish dissidents is a long-standing one. Their republican movement goes back to the partition of Ireland in 1921, with most of the island – mainly Roman Catholic by faith – becoming the independent Irish Free State but with six northern counties, characterised by large Protestant populations, remaining in the union with Great Britain. The decades since have been scarred by violent conflict and terrorist bombings, pitting the Catholics of groups such as the Irish Republican Army (IRA) against the British army and Protestant loyalists or unionists such as the Ulster Volunteer Force. Supposedly, peace was finally achieved (not least because of the help of the United States) with the Good Friday agreement of April 10th 1998 between the UK, Ireland and the main parties of Northern Ireland.

In practice, although Sinn Fein, the political arm of the republican movement, and its unionist counterparts have abided by the power-sharing laid out in the Good Friday agreement, some recalcitrant republicans remain committed to an armed struggle to secede from the UK. Historically, the lead actor was the IRA, but when in 1969 it recognised the parliaments in London, Dublin and Belfast, angry republicans broke away to form the Provisional IRA, continuing a campaign of bombings and assassinations in defiance of the 1972 ceasefire by the Official IRA. Now the Provisionals, having accepted the Good Friday agreement, find themselves supplanted by groups such as the Real IRA and the Continuity IRA.

The danger posed by the Continuity IRA and similar dissident republicans (such as Óglaigh na hÉireann, or ONH – soldiers of Ireland in Irish Gaelic) is real enough. In 2014 letter bombs were sent to targets in both England and Northern Ireland; pipe bombs were discovered; and at least two dissident republicans were murdered, possibly as a result of internecine squabbles within the republican movement. One complication is that the republican dissidents are matched by paramilitary loyalists, such as the Ulster Volunteer Force and the Ulster Defence Association. Though the loyalists have, at least in theory, given up their weaponry, the suspicion remains that many are involved in gangsterism – as are many republicans. As in Latin America, political objectives easily become tainted by money-raising activities such as protection rackets and drug-trafficking. For the moment, the British government has proscribed as terrorist organisations some 14 Northern Irish groups, the majority of them republican.

In the popular view – shared also by the UK's politicians and security forces – a much greater threat than Irish extremism is that of Islamist extremism. British citizens have been kidnapped or executed by Islamist groups abroad, for example in recent years by Boko Haram and its sympathisers in northern Nigeria and by Somalia's al-Shabab guerrillas in Kenya. British ships and crew have also frequently been the targets of Somali pirates. The pirates' motives are mercenary rather than inspired by a fundamentalist reading of Islam, but British participation in the international maritime force formed to bring security to the Indian Ocean is bound in some minds to increase al-Shabab's zeal for revenge on Britons abroad.

In reality, though, the greater danger is at home. The legacy of the UK's imperial sway and then the need for imported labour as the UK economy recovered in the aftermath of the second world war meant an influx of Muslim workers in the 1960s from the Indian subcontinent, especially from Pakistan and what became Bangladesh. By the time of the 2011 census they and their descendants, joined by migrants from elsewhere in the Muslim world, numbered 2.7 million, almost 5% of the population in England and Wales and some 9.1% of children under the age of five. A small minority of that population has been radicalised, some by fundamentalist preachers such as Abu Hamza al-Masri (deported in 2012 to the US for trial on terrorism charges) and Abu Qatada al-Filistini (deported to Jordan for trial in 2013). Abu Hamza was sentenced to life imprisonment in 2015; Abu Qatada was acquitted in 2014. Other British Muslims have been radicalised while in prison, and others still by extremist sites on the internet. Significant in this process has been the money and influence of Wahhabi and Salafist interpreters of Islam, especially in Saudi Arabia.

Add to that the view held by many Muslims that the US and the UK have declared war on Islam by the invasions of Afghanistan and Iraq, and the result is a readiness to strike back with the typical weapons of modern asymmetric warfare. The worst example was on July 7th 2005 when a co-ordinated attack by four separate British-born Muslim suicide bombers killed 58 people (including themselves) in London and injured another 700. Three of the suicide bombers were born in the UK to Pakistani immigrant parents; the fourth was a convert to Islam born in Jamaica. Two years later a British-born doctor of Iraqi descent and an Indian colleague launched a suicide attack on Glasgow airport in Scotland (the Indian died but the doctor survived to be sentenced to imprisonment for life). In 2013 two young Britons of Nigerian descent who had converted to Islam murdered a British soldier, Lee Rigby, in London (attempting in their attack to decapitate him). The assailants made no attempt to flee, with one of them declaring:

> The only reason we have killed this man today is because Muslims are dying daily by British soldiers. And this British soldier is one ...
> By Allah, we swear by the almighty Allah we will never stop fighting you until you leave us alone.

The UK government has proscribed well over a score of Islamist groups, from al-Qaeda to Tehrik-e Taliban Pakistan, but though several of these organisations have carried out operations in the West, the security forces must also cope – as with the killing of Rigby – with extremists who have no connection with or direction from an organised group. As MI5, the British security service, puts it:

*There are several thousand individuals in the UK who support
violent extremism or are engaged in Islamist extremist activity.*

A greater worry for MI5 is that their number will be increased by
young Britons going to join the *jihad* in a turbulent Middle East. In
2014 the government estimated that some 500 British citizens were
fighting in Syria in the struggle to topple President Bashar al-Assad,
and many of them would be in the ranks of Islamist groups such as
Jabhat al-Nusra. The reality, too, is that many have joined – and will
join – the even more extreme Islamic State in Iraq and Sham (ISIS)
in an attempt to establish an Islamic caliphate (hence ISIS's change
of name to Islamic State) in both Syria and Iraq. Some of the young
jihadists would argue that their fight in Syria is akin to that of the
International Brigades fighting Franco in the Spanish civil war of the
1930s. The argument does not impress the British authorities: they
fear that young British Muslims going to the Middle East will return
as battle-hardened extremists, ready to commit terrorist acts in the
UK – which in turn will prompt an anti-Muslim backlash. In short, the
present and the future are both unsettling.

France

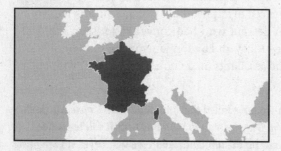

The French Republic is in many ways a carbon copy of the UK. It,
too, has just over 63 million citizens; it, too, is a nuclear power and
permanent member of the UN Security Council; and it, too, has
the capacity and willingness (unlike others in the EU) to exert its
military power beyond its borders. The other similarity is a proud
imperial history, with the French empire established by Napoleon
and his successors stretching from the West Indies through Africa to

South-East Asia. Ironically, given that the UK and France have been close allies for more than a century and signed a defence co-operation treaty in 2010, in much of their imperial histories the two countries were at war with each other.

For the French, however, the salient fact is a long history of military prowess. According to heroic calculations by Niall Ferguson, a British historian at Harvard University, France has fought in 168 major European wars since 387 BC, winning 109, drawing 10 and losing 49. Modern cynics will note that France was conquered twice by Germany in the 20th century, lost its territorial possessions – violently in the case of Algeria – in north Africa, and was forced out of Indochina in 1954 by its catastrophic defeat at Dien Bien Phu at the hands of Vietnamese revolutionaries.

France, like the UK, aspires to punch above its weight, but what has distinguished it since the days of General Charles de Gaulle – first as leader of the Free French in the second world war and then as founder and president of the Fifth Republic – is France's determination to preserve its military independence. For De Gaulle, this meant withdrawing France from NATO's military structure in 1966, while remaining in its political councils, and ordering American troops to leave French soil. Some four decades later De Gaulle's decision was set aside by the more Atlanticist President Nicolas Sarkozy, who declared that henceforth France would fully participate in NATO operations.

Nonetheless, the idea of France's independent military identity is fundamental. France volunteered to help the US in its post-9/11 assault on Afghanistan but refused to take part in the 2003 invasion of Iraq (prompting a popular American gibe that the French were "cheese-eating surrender-monkeys"). In retrospect, France's politicians can boast that their stance on Iraq was justified, even if it had a hint of Gaullist anti-Americanism. The military question is what is France's military strength, and the answer – as with the UK – is that its capabilities are being eroded by budget constraints. A 2013 defence white paper envisaged cutting the operational strength of the army from 88,000 to 66,000; the possibility of a new aircraft carrier for the navy was abandoned; and the air force and navy were to reduce their 300 fast-jet combat aircraft to no more than 225. Not surprisingly, in

2014 several defence chiefs said they would resign if still more cuts were demanded.

Yet whatever the budgetary limits, in the right circumstances – notably in developing countries – France's military forces (which in total number around 222,000, including the fabled Foreign Legion) still wield a powerful punch, with some 20,000 troops based abroad either on French operations or in multinational peacekeeping efforts. In 2011 France was a leading member of the UN-sanctioned multinational intervention in Libya that led to the overthrow of Qaddafi. That deployment was ordered by the centre-right President Sarkozy, but his socialist successor, François Hollande, has proved still more bellicose. In January 2013 he sent more than 4,000 French troops to Mali to halt an advance on its capital by Islamist rebels. By the end of 2013 President Hollande had also committed more than 1,000 troops to intervene in a sectarian civil war, pitting Muslims against Christians, in the Central African Republic (CAR).

It is tempting to see such interventions as a continuation of the *Françafrique* policy under which successive administrations in France fostered close relations with the dictators and other strongmen of their former colonies (the support, later withdrawn, for the CAR's Jean-Bédel Bokassa in the 1970s is a case in point). In 2008 President Sarkozy announced that France would concentrate less on its bilateral defence ties with its former African colonies and more on combating an arc of instability running across north Africa to the Horn of Africa and the Gulf. Accordingly, he closed one French garrison in Senegal and opened another in Abu Dhabi.

So much for the geopolitical priorities of the day. The spread of al-Qaeda-linked Islamism and sectarian conflict in the Sahel region has reordered French thinking. In 2014 President Hollande announced "Opération Barkhane" (Operation Sand Dune), a permanent, 3,000-strong counter-terrorism force headquartered in the Chadian capital, N'Djamena, and spanning not just Chad but also Mali, Burkina Faso, Niger and Mauritania.

The reason for the deployment is clear enough: just as the UK fears that Muslim Britons going to fight in the Middle East may return to commit terrorist acts at home, so too France worries about the French-born Muslim offspring of its former colonies. In 2012 Mohammed

Merah, a Frenchman of Algerian background, killed seven and injured five in south-west France, apparently in protest over the plight of the Palestinians and France's role in Afghanistan. Worse was to come in January 2015, when two French brothers of Algerian descent, claiming allegiance to al-Qaeda's branch in Yemen, attacked the Paris offices of *Charlie Hebdo*, a satirical weekly magazine that had caricatured Islam. They killed 11 in the building and a policeman outside. In a related incident, a French Muslim of Malian descent who had pledged himself to ISIS attacked a Jewish kosher supermarket in Paris, killing four of his hostages.

In January 2014 President Hollande said that up to 700 French citizens had joined the fighting in Syria (a year later the estimate was 1,200). In that context, France is understandably keen that none of its former African colonies should become a "jihadistan" with the potential to launch attacks on France itself. Although the French state, on the grounds that in a secular republic all French men and women are equal, collects no statistics of race or religion, there are reckoned to be around 5 million Muslims in France and perhaps 480,000 Jews. This means that it has the largest Muslim and Jewish communities in Europe, and both are sensitive to events in the Middle East.

It is, of course, possible that Opération Barkhane could backfire. In 2013 al-Qaeda in the Islamic Maghreb (AQIM) declared French interests legitimate targets because of France's occupation of Mali, and six months later the group kidnapped and killed two French journalists. As Europol pointed out in its 2014 annual report, France – with 63 terrorist attacks on its soil – had suffered more acts of terrorism in 2013 than any other EU country.

Not all of these incidents were by Muslim extremists. In January 2013 three Kurdish political activists, all of them women, were assassinated in the Kurdish Institute of Paris. Since two of the three were members of the PKK (Partiya Karkerên Kurdistan, or Kurdistan Workers' Party), the assumption was that the killings were connected with the struggle for Kurdish rights or independence. The PKK is considered a terrorist organisation by the US and the EU, but it has attracted many sympathisers (and collected plenty of funds) in Europe.

Meanwhile, France continues to confront two old domestic

challenges: Basque separatism and Corsican separatism. Basque separatism in south-west France has never been particularly strong. One reason is that during the decades of the Franco dictatorship in neighbouring Spain, France was a welcome refuge for many members of ETA (Euskadi Ta Askatasuna, or Basque Homeland and Liberty), the armed group seeking the Basque region's secession from Spain. Obviously, ETA operatives did not want to jeopardise France's tacit acceptance of them on French soil. This acceptance was extended through and beyond the 1980s, a period in which the Spanish state was implicated in attacks on ETA by paramilitary death squads. As a result, ETA violence in France has been relatively rare (a French gendarme was killed in a shoot-out with an ETA group near Paris in 2010 and another gendarme manning a roadblock was shot by two ETA members in 2011).

These incidents reflected not ETA attacks on France but the close co-operation that has prevailed in recent years between France and Spain, with the French helping to track down ETA members. In 2013, for example, the French authorities arrested six suspected members of ETA.

The likelihood is that Basque separatism is now a thing of the past in France. Though the group has yet to disband, as France and Spain have demanded, in October 2011 ETA had announced a definitive end to its armed activities. Moreover, at the start of 2013 Batasuna, a Basque nationalist party regarded as the political arm of ETA, announced it was dissolving itself in France. Batasuna had grown out of Herri Batasuna (Unity of the People), a political party founded in 1978. With its abbreviated name, Batasuna was allowed to operate in France as an association rather than a political party, but it had been declared illegal in Spain in 2003. Its decision to dissolve itself in France came, it said, after a period of political reflection.

Is Corsican separatism similarly a vanishing threat? Probably not completely, given the fundamental strength of the Corsican identity, with its own language and its sense of cultural separation from France. (The history books show that in the 18th century Corsica freed itself from control by Genoa and established an independent republic, only to be conquered by France in 1769.) The birth of modern Corsican nationalism coincided with the struggle for independence by France's colonies in the 1950s and 1960s. The loss of the colonies meant that there were fewer opportunities for Corsicans to find jobs in the colonial administration, where they had constituted 20% of the workforce.

Economic pressure on the Corsicans, made worse by an influx of *pieds noirs* (French settlers) from Algeria, prompted Corsican activists in 1976 to form the National Liberation Front of Corsica (Fronte di Liberazione Naziunale Corsu, or FLNC, in the Corsican language). This was a merger of two earlier organisations, the Ghjustizia Paolina and the Fronte Paesanu Corsu di Liberazione, and the result was four decades of some 10,000 acts of violence – mainly bombs against government institutions – aimed at the French state, both in Corsica and at times on the French mainland. In just one day in 1979, for example, the FLNC – which can count on some 600 militants – bombed 20 banks in Paris. Attacks on holiday homes on the island owned by French mainlanders have been a constant target, but the killings of individuals have been relatively rare, with only around 40 murders linked to the group. The most politically important of these was the assassination in 1998 of Claude Érignac, who, as the island's *préfet*, was the highest representative of France in Corsica. The uproar that followed increased the tendency for feuds within the FLNC.

These internal squabbles may well cast doubt on the 14-page declaration by the FLNC in June 2014 asserting that "without further notice or conditions" it would "unilaterally begin a demilitarisation process and a gradual exit from clandestine activities". The decision may have been spurred by a vote in the island's regional assembly to give priority to Corsicans in property purchases. Four days later, however, a holiday home belonging to a French mainlander was attacked.

Whatever the identity of the attackers, the parallel with Northern Ireland is clear: the separatist movement is often connected with crime, not least to finance itself, and is prone to splintering because of both personalities and tactics. As Gilbert Thiel, a prosecutor in several trials against FLNC members, told Agence France-Presse:

> If the FLNC has really abandoned its armed struggle, then this is really the end of terrorism in Corsica.

But he added:

> *We have to hope that this announcement doesn't cause a more radical wing to emerge, as happened during the peace process in Northern Ireland.*

Georgia

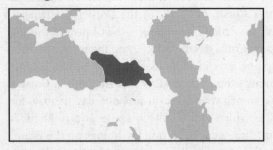

Situated between Russia and Turkey and with a strategic coastline on the Black Sea, Georgia has historically been coveted by its larger neighbours. During most of the 20th century this meant control by Moscow as part of the Soviet Union – indeed, in some ways an honoured part, given that Joseph Stalin was a Georgian. Independence came in April 1991 as Georgian nationalists (there had been anti-Soviet demonstrations three years earlier) took advantage of the accelerating collapse of the Soviet Union.

But independence for the 4.9 million population has been marked by continuing tensions, at times violent, between the Georgian government in Tbilisi and the Russian government in Moscow. In common with several former satellite states of the Soviet Union, Georgia has sought closer relations with the West, both with NATO and the EU. One aspect of this is the country's membership since 1994 in the Partnership for Peace, a programme offered by NATO to improve trust between western European countries and former communist states. Another aspect is Georgia's desire to join the EU, which has responded by first in 2006 including Georgia in its European Neighbourhood Policy and then in 2014 signing an association agreement with it to deepen both economic and financial links. Neither initiative has endeared Georgia to the Russia of Vladimir Putin.

The proof was the five-day Russo-Georgian war of 2008. This had its origins in Georgia's wish to reassert its authority over the provinces of South Ossetia and Abkhazia. The former had declared its independence from Georgia in 1991 (ironically three months before Georgia's declaration of independence) and the latter in 1992. The outcome of these clashes of rival ethnicities and nationalisms in the Caucasus was defeat for Georgia by the mid-1990s and the installation in both South Ossetia and Abkhazia of Russian troops as peacekeepers.

Tensions with Russia lessened after Eduard Shevardnadze, the Georgian-born former Soviet foreign minister, took charge from 1992 onwards of the government in Tbilisi. But Shevardnadze was ousted – peacefully – in the "Rose revolution" of 2003 and replaced by the US-educated and aggressively pro-Western Mikheil Saakashvili. The relationship with Russia, which even in the days of Shevardnadze had accused Georgia of harbouring Chechen rebels seeking to secede from Russia, almost immediately became fraught. In 2006 Georgia demanded that Russian peacekeepers in South Ossetia should have visas; in April 2008 it accused Russia of shooting down an unmanned drone over Abkhazia. Things finally came to a head in August 2008 when South Ossetian separatists fired on Georgian peacekeepers: Georgia reacted by sending its troops into South Ossetia; and Russia reacted by invading Georgia and launching air raids as far as the Black Sea port of Poti.

If Saakashvili had expected the West to come to his aid, he was soon disillusioned. For all his rhetoric, and despite the close co-operation in training exercises between the American and Georgian military, the fact is that Georgia's military, with active personnel of some 37,000, could never be a match for Russia's – and Georgia's Western allies had no intention of being drawn into military involvement. In a five-day conflict Georgia lost 170 servicemen, 14 policemen and 228 civilians; Russia lost 67 servicemen; and some 365 South Ossetians, both soldiers and civilians, were killed. After a ceasefire brokered by President Nicolas Sarkozy of France, South Ossetia and Abkhazia were recognised by Russia (along with Venezuela, Nicaragua and tiny Nauru) as independent republics.

One significant outcome of Russo-Georgian war is that it has very much dampened any enthusiasm in NATO to offer membership to nations, such as Ukraine, that Russia considers should be in its sphere of influence. At the same time the West is conscious of Georgia's strategic importance as a transit route for gas exports from Azerbaijan to Turkey. The reality is that as part of the fault line between Europe and Asia, Georgia is never likely to be relaxed about its position in the world. In March 2014 the Georgian parliament condemned Russia's annexation of Crimea – prompting the claim by one Western source that Russia then flew its jet fighters and military helicopters over Georgia in contravention of the accord negotiated by President Sarkozy.

Greece

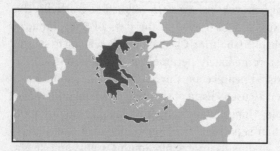

For all its history as the birthplace of democracy, Greece – or more properly the Hellenic Republic – is relatively young as a stable, modern democracy. The military junta that took power in 1967 and forced King Constantine to flee was not ousted until 1974, when democratic elections led to the creation of a parliamentary republic. That, in turn, led to entry into the European Union (or European Community, as it then was) in 1981. Being in this European family meant economic and political comfort and support (including acquiescing, for the most part, in Greece's insistence that the new Republic of Macedonia should be called the Former Yugoslav Republic of Macedonia); in military matters, as a member of NATO since 1952, Greece already had those helpful benefits.

For successive Greek governments, NATO membership has been a means of handling the country's often tense relationship with Turkey, which also joined the alliance in 1952. Without the NATO umbrella over both countries, complex disputes over territory and maritime issues in the Aegean could easily have led to military conflict, and Greece's active military personnel of just over 177,000 would be no match for Turkey's 410,500. When Turkish troops landed in Cyprus in 1974 to forestall the Greek Cypriot desire for *enosis* or union with Greece, so creating the division of the island between the Turkish Cypriot north and the Greek Cypriot south, Greece was in no position to intervene; indeed, it was Greece's powerlessness to help fellow Greeks that accelerated the fall of the military junta.

The nervous relationship with Turkey can be traced all the way back to the centuries (from the 15th to the early years of the 19th) in which Greece was part of the Ottoman empire; modern instances of internal conflict have their origin in the civil war between communists and anti-communists that followed the second world war (guerrilla groups from across the political spectrum had resisted the Nazi occupation). By 1949 the communists had been defeated, with both the US and the UK supporting the government. Nonetheless, the tensions between left and right helped bring the military junta to power in 1967. After the junta collapsed in 1974, the leftists who had opposed the colonels formed several groups prepared to use extreme violence to combat Western interests in Greece, the two most notable being the Revolutionary Organisation 17 November (17N) and Revolutionary Popular Struggle (ELA, in its Greek abbreviation).

The first major action by 17N (named after the date in 1973 of an uprising against the military junta by students at Athens Polytechnic) was to assassinate the CIA station chief in Athens in 1975. Before disbanding in 2002 it had carried out more than 100 attacks on Greek, British, American and Turkish targets, killing 23 people. For its part, ELA was responsible for around 250 attacks between 1975 and its last operation in 1994. But despite the efforts of the authorities (desperate, for example, to prevent any disruption of the 2004 Athens Olympics), the threat of radical left-wing terrorism has never totally vanished.

The main groups now are Revolutionary Struggle (EA), Sect of Revolutionaries (SE) and the anarchist Conspiracy of Fire Nuclei (SPF). All are perversely benefiting from the collapse of the Greek economy following the global financial crisis of 2008. During 2010 the Greek security forces arrested six EA members with a large cache of weapons and explosives; SE assassinated a Greek journalist in Athens; and SPF waged a parcel-bomb campaign against Western and international targets outside Greece.

Such extremism is likely to continue, at least until Greece regains economic and political stability. Though 17N was supposedly crushed in 2002, one of its leaders escaped from prison in January 2014. Later in the year two members of Golden Dawn, a new far-right political party, were killed outside the party's headquarters in Athens. A previously unknown group, the Militant Popular Revolutionary Forces (Mahomenes Laikes Epanastatikes Dynameis), claimed responsibility for what it called political executions of the fascist members of the neo-Nazi Golden Dawn party.

Italy

With a population of just over 60 million Italy is almost on a par with the UK and France in demographic and economic weight. The same, however, is not true in terms of its military clout. Even though Italy has some 180,000 active military personnel (plus a territorial force of 109,000 *carabinieri*), compared with 159,000 for the UK and 204,000 for France, it is instinctively far less bellicose.

This does not mean it is inactive. As a founder member of NATO and the European Union, Italy willingly sends its troops to take part in UN peacekeeping missions from Lebanon to South Sudan and in EU missions from Bosnia to Mali. However, Italy did not engage in the US-led 2003 invasion of Iraq. Instead, its troops arrived towards the end of that year only after President George W. Bush had declared an end to major combat operations – and those 3,200 troops were withdrawn in 2006.

This relative reticence doubtless owes much to Italy's history as a modern country (unification as the Kingdom of Italy occurred only in 1861 and the Republic of Italy was declared only in 1946 in the wake of Italy's defeat in the second world war). As fears grew in the aftermath of the first world war of a communist revolution in Italy along the lines of the Russian one, the country turned to fascism and the rule of Benito Mussolini, first as prime minister in 1922 and then from 1925 as outright dictator. Mussolini's expansionist zeal in 1935 added Ethiopia as a conquered possession to join Libya, which Italy had seized from Ottoman Turkey in 1912. As with Germany, the disastrous experience of fascism and defeat in the second world war has left Italy with a mistrust of militarism.

Another legacy was a powerful Italian communist party, which in the 1970s commanded the support of a third of the electorate before, in 1991, it evolved into the less radical Democratic Party of the Left (PDS). At the same time, the corruption of Italian politics and the clear support by the United States of the Christian Democrats bred an extra-parliamentary extremism dedicated to violent revolution.

The most prominent of the extremists have been the Red Brigades (Brigate Rosse), a Marxist-Leninist group formed in 1970 and willing to use kidnapping, bombings, bank robberies and assassination as the means to its revolutionary ends. The group took its inspiration from the liberation movements in Latin America, especially the Tupamaros of Uruguay, and in its tactics was similar to the Baader-Meinhof gang (also known as the Red Army Faction) in Germany.

The Red Brigades' most famous exploit was the kidnapping in 1978 of Aldo Mori, a long-serving former Christian Democrat prime minister. Mori had been trying to effect a historic compromise in Italian politics that would have brought the Communist Party of Italy (PCI) into government with the Christian Democrats. That idea (which did not please the United States, worried by Soviet influence over the PCI) died with Mori's execution by the Red Brigades after 54 days in captivity. Another exploit was the kidnapping in December 1981 of an American brigadier-general who was stationed in Italy as a senior figure in the NATO command (after being held for 42 days the general was rescued by an Italian anti-terrorism team).

Not much of the Red Brigades' power still survives. In the 1980s its ranks were depleted by pressure from the police and security forces (in 1980 some 12,000 left-wing extremists were arrested and several hundred fled abroad, principally to Latin America and France, where many French intellectuals rallied to their defence and where in 1985 President François Mitterrand guaranteed asylum to any who had rejected violence). There were also internal conflicts, with the organisation splitting into the Red Brigades Communist Combatant Party (Red Brigades–PCC) and the smaller Red Brigades Union of Communist Combatants (Red Brigades–UCC). Several Red Brigades-PCC operatives were arrested in 2003 and 2005 for killing an adviser to the prime minister, Massimo D'Alema, in 1999 and an adviser to the prime minister, Silvio Berlusconi, in 2002. Since then, the organisation has been barely active.

But it would be naive to suppose that extremist tactics are about to disappear in Italy. Though present in several European countries, the Informal Anarchist Federation (Federazione Anarchica Informale, or FAI) has been particularly active in Italy. Opposed to both the present European system of government and Marxism (which it views as an authoritarian alternative to authoritarian capitalism), the FAI is believed to co-operate with the remnants of the Red Brigades. In 2013 the police arrested two FAI members on charges of committing 13 attacks on property in the previous three years. The FAI was also responsible for several letter bombs, including one to a journalist in Turin in 2013 that would have detonated as soon as he inserted the enclosed USB stick into his computer.

Apart from all this, the Italian state must also cope with occasional right-wing extremism – for example, an alleged plot in 2014 to promote Venetian independence from Italy by mounting an attack on St Mark's Square with a home-made tank. But most of all, it must confront the continued violence of the country's various Mafia organisations. Though groups such as the Cosa Nostra, Camorra, Sacra Corona Unita and 'Ndrangheta are not attempting revolution, they nonetheless undermine the state's institutions and so jeopardise its ability to counter political extremism.

Nagorno-Karabakh

The Nagorno-Karabakh Republic, a landlocked region of only 140,000 people sandwiched between Armenia and Azerbaijan, is a prime example of the problems that have arisen since the collapse of the Soviet Union. Under Soviet rule, Nagorno-Karabakh in 1923 was declared an autonomous *oblast* (region) within the Soviet Socialist Republic of Azerbaijan. But the majority of Nagorno-Karabakh's population are ethnically Armenian and religiously Christian, in contrast to Azerbaijan's mainly Turkic and Muslim population. In 1991, after some three years of conflict with Azerbaijan, Nagorno-Karabakh organised a referendum in which its population voted overwhelmingly for independence. The war, in which around 30,000 were killed, eventually ended in a ceasefire in 1994 signed not just by Armenia and Azerbaijan but also by the Nagorno-Karabakh Republic – a de facto recognition of its independent status.

The ceasefire, however, has been far from perfect, with hundreds of violations reported each month and with Armenia – supporting its ethnic brethren in Nagorno-Karabakh – occupying some parts of Azerbaijan bordering the new republic. The Organisation for Security and Co-operation in Europe (OSCE) in 1992 formed the Minsk Group, led by France, Russia and the United States, to work towards a peaceful settlement of the Nagorno-Karabakh issue. Its efforts have been in vain: Nagorno-Karabakh remains a frozen conflict – similar to the cases of South Ossetia and Abkhazia – in the Caucasus following the dissolution of the Soviet Union. Significantly, official recognition of the Nagorno-Karabakh Republic has come only from South Ossetia, Abkhazia and Transnistria (which declared its independence from Moldova in 1990).

The risk that frequent clashes (for example, several soldiers on both sides were killed in April 2015) will evolve into full-scale war cannot be dismissed. Nor can the possibility that such a war would involve directly or indirectly the neighbouring powers of Turkey, Iran and Russia. Pessimists cite the sheer amount of bitterness between Armenia and Azerbaijan. In 2012, for example, Armenia was furious that when Azerbaijan obtained the release of Ramil Safarov, an army officer serving a prison sentence in Hungary for killing an Armenian officer on a NATO-led language course, the Baku government – far from making Safarov complete his term in an Azerbaijani prison – hailed him as a hero and gave him a promotion.

The tensions are reflected in military preparations. Both Armenia and Azerbaijan have increased their military budgets (Armenia spends some 3.5% of its GDP on defence; Azerbaijan around 2.6%). Yet it is hard to see Armenia as the winner in any proper war: it has only 41,000 active military personnel, compared with Azerbaijan's 72,000, and has only a third of Azerbaijan's complement of tanks, combat aircraft and attack helicopters.

Meanwhile, a complicating factor is the role of Russia, as President Vladimir Putin works to assert Russian power in the region. In 2013, for example, the Kremlin raised the price of gas supplied to Armenia and increased the delivery of weapons to Azerbaijan – an effective way of persuading Armenia to backtrack on its desire for an association agreement with the EU. As usual in the Caucasus region, all players need to keep an eye on Russia.

Russia

Stretching from the Baltic Sea in the west to the Pacific Ocean in the east, the Russian Federation (as Russia is now officially known) is the world's largest country. Not surprisingly, perhaps, Russia, with a population of 143 million, is also a giant both militarily and politically: it has around 7,500 nuclear warheads (and is said to have had the world's largest stock of biological and chemical weapons during the Soviet era); it is a permanent member of the UN Security Council; and it vies with the United States as the world's biggest producer of oil and gas. In short, Russia is a power to be reckoned with, and has been for centuries, from the empire created by Peter the Great in the 18th century to the Soviet bloc ruled over by Joseph Stalin and his successors in the 20th century.

That power is also characterised by a capacity for endurance: in the second world war (which the Soviet Union entered in 1941 and termed the Great Patriotic War) the Soviet Union was instrumental in the defeat of Hitler's Germany, and was willing to accept a military and civilian death toll estimated by some historians at around 25 million.

Yet for the rest of the 20th century Russia's leaders were reluctant to wage war directly. In the Korean war of 1950–53, for example, the Soviet Union provided weapons and aid to its Chinese and North Korean allies, but did not commit troops. The basic reason was the balance of terror that existed in the wonderfully named cold war between the Soviet Union, intent on spreading communism around the world, and the United States, intent on spreading capitalism. Since both were superpowers with thousands of nuclear-armed missiles, both were conscious that any conflict leading to one or the other pressing the nuclear button would mean mutually assured destruction – a prospect that seemed horribly possible in the Cuban missile crisis of 1962, until President John Kennedy convinced Nikita Khrushchev to withdraw Soviet missiles from the island. The existence of what Churchill termed the iron curtain, dividing the communist Soviet bloc from the West, meant that Russian troops could invade Hungary in 1956 to put down the uprising against Soviet control and could invade Czechoslovakia in 1968 to quell the reform movement – on both occasions without any reaction by NATO.

The consequence of this superpower rivalry of the 20th century was a plethora of wars, rebellions and coups by proxy, be they in Latin America, Africa, Asia or the Middle East. But there is one exception, on the Russian side at least, to this conflict by proxy: the December 1979 Soviet invasion of Afghanistan, intended to preserve communist rule against the increasing threat of the *mujahideen* insurgents (a *mujahid* is someone performing *jihad*, which means struggle but which is often – and not always accurately – translated as holy war).

The rationale for the Soviet intervention was the Brezhnev doctrine, a decision by the then leader that once a country had joined the socialist camp it could never leave it (the Soviet Union had supplied arms to Afghanistan since 1955 and the country had turned to communism in 1978). The occupation was a decade-long disaster – Russia's Vietnam, as the headline writers like to say. Apart from the toll of death and destruction wreaked on Afghans, 13,310 Soviet troops were killed, 35,478 were wounded and 311 were reported missing by the time Mikhail Gorbachev ordered the withdrawal of troops in February 1989.

In retrospect, the Afghanistan war, coupled with Ronald Reagan's determination to surpass Russia in defence spending and capability, was clearly a factor in the collapse of the Soviet Union. Yet it has also been a factor in the Islamist extremism that threatens both Russia and the West today: the victorious *mujahideen* had been supported with weapons and money by several outside powers, notably the United States and Saudi Arabia, and among their recruits were many foreign Muslims, the most famous of them being a certain Osama bin Laden, founder of al-Qaeda.

In the 21st century, Russia's reaction to the demise of the Soviet Union has become markedly forthright under Vladimir Putin, a former KGB officer who assumed power in Russia in 1999 after the chaotic era of Boris Yeltsin (the successor to Mikhail Gorbachev and the first president of the Russian Federation). Putin was Russia's president until 2008, when he was constitutionally obliged to step down after two successive terms in office. But he remained the real power in the land as prime minister to President Dmitry Medvedev until 2012 – at which date he was again elected president.

Throughout his tenure in the Kremlin, Putin's ambition has been to restore Russia's status in the world, famously telling the Russian nation in 2005 (in the official translation):

> *Above all, we should acknowledge that the collapse of the Soviet Union was a major geopolitical disaster of the century. As for the Russian nation, it became a genuine drama. Tens of millions of our co-citizens and co-patriots found themselves outside Russian territory. Moreover, the epidemic of disintegration infected Russia itself.*

What that meant in 2008 was an invasion of Georgia in support of the separatists in South Ossetia and Abkhazia, both of which had favoured closer links with Russia. In 2014 it meant the threat of military force to help local pro-Russian forces accomplish the annexation of Crimea – a majority of whose population are ethnically Russian – from Ukraine. In the same year pro-Russian forces in eastern Ukraine could rely on the political – and potentially military – backing of Russia in their effort to secede from Ukraine and join Russia.

Western governments professed outrage at the plight of Ukraine and the loss of Crimea, not least because in 1994 in the Budapest memorandum the US, the UK and Russia agreed to be joint guarantors of Ukraine's territorial integrity. Yet the situation is more complex than the headlines criticising Russian aggression presume. Crimea, for example, became part of the Russian empire in 1783 and remained part of Russia until Nikita Khrushchev (hoping to consolidate his power at a time of Communist Party infighting) donated it to Ukraine in 1954. Crimea also contains the port of Sevastopol, a base for

Russia's Black Sea navy giving it access to the Mediterranean. It is also clear that most Crimeans did want to join "mother Russia", given that in a referendum held in March 2014 and denounced as illegal and one-sided by the Ukraine government some 97% of the vote was for Crimea to become part of Russia.

It may well be true, also, that a majority of the population in the eastern part of Ukraine wish their region to be part of Russia, especially after the Ukrainian parliament in February 2014 voted to annul a law that has allowed 13 of Ukraine's 27 regions to use Russian as a second official language (the parliament's decision was not signed into law). Putin, with Russian troops poised to cross the border if needed by the pro-Russian rebels, argues that the West is backing a regime in Ukraine that came to power illegally after demonstrations in Kiev forced President Viktor Yanukovych in early 2014 to flee into exile. The background to this crisis was a competition for influence between the West, in the shape of the EU, and Russia. Ukraine had been about to sign an association agreement with the EU, but Yanukovych abruptly rejected the EU proposal in favour of a loan from – and closer links with – Russia.

That competition has its roots in the decision during the Clinton presidency in the United States to offer NATO membership – or the prospect of membership – to former members of the Warsaw Pact (the mutual defence pact between the Soviet Union and its satellite states). That membership was eagerly embraced by Poland, Hungary, Czechoslovakia (as it then was), Romania, Bulgaria and the Baltic states of Lithuania, Estonia and Latvia. When other states in the former sphere of influence of the Soviet Union were invited to join NATO's Partnership for Peace, Russia saw this as an attempt to spread Western power at its expense – hence its invasion of Georgia when an invitation for Georgia to join NATO itself seemed on the cards.

The consequence now is the threat of a renewed cold war, and the possibility – if only by accident – that it might become hot. In 2014 the Baltic states in particular, because of their large Russian minorities, feared Putin's intentions and clung to the hope that NATO's mutual defence pact (an attack on one is an attack on all) would not have to be put to the test. So, too, did Poland, with its shared border with Russia and its memories of Soviet rule. Evidence of the changing temperature was the exchange of sanctions between the West and Russia, with the US and the EU imposing financial constraints and travel bans on Russian individuals and with Russia banning food imports from the EU, the US and some other Western countries. Pessimists recalled that the first world war, 100 years earlier, had been the improbable consequence of the assassination in Sarajevo of Archduke Franz Ferdinand, heir to the Austro-Hungarian throne.

In purely military terms Russia is no match for NATO, or for the US, NATO's leading force. With 766,000 active military personnel, Russia's armed forces are only half the size of the US's and a fifth of the NATO total of 3.37 million. But such numbers would hardly be relevant if NATO's political will to combat Russia were lacking. Certainly, there was no appetite in the West to intervene in the Georgian conflict on Georgia's behalf. And certainly, Putin is keen to reinforce and even increase Russia's military power, hence not just the determination to keep the Sevastopol base in Crimea and the naval facilities at Tartus in Syria (where Russia opposed the West's desire for regime change) but also a desire, outlined by Russia's defence minister in early 2014, to establish bases in a number of foreign countries which are not former Soviet republics, from Vietnam and Cuba to the Seychelles and Nicaragua. As Putin is well aware, in Soviet times Russia had a large naval base in Vietnam and a radar facility in Cuba, but both were closed down for financial reasons.

Yet for all Russia's concern with the West, its most immediate problems are nearer home, with the growth of separatism and Islamic extremism in the North Caucasus region, home to nominally autonomous and predominantly Muslim Chechnya, Ingushetia, Dagestan, North Ossetia, Kabardino-Balkaria and Karachay-Cherkessia. The break-up of the Soviet Union encouraged separatists to seize their opportunity. In 1991 Chechnya declared itself the independent Chechen Republic of Ichkeria. Three chaotic years in Russia later, President Yeltsin sent in Russian troops to reclaim Chechnya; but after 18 months of savage fighting, with the Chechen capital, Grozny, heavily bombarded, the Russian forces withdrew, accepting Chechnya's de facto independence.

Succeeding Yeltsin in power, Putin had other ideas, launching a second Chechen war in 1999 after Shamil Basayev, a Chechen Islamist opposed to Chechnya's secular leadership, led his International Islamic Brigade in an invasion of neighbouring Dagestan – the start of what Putin feared could become a regional Islamist revolt. By April 2000 Russia declared a military victory, but combating the continuing insurgency would tie down Russian troops and their Chechen allies for another nine years. Moreover, quelling the twin forces of separatism and Islamism had come at a heavy price. By one account Russia lost more tanks in the first Chechen war than in the battle for Berlin in 1945, and in 2003 the UN described Grozny as the most destroyed city on earth. As to the loss of life, one Chechen official in 2005 said the total number of dead – be they Russian Federation troops, Chechen rebels or civilians – had reached up to 160,000.

A decade after the first Chechen war, despite the enormous loss of life, and despite installing in Grozny a pro-Russian prime minister (first, an ex-separatist, Akhmad Kadyrov, and then, after his assassination, his son Ramzan), Russia can still not regard the North Caucasus region with complacency. Chechnya and its neighbours are poor and corrupt, which means they are fertile ground for Islamist extremism, with an increasing number of the region's Muslims turning from more moderate Sufism to Salafism, an austere brand of fundamentalist Islam. In 2007, for example, Dokka Umarov, the former president of the Chechen Republic of Ichkeria, announced the establishment of the Caucasus Emirate, with a goal of expelling Russia from the region and creating an Islamic emirate.

Umarov (who is believed to have died, perhaps by poison or perhaps in combat, in 2013) was an advocate of terrorism as a means of putting pressure on Russia. So too was Basayev. Between 1991 and his death in 2006, Basayev was responsible for hijacking an airline, taking a whole hospital hostage and launching suicide bombers in Moscow itself. Perhaps the most notorious of his operations was the seizure by Ingush and Chechen militants of a school at Beslan in North Ossetia in 2004. When the siege, with around 1,200 held hostage, ended three days later, some 334 people were dead, including 186 children. Umarov's operations included the derailing of an express train in 2009, claiming 28 lives; two suicide attacks in the Moscow subway in 2009, with 40 deaths; and a suicide-bomb attack on Moscow's Domodedovo airport in 2011 that killed 35.

Will the threat of Islamist violence recede? Perhaps marginally (there were no terrorist incidents to upset the 2014 Winter Olympics in Sochi), but surely not entirely. Despite brutal counter-terrorism tactics by the state, Russia still recorded 661 terrorist offences in 2013, of which it classified 31 as fully fledged terrorist attacks. Moreover, one feature of Chechen separatism was the number of Chechen fighters who had returned from fighting in Afghanistan, forging links with the Taliban and with the beginnings of al-Qaeda. With the Arab world in turmoil, up to 1,500 jihadists with Russian passports were said to be fighting in Syria and Iraq in early 2015 – and doubtless some will return and attempt to create havoc.

Spain

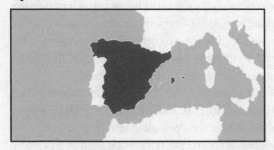

For most of the 16th and 17th centuries Spain was Europe's leading imperial power, with its colonies stretching across the globe from Latin America in the west to the Philippines in the east. Yet in modern times it is the UK and France that retain a taste for overseas military adventure. Spain, with a population of 47 million, contributes to UN, EU and NATO peacekeeping missions from Haiti to Lebanon, and it has given its air support to NATO operations in the Balkans and in the Libyan civil war that ousted Qaddafi in 2011. Yet, for all that, it is far less bellicose than its British and French allies.

An example is Spain's commitment of at one point 2,500 troops to the NATO-led war in Afghanistan, "Operation Enduring Freedom". The troops, though in dwindling numbers, stayed until 2013, but the Spanish parliament's mandate allowed them to engage the Taliban only if first attacked by the Taliban. As for the US-led invasion of

Iraq in 2003, popular opposition in Spain to the so-called "Operation Iraqi Freedom" compelled a new Socialist government in Madrid to withdraw Spain's 1,400 troops after less than a year. Significantly, the new government was elected in March 2004 just three days after an al-Qaeda-linked attack on four commuter trains in Madrid killed 191 and injured more than 1,800. The motive for the attack remains unclear, but many have linked it to Spain's role in Afghanistan and argue that the presence in Spain of over 1 million Muslims – mostly immigrants from Morocco – provides a reservoir in which Islamist extremism can breed.

One factor in Spain's military shyness is perhaps the memory of the savage civil war of 1936–39 that led to the dictatorship of General Francisco Franco. The general kept Spain neutral during the second world war but was clearly sympathetic to the fascist regimes of German and Italy that had helped his nationalists overcome the Soviet-supported republicans. Indeed, although Spain was officially not involved in the war, Franco organised a volunteer force of almost 50,000 to fight for Germany on the eastern front against the Soviet Union.

A second factor is that most of Spain's colonial possessions had achieved independence a century or more earlier. One big exception was the Spanish Sahara, where the Polisario guerrilla group began its fight for Sahrawi independence in 1973 with a raid on a Spanish post manned by Sahrawi auxiliaries. But with Franco ailing, Spain was in no mood for a fight. When he died in 1975, Spain celebrated the transition to democracy by summarily withdrawing from what most outsiders would now call the Western Sahara, but which would be claimed as part of Morocco by the Moroccan government.

Spain still retains, over Moroccan protests, some small possessions in north Africa, notably the coastal enclaves of Ceuta and Melilla and a few tiny islands. The minute and deserted island of Perejil, just off the coast of Morocco, was the scene of a bloodless clash between Spain and Morocco in 2002, when Spain sent in troops to dislodge a small Moroccan force that had taken a presumably symbolic possession of Perejil. A more serious problem for both governments is the flood of migrants, many from south of the Sahara, attempting to scale the barbed-wire defences of Ceuta and Melilla in the hope of finding a better life in the EU.

The Spanish presence in north Africa is one source of occasional tension with a neighbour, in this case Morocco, but a better-known dispute is with the UK over its possession of Gibraltar, at the southern tip of the Iberian peninsula, which was ceded to the UK in perpetuity by Spain in the 1713 Treaty of Utrecht. Though almost all of Gibraltar's 30,000 population clearly wish to remain British citizens (98% in a 2002 referendum), Spain accuses Gibraltar of being a haven for financial fraudsters and tobacco smugglers. The tensions arising with Spain's claim to the territory at times lead to delays for Gibraltarians at the frontier, and even to occasional Mexican stand-offs between Spanish and British naval ships – but it is inconceivable that Spain and the UK will come to actual blows.

By contrast, the real threats to the Spanish state are separatism and Islamist terrorism, neither of which can be solved merely by a military response from armed forces that number 123,300 active personnel.

Outsiders might question the desire for any region of Spain to secede, given the large degree of autonomy given to the country's 17 regions under the 1978 constitution that consolidated the transition to democracy after the Franco era. But Catalonia, whose 7.5 million people provide the economic powerhouse of the Kingdom of Spain, and the Basque Country both have strong separatist movements, with their populations proud of their cultural identities and of having languages distinct from Spanish.

The Catalan quest for secession was not always peaceful. Terra Lliure (Free Land), a Marxist group formed in 1978 with the goal of establishing an independent Catalonia that would also include Valencia, waged a bombing campaign against foreign banks and other property. However, Terra Lliure's tactics never inspired popular support and in 1991 it publicly abandoned violence before dissolving itself in 1995. Today's Catalan separatists believe in democratic politics rather than violence.

Will that be true of the Basque Country and its 2 million residents? The answer depends on Euskadi Ta Askatasuna (Basque Homeland and Liberty), known normally as ETA and responsible for well over 800 deaths since it killed a *Guardia Civil* (Spanish gendarmerie) member at a roadblock in 1968. ETA's origins lie in the Basque Nationalist

Party (Partido Nacionalista Vasco, or PNV), founded in 1895. In 1959, frustrated by the PNV's refusal to adopt armed struggle as a strategy, some younger members broke away to found ETA, which in 1966 split into the more moderate ETA-V and the ideologically Marxist ETA-VI, which favoured a policy of sabotage and assassination. There were several subsequent splits, but by the end of the 1970s ETA was reunified as an underground military organisation.

As such it had some success, provoking the authorities into secretly forming death squads to assassinate ETA members and supporters. The first of these was the right-wing Batallón Vasco Español (Basque Spanish Battalion, or BVE) in 1975–81 and then, when the Spanish Socialist Party came to power in 1982, the Grupos Antiterroristas de Liberación (GAL). Both the BVE and the GAL carried out most of their assassinations in France, where ETA militants enjoyed sanctuary because of the French government's distaste for Spain's tactics. When the GAL was disbanded in 1987 and the so-called dirty war ended, France began to co-operate with Spain, not least by refusing asylum to ETA members and by extraditing them back to Spain.

Such cross-frontier collaboration, popular uproar – including in the Basque Country itself – at some of ETA's operations and heightened anti-terrorist pressure everywhere after the 9/11 attacks in the US combined to force ETA into announcing several ceasefires, the last being in September 2010. This was followed in January 2011 by a declaration that the ceasefire would be permanent and in October by an announcement from ETA of a definitive end to its armed struggle.

Perhaps as significant as ETA's abandonment of violence was the decision by Batasuna (Unity – originally Herri Batasuna, or Unity of the People), a banned political party that had acted as the political arm of ETA, to announce its dissolution in January 2013. Given that Batasuna, in its various legally accepted guises, could command around 15% of votes to the Basque Autonomous Community, its disappearance and the laying down of arms by ETA should mean the end of Spain's long and violent conflict with Basque separatism. Yet the lure of nationalism for the Basques is not about to vanish, and the example of those extremists in Northern Ireland who still reject the Good Friday agreement is a sobering warning for the Spanish government that peace cannot be taken for granted.

At least as sobering, given the Madrid train bombings of 2004 (which were initially – and wrongly – blamed on ETA), is the threat of Islamist violence in Spain. In the decade after the Madrid bombings, the Spanish authorities arrested some 472 suspected Islamist militants. In 2012 the security forces seized three suspected members of al-Qaeda to forestall alleged plots to bomb a shopping mall near Gibraltar and attack a Spanish naval base at Rota that supports the US navy.

Given the perennial turmoil in the Middle East, the authorities are bound to fear more such plots, especially as Spanish jihadists – battle-hardened and ideologically driven – return home from the conflicts in Syria and Iraq. In May 2014 the police in Melilla arrested six Spanish citizens on suspicion of sending 26 Islamist militants to fight in Syria, Iraq and Libya. Two months later ISIS released a video promising to extend the Islamic State, or caliphate, throughout all of Islam's historical territory, including Spain's Andalusia. A few weeks later Spanish and Moroccan police combined to seize a nine-member ISIS recruitment cell in northern Morocco, making it clear that the Spanish authorities are taking the threat of Islamist violence seriously, not just from al-Qaeda but also from the better organised, better financed and even more violent ISIS.

Turkey

Nominally European, due to the small part of its territory on the western side of the Bosphorus strait and the European leanings of its founding father, Kemal Ataturk, the Republic of Turkey, with a population of 81 million, has the largest armed forces – some 410,000

active frontline personnel – of any NATO member other than the United States. It is also NATO's only Muslim state (an identity that will probably delay indefinitely its progress towards membership of the EU), and was the first Middle Eastern state to have an alliance (often strained by the issue of Palestine) with Israel. Geopolitically, Turkey's governments – especially since the election of the AK Parti (Adalet ve Kalkınma Partisi, or Justice and Development Party) in 2002 – have seen their country as a bridge between Europe and the Arab Middle East. To Turkey's Western allies, the AK Parti, which is founded on a moderate version of Islam and led by Recep Tayyip Erdogan, is proof that Islam and democracy can coexist.

But the rise of modern Turkey from the collapse of its Ottoman empire (Turkey foolishly sided with the losers in the first world war) has not been without its problems. Possibly as many as 1.5 million of Turkey's Armenian population (who were both Christian and accused of betraying the country) perished during the first world war, as the Turkish authorities carried out a campaign of ruthless Turkification. This has led to Armenian claims, accepted by many outsiders, of genocide and to periods of tension with modern Armenia that were only increased by Turkey's support for Azerbaijan over the Nagorno-Karabakh issue. In 2009 Swiss mediation produced an agreement for Turkey and Armenia to establish diplomatic relations, but by mid-2015 neither country had ratified the accord.

Whereas the AK Parti's predecessors (several of them military governments) looked very much westwards in foreign policy, Erdogan's pledge has been zero problems with the neighbours and an emphasis on strategic depth, by which Turkey would be a stabilising influence in the Middle East. In practice, the formula has been found wanting: relations with Israel have been strained by devastating Israeli bombardments of Gaza in 2008, 2012 and 2014; the Muslim Brotherhood, with which Turkey sympathises, has been banned in Egypt; and notwithstanding the aid and sanctuary they receive from Turkey, Syria's rebels have failed to dislodge Bashar al-Assad. In a mockery of zero problems with the neighbours, there have been several clashes on the border with Syria and in 2012 Syrian artillery shot down a Turkish jet fighter that had accidentally strayed into Syrian airspace. In short, the chaos that has followed the Arab spring of 2011 continues, with the establishment in much of Syria and Iraq in 2014 of a new caliphate by the self-proclaimed Islamic State threatening yet more turmoil.

Turkey's most enduring differences, however, are with Greece, with a plethora of maritime and territorial disputes that may become more fraught with the discovery of petroleum reserves in the eastern Mediterranean. (Historians will note that when the Turkish republic was formed in 1923, the Lausanne Treaty organised or coincided with a massive transfer of populations, with 1.1 million Greeks leaving Turkey for Greece and some 380,000 Muslims leaving Greece for Turkey.) In 1974 Turkish troops parachuted into Cyprus to protect Turkish Cypriots after a coup carried out by Greek Cypriots wanting *enosis* (unity) with Greece. The resulting division of the island has yet to be mended, with Turkey being the only country to recognise the establishment in 1983 of the Turkish Republic of Northern Cyprus.

Happily, both Turkey and Greece are members of NATO and both have been staunch allies of the United States (which has two large air-force bases in Turkey) ever since the cold war pitted the West against the communist Soviet Union. The consequence is that tensions between the two have usually been kept under control. Though military pilots from both countries sometimes indulge in mock dogfights, it is difficult to see the two coming to blows in the 21st century.

The greater threat for Turkey comes from internal dissent. Nationalism verging on jingoism has been an underlying feature of the Turkish republic ever since the days of Ataturk (whose name means father of the Turks), with the armed forces so keen on preserving his secularist ideas that they mounted coups in 1960, 1971, 1980 and 1997 (the last with a set of recommendations that the government had no choice but to accept).

Although the Erdogan governments have tamed such military adventurism, ultra-nationalism still exists in the form of extremists of left and right. The Grey Wolves (Bozkurtlar), regarded as the militant branch of the far-right Nationalist Movement Party (Milliyetçi Hareket Partisi, or MHP), was responsible, according to the authorities, for 694 killings between 1974 and 1980 – and it won global notoriety with the attempted assassination in 1981 of Pope John Paul II by one of its members, Mehmet Ali Agca. At the other end of the political spectrum are several far-left groups, such as the Revolutionary People's Liberation Party–Front (Devrimci Halk Kurtulus, Partisi–Cephesi, or DHKP/C), which was responsible in the 1980s and 1990s for several assassinations, including of imperialist Americans and one Briton. In 2013 a DHKP/C suicide bomber attacked the US embassy in Ankara and in the same year other DHKP/C activists twice attacked government and AK Parti installations in the capital. A DHKP/C suicide bomber claimed responsibility in January 2015 for the death of an Istanbul policeman and the wounding of another, apparently in retaliation for the death of a 15-year-old demonstrator at an anti-government protest in 2013.

But the defining struggle for the Turkish authorities has always been with the Kurdistan Workers' Party, the PKK (Partiya Karkerên Kurdistan), founded in 1978 with the goal of establishing an independent Kurdistan for the 30 million or so Kurds – 14 million of them in Turkey – living in an area that encompasses the south-east of Turkey and parts of Syria, Iraq and Iran. The PKK, which abandoned its Marxist-Leninist roots at the end of the 20th century, began its armed struggle in 1984, with a full-scale insurgency that lasted until it declared a unilateral ceasefire in 1999 and withdrew many of its fighters into northern Iraq.

That ceasefire was never complete or likely to endure: Turkish troops raided PKK bases, including in Iraq, and some PKK guerrillas broke away to carry on fighting in groups such as the Marxist-Leninist Revolutionary Party of Kurdistan (PSK) and the Kurdistan Freedom Falcons (Teyrênbazê Azadiya Kurdistan, or TAK). By 2004 the PKK's insurgency had resumed and continued until 2012, interrupted only by a ceasefire in 2009 that ended a year later. Yet in April 2013, Murat Karaliyan, the military leader of the PKK, announced that all his fighters would be withdrawn to northern Iraq the following month – a decision prompted by a call for a ceasefire and negotiations with the government from Abdullah Ocalan, the founder of the PKK who is serving a life sentence in prison after being arrested (with CIA help) in Kenya in 1999.

In theory this should presage the end to Turkey's three-decade-long conflict with its Kurdish minority, a struggle in which the PKK – with at most 10,000 active guerrillas (and thousands more part-time) and using tactics from ambush to sabotage and suicide bombings – were never crushed by NATO's largest European army. The total killed on both sides has been estimated at 45,000 and there have been dreadful human-rights abuses by both the Turkish armed forces and the PKK.

Yet one reason for optimism is the conciliatory approach of the AK Parti under President Erdogan, with the government having talks with the imprisoned Ocalan (who, having been sentenced to death, was spared when Turkey abolished the death penalty as part of its bid to join the EU). In 2013 Erdogan's government relaxed some of the restrictions on the use of the Kurdish language and in 2014 a political party, Turkey's Kurdish Democratic Party (T-KDP), was allowed to use the word Kurdish in its title, some 49 years after it first applied for a licence to operate legally. Similarly, the government in 2012 approved the formation of the pro-Kurdish and anti-capitalist People's Democratic Party (Halklarin Demokratik Partisi, or HDP), despite allegations of links with the PKK. Those links may well explain the twin bomb attacks on HDP offices in Mersin and Adana in May 2015, injuring several party workers.

Though Turkey's relationship with its Kurdish minority has undoubtedly improved, its attitude towards the Kurds led it to adopt policies towards the civil war in neighbouring Syria that in late 2014 put it at odds with its Western allies, especially the United States. Not only was it clear that Turkey was doing little to intercept European would-be jihadists from crossing into Syria to join Islamist groups such as ISIS and Jabhat al-Nusra, but it stood by while the Kurdish town of Kobane (Ayn al-Arab in Arabic), just inside Syria, was under a prolonged siege by ISIS fighters. The reason was that the defence of Kobane involved the YPG (the People's Protection Units), acting as the armed wing of the Kurds' Democratic Union Party (PYD) – and Turkey regards the PYD as the Syrian arm of the PKK. Eventually, American arm-twisting forced Turkey to allow Peshmerga guerrillas from Iraqi Kurdistan to pass through Turkish territory to help defend Kobane. That, and US-led aerial bombardments of ISIS targets, finally lifted the Kobane siege in March 2015.

Some four months later, the Ankara government modified its tactics still further. Following an ISIS suicide bomb that killed 32 in the Turkish town of Suruc in July 2015, Turkey launched air attacks on Islamic State targets in Syria and finally allowed US jets to use Turkish air bases for their raids on Syria. Yet, putting at risk the improved relations with its Kurdish citizens, Turkey also sent jets to strafe PKK facilities in northern Iraq, perhaps in retaliation for the killing by the PKK of two Turkish policemen, accused by the PKK of collaborating with ISIS.

In the end, though, the decisive factor in resolving Turkey's Kurdish problem may be the fate of Iraqi Kurdistan, which since the fall of Saddam Hussein has operated officially as an autonomous region of Iraq but increasingly as an independent entity. Sandwiched between Iran, Turkey and the self-proclaimed caliphate of the Islamic State, Iraqi Kurdistan's future is by no means assured. If it stays within its boundaries, its neighbours will wish it well. But if it seeks to expand, all of them – including Turkey – will react militarily.

Ukraine

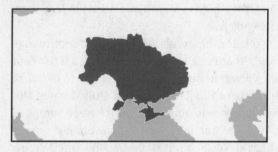

Ukraine, once the breadbasket of the Union of Soviet Socialist Republics (USSR), proclaimed itself an independent state in August 1991, following the collapse of the Soviet Union. Yet in the second decade of the 21st century independence has become an ambiguous concept, with Ukraine's future a prize to be contested between Russia to its east and the EU to its west – and with the contest resurrecting fears of a new cold war between the United States and Russia.

For Ukraine's 44 million population the promise that came with independence was first tarnished by rampant corruption; now it has given way to destructive differences defined partly by language and partly by the competing lures of the capital, Kiev, and Moscow. Whereas three-quarters of the population are ethnically Ukrainian, around 17% – mainly in the east of the country – are ethnically Russian and around 30% of the population say Russian is their first language.

Some 2 million of these Russian-speaking Ukrainians instantly became Russian citizens on March 18th 2014 when Crimea, which had been made part of Ukraine by Nikita Khrushchev in 1954 (this generous gesture reflected Communist Party infighting in the Soviet Union), was formally annexed by Russia – the first time that a Russian government had expanded the country's borders since the second world war. The loss of Crimea was compounded by a well-armed pro-Russia separatist movement in eastern Ukraine, which has led to months of heavy – but inconclusive – fighting with government forces.

By the summer of 2015 this conflict in eastern Ukraine had claimed more than 6,000 lives since pro-Russian activists in early April 2014 seized government buildings in Donetsk, Luhansk and Kharkiv. In the succeeding months both the violence and the rhetoric mounted: Russian troops were stationed intimidatingly close to the border and the US and the EU imposed economic sanctions on Russia and travel bans on senior Russian associates of President Vladimir Putin. In one hyperbolic outburst, Ukraine's prime minister, Arseniy Yatsenyuk, in late April 2014 accused Russia of seeking to trigger a third world war; in June Russia's Gazprom cut off gas supplies to Ukraine and said any future supplies would have to be paid for in advance by the near-bankrupt Ukrainian authorities. In a particularly troubling incident in July 2014, Malaysian Airlines flight MH17, with 298 people on board, was shot down over eastern Ukraine by a missile allegedly (and presumably mistakenly) fired by a rebel.

Russia's involvement in the Ukraine crisis is a matter as much of opinion as of fact. The Kremlin denies any participation by Russian troops in the fighting, while Ukraine's President Petro Poroshenko said in January 2015 that Russia had sent 9,000 troops and 500 tanks and armoured vehicles to support the pro-Russian separatists. What is undeniable is that in August 2014 Ukraine handed ten captured Russian paratroopers, who claimed they had crossed the border by accident, back to Russia and Russia handed 63 Ukrainian troops, who had crossed into Russia to escape separatist attacks, back to Ukraine.

The tensions with Russia emphasise Ukraine's troubled history since independence. With the country set free from the command economy of the Soviet Union, Ukraine suffered deep economic recession and high inflation under the first president, Leonid Kravchuk (a long-time Communist Party functionary belatedly embracing nationalism). His successor in 1994, Leonid Kuchma, attempted to stabilise the economy by fostering closer links with Russia while also adopting pro-market reforms (economic growth did not finally resume until 2001).

An important feature of Kuchma's first year as president was his signature, along with those of the US president, Bill Clinton, the Russian president, Boris Yeltsin, and the UK prime minister, John Major, on the Budapest memorandum, under which Ukraine agreed to give up its Soviet-era nuclear warheads (the world's third-largest nuclear arsenal at the time) and transfer them to Russia. In return, the other signatories pledged to "respect the independence and sovereignty and the existing borders of Ukraine" and to "refrain from the threat or use of force against the territorial integrity or political independence of Ukraine". It is this agreement that the West accuses President Putin of flouting in his annexation of Crimea and support for the separatists in eastern Ukraine.

But the Kuchma presidency was also marked by corruption, cronyism and censorship; worse still, audio tapes were found that appeared to implicate him in the murder in 2000 of a dissident journalist (in 2011 a court dismissed the prosecution case). Cleared by the Constitutional Court to run for a third term in 2004, Kuchma decided instead to endorse his prime minister, Viktor Yanukovych, who also had the backing of Putin. Yanukovych's opponent was Viktor Yushchenko, who argued for a close relationship with the EU – and who fell victim to a mysterious illness. This turned out be caused by dioxin poisoning and left him with a badly pockmarked face. Amid accusations by independent observers of electoral fraud, Yanukovych was declared the winner in the election's second-round run-off in November. This immediately provoked the pro-West "Orange revolution" of 2004, with demonstrators in mass protests wearing orange, the campaign colour of Yushchenko. In December the Supreme Court ruled that the November run-off had been invalid and ordered a second one, which was won on December 26th by Yushchenko.

The following month President Yushchenko appointed Yulia Timoshenko, his foremost ally in the Orange revolution, as his prime minister – and within months was at odds with her. By 2008, with the country suffering not just from endemic corruption but also from the impact of the global financial crisis, Yushchenko was locked in a bitter power struggle with Timoshenko. In the presidential election of January 2010 Yushchenko received only 5% of the vote, leaving the February run-off to be decided by Timoshenko and Yanukovych.

Victory went to Yanukovych, and Timoshenko immediately claimed the result had been rigged. No matter: the pro-Putin Yanukovych was in the presidential palace and by June 2011 Timoshenko was on trial on charges of abuse of power during her two periods as prime minister, notably over a 2009 deal to purchase gas from Russia at an inflated price. In October 2011 she was sentenced to seven years in prison, and then in November she faced new charges of embezzlement and tax evasion allegedly dating back to the 1990s.

Whereas Yushchenko had seen Ukraine's future in a close alliance with the EU (hence negotiations that began in 2007), Yanukovych – born in eastern Ukraine and instinctively pro-Russian – looked towards Russia. In April 2010, in exchange for a lower price for Russian gas, he extended Russia's lease on its naval base in Sevastopol, in Crimea, to 2042, but then enraged many in Ukraine by declaring that the Soviet-era famine of 1932–33, in which perhaps 5 million Ukrainians died, was not – as Yushchenko had charged – a Soviet-inspired genocide.

Ukraine's descent into chaos and war began in November 2013, when President Yanukovych backed out of a trade and co-operation agreement with the EU just days before it was due to be signed, arguing that Ukraine would be better off in the Eurasian Economic Union advocated by Putin (the EEU came into force in January 2015 with Russia, Armenia, Belarus and Kazakhstan as its founding members).

The immediate result of Yanukovych's apparent abandonment of the dream that one day Ukraine might be part of the EU was a swelling tide of popular demonstrations and the occupation by thousands of pro-West protesters of Kiev's central Maidan Nezalezhnosti (Independence Square). After weeks of protest, around

100 Maidan demonstrators were shot dead on February 18th–20th 2014, apparently by government snipers. On February 22nd, a day after Yanukovych fled from Kiev, parliament voted to end his presidency and Timoshenko was freed from prison.

On the face of it, the pro-EU and pro-Western forces that a decade earlier had triumphed in the Orange revolution had triumphed once again. As Yanukovych retired to safety in Russia, his private residence outside Kiev was opened to the public to see its extraordinary opulence and the interim government issued a warrant for his arrest for mass murder.

Yet Russia and its allies have a different view. They see the Orange revolution as the continuation of a campaign by the US government and Western non-governmental organisations (NGOs), such as the Open Society Foundations of George Soros, to seduce countries that once were in the Soviet orbit – for example, Serbia and Georgia – into the economic and political embrace of the West. In the same vein they see the ousting of Yanukovych as an illegal coup engineered by the West and favouring Ukrainian fascists (Svoboda, a political party tainted by anti-Semitism and with pro-Nazi origins, played a prominent role in the Maidan demonstrations). This coup d'état meant that it was the West, not Russia, that was reneging on the Budapest memorandum.

This does not, of course, legitimise the annexation of Crimea, but in March 2014 President Putin, accusing the West of double standards, offered Kosovo's independence in 2008 as a parallel and self-determination as a justification:

> Our Western partners created the Kosovo precedent with their own hands. In a situation absolutely the same as the one in Crimea they recognised Kosovo's secession from Serbia legitimate while arguing that no permission from a country's central authority for a unilateral declaration of independence is necessary.

Whatever the legal validity of Crimea's secession, it was achieved with the loss of only two lives. The reason was that any Ukrainian military resistance would have been futile, since under its lease agreement for its Sevastopol base Russia was allowed to station up to 25,000 troops in Crimea. By contrast, government forces have fiercely opposed the separatists in eastern Ukraine. In March 2014 pro-Russia militias in the Donetsk and Luhansk *oblasts* (regions) seized government buildings and pro-Russia and pro-government demonstrations became increasingly violent. By early April pro-Russia separatists had declared the People's Republic of Donetsk and the goal of unification with Russia. Later in the month separatists declared the People's Republic of Luhansk, which in May merged with its Donetsk equivalent to form the confederation of Novorossiya (recognised only by South Ossetia, the barely recognised pro-Russia republic that seceded from Georgia in 1990).

Ukraine's armed forces began their counter-offensive in mid-April 2014. With around 160,000 frontline personnel and almost 3,000 tanks, as well as helicopters and aircraft, on paper they should have had no problem in reasserting the government's control over the east. Much of the army, however, is composed of conscripts with no wish to risk their lives – hence growing numbers of defections – and recruits mobilised in 2014 and 2015 were described by one government adviser as "alcoholics and dodgers, drug addicts and morons". Moreover, despite its denials, it was clear that Russia was supplying the separatists with arms – and quite possibly with trained soldiers, too. The result has been a military stalemate, marked by ineffectual ceasefires and coinciding with an increasingly acute economic crisis and the massive destruction of many towns in eastern Ukraine.

The challenge for Petro Poroshenko, elected president in May 2014, is somehow to find a solution that will leave Ukraine intact, at least in principle if not in practice. Poroshenko's pro-West stance is not in doubt, and was confirmed on June 27th 2014 – just 20 days after his inauguration – by his signature on the EU–Ukraine Association Agreement that Yanukovych had rejected. His pro-West policy is also of long standing: he was a billionaire supporter of the Orange revolution (his fortune comes from control of a business empire that includes a confectionery company – hence his nickname "the chocolate king") and he served as President Yushchenko's foreign minister. He also served as trade minister for President Yanukovych, but he was trying, he says, to move Ukraine closer to the EU despite Yanukovych's opposition.

Despite his impressive curriculum vitae, any solution must clearly be agreed by players much more powerful than Poroshenko, who has not helped his cause by declaring in December 2014 that Ukraine should hold a referendum on joining NATO – precisely the opposite of what Putin has in mind. In February 2015 marathon talks in the Belarus capital, Minsk, involving Poroshenko, President Hollande of France, Chancellor Merkel of Germany and, of course, President Putin, yielded a ceasefire under which both the Ukrainian government and the separatists would withdraw their heavy weapons and leave a wide security zone between them; all foreign troops and mercenaries would depart; militias would disarm; and Ukraine would recover control of its borders after the holding of local elections.

Optimists were encouraged by the Minsk agreement; realists have remained sceptical, not least because Poroshenko's date for the local elections was a distant October 2015. The level of violence certainly diminished in the wake of the Minsk ceasefire, but not the level of rhetoric, with Russia particularly criticising the dispatch to Ukraine in April of American paratroopers on a six-month mission to train Ukrainian troops. In short, Ukraine's crisis has all the features of a post-Soviet frozen conflict, with the country trapped between West and East, or as cynics might say, between a rock and a hard place.

5 The Americas: faith, drugs and revolution

IMAGINE THE ABSENCE of the United States and to many casual observers the Americas become a caricature in three parts: peaceful (some of its citizens might even say boring) and socially responsible Canada; the laid-back but crime-ridden islands of the Caribbean; and turbulent, socially divided Latin America.

As with most caricatures there is an element of truth in these sweeping generalisations. But the reality is, of course, much more complex: Chile is very different from Mexico; communist Cuba is not the same as the British overseas territories of Anguilla or the Turks and Caicos Islands; Portuguese-speaking Brazil is an economic giant whereas Spanish-speaking Paraguay is an economic pygmy. What is common to all is the looming influence of the US. Ever since President James Monroe declared in 1823 that "the American continents ... are henceforth not to be considered as subjects for future colonisation by any European powers", the US has considered Latin America and the Caribbean as its own backyard – a view bolstered by its overwhelming economic and military power. For Canada to its north, the US is its most important trading partner; for the countries to its south, the US is a seemingly irresistible magnet for migration (much of it illegal) and a huge market for drugs such as cocaine, heroin and marijuana.

Not surprisingly, therefore, the influence of the US is a thread running through the continent's politics and conflicts, especially during the cold war, with the US determined to oppose communism and socialism. This was shown most obviously in the CIA-plotted overthrow of Chile's socialist president, Salvador Allende, in 1973 and the US invasion of tiny Grenada (a member of the British Commonwealth) to oust the leftist regime of the New Jewel Movement in 1983. Most remarkable (indeed egregious) was the Iran–Contra affair of the 1980s, when in defiance of Congress the US government channelled funds to the Contra rebels seeking to overthrow the left-wing Sandinista regime in Nicaragua (the funds were acquired by selling arms to Iran, in the vain hope that Iran would arrange the release of American hostages held by Shia groups in Lebanon). Most durable has been the US opposition to the communist regime of Cuba, complete with assassination attempts on Fidel Castro and support for the abortive Bay of Pigs invasion in 1961 by Cuban rebels.

There are also tensions that have nothing to do with the US.

Border disputes in Central and South America are relatively common: Nicaragua has maritime or territorial claims that annoy Colombia, Costa Rica, Panama and Jamaica; Bolivia and Peru are in dispute with Chile; El Salvador, Guatemala, Venezuela, Colombia and Guyana have all resorted to sabre-rattling with their neighbours. But actual wars have been rare. Ecuador and Peru came briefly to blows in 1995 (the disputed border was not definitively agreed until 1998); and Honduras and El Salvador famously engaged in 1969 in their short-lived football war (so-called because both were attempting to qualify at the time for the 1970 World Cup) in what was essentially a dispute over the effects of large-scale Salvadoran migration to Honduras. By contrast, Brazil and Uruguay have not come into conflict over their rival claims to an island in the river between them; nor have Belize, Guatemala and Mexico let their various territorial issues escalate into warfare.

Ironically, the region's worst war in the 20th century involved not Latin American neighbours but an outsider: Argentina's 1982 invasion of the UK's Falkland Islands – or Las Malvinas, as Argentina calls them – brought a British response that led to the deaths of 649 Argentine military personnel, 255 British servicemen and three Falkland Islanders. The Argentine surrender after the ten-week war led to the overthrow of the military dictator, General Leopoldo Galtieri, and the country's transition to democracy.

God and drugs

There are two other threads running through Latin America's violence. One is the influence, beginning in the 1960s and prevalent in the 1980s, of liberation theology: a radical interpretation of scripture seeking to reconcile Christian faith and practice with the realities of poverty and inequality. The victims of these realities were both the slum dwellers of the cities and the peasantry of the countryside, and indigenous peoples everywhere were disfavoured. Brazilian theologians (and brothers) Leonardo and Clodovis Boff asked the question: "How are we to be Christians in a world of destitution and injustice?" Their reply was:

There can be only one answer: we can be followers of Jesus and true Christians only by making common cause with the poor and working out the gospel of liberation.

The implication to many, not least in the priesthood, was that a modern Jesus would have been a Marxist, striving to end the social disparities in which Latin America's wealthy and politically powerful Roman Catholic Church was complicit. This obvious threat to the church establishment was denounced by Pope John Paul II (who had been raised in communist Poland), whose argument was that Christianity must not be transformed into a secular political movement – the church should champion the poor, but not with revolutionary violence. In a sermon in Mexico in 1990 the pope declared:

When the world begins to notice the clear failures of certain ideologies and systems, it seems all the more incomprehensible that certain sons of the Church in these lands – prompted at times by the desire to find quick solutions – persist in presenting as viable certain models whose failure is patent in other places in the world. You, as priests, cannot be involved in activities which belong to the lay faithful.

There were plenty of priests, monks and nuns who were prepared to defy papal authority. In Nicaragua, for example, many priests and Catholic congregations sided with the Marxist Sandinistas in the 1979 overthrow of the US-backed dictatorship of Anastasio Somoza Debayle. Indeed, four Roman Catholic priests took positions in the Sandinista government. In the annals of liberation theology Oscar Romero, an archbishop of El Salvador assassinated in 1980, is often considered a martyr to the movement for his support of the poor peasantry in a Salvadoran civil war in which the US was sending aid to bolster the military-backed government. Ironically, given the left's eulogies for the dead archbishop, John Paul II was also full of praise for Romero, embracing calls for the beatification finally carried out under Pope Francis in May 2015.

The remaining thread in the violent conflicts of the region is the production and export of illegal narcotics. Estimates of the US market for illegal drugs vary from $100 billion to $750 billion a year. Behind that absurdly wide range of figures is the reality that drug-traffickers in poor countries in Latin America and the Caribbean can earn huge sums by satisfying US (and, indeed, European) demand, whether for marijuana, heroin or – most commonly – cocaine. The Andean nations of Colombia, Peru and Bolivia are the world's biggest producers of cocaine; and Central American nations such as Mexico and Caribbean islands such as Jamaica have long provided the main supply routes to the US and Europe.

In response, the US has for decades waged what is commonly known as its war on drugs. Domestically, this has meant increased penalties for illegal drug use (though a decriminalisation and even legalisation movement has had an impact at the level of individual states such as Colorado). Abroad, this has meant crop-eradication schemes – often by aerial spraying – and aid, both financial and military, to Latin American governments fighting guerrilla groups that support themselves through the drug trade.

All too often the consequences are perverse: poor farmers, deprived of their crops, join the guerrillas or the "narco gangs"; government forces abuse their power; murder and crime rates become the highest in the world; and individual politicians and military officers become corruptly involved in the trade they are supposed to be combating. Panama's military dictator, Manuel Noriega, for example, was a leading drug-trafficker until in 1989 US troops invaded Panama to oust him and then prosecute him for racketeering, drug-smuggling and money-laundering. Students of realpolitik will note that Noriega had been protected for years by the CIA in the full knowledge of his activities.

The factors that lead to conflict will not disappear overnight. Indeed, the ethnic tensions and disparities of wealth in Latin American society have spawned Bolivarianism, a socialist, anti-US political platform named after Simon Bolivar, a 19th-century independence leader. The best-known advocate of a Bolivarian revolution was Venezuela's late president, Hugo Chavez, but the anti-imperialist tone strikes a sympathetic chord in many other countries in the region.

That does not necessarily imply conflict. Some guerrilla movements, such as the Tupamaros (urban guerrillas in Uruguay who took their name from Tupac Amaru II, leader of an indigenous revolt in the 18th century against Spanish control of Peru), have long ago been defeated. Others, such as Peru's Shining Path (Sendero Luminoso) are struggling to survive. Similarly, as Latin American democracy becomes ever more firmly rooted, a plethora of anarchist groups is finding it hard to gain adherents. Yet while drug-trafficking, corruption and staggering social inequalities continue to exist, so will conflict – which means that the region's optimists and pessimists alike have plenty of current conflicts to mull over.

Chile

During the 1973–90 dictatorship of General Augusto Pinochet, several left-wing extremist groups – often benefiting from training in Cuba and Nicaragua – waged armed attacks against the regime. Prominent among these groups were the Movement of the Revolutionary Left (Movimiento de la Izquierda Revolucionária) and the Patriotic Front of Manuel Rodríguez (Frente Patriótica Manuel Rodríguez, an affiliate of the Chilean Communist Party named after a hero of Chile's struggle for independence from Spain in the early 19th century).

Following the post-Pinochet transition to democracy, however, such groups have more or less disappeared. In their place is now the Arauco-Malleco Coordination Group (Coordinadora Arauco-Malleco, or CAM), a radical group demanding the return of the traditional lands of the indigenous Mapuche community, which makes up about a tenth of Chile's population. The CAM declared war on the Chilean state in 2009, and the government in retaliation has used anti-terrorism laws inherited from the Pinochet era. According to the Chilean government:

> *We are in the presence of an organised terrorist group, with terrorist methods, with international links that provide them with training, with skills and with contact with the Revolutionary Armed Forces of Colombia (FARC).*

Those methods have included a string of arson attacks in southern Chile. According to the Colombian government, in a dossier handed to Chile, the CAM had also had training at a FARC camp in Ecuador.

A more recent problem for the government to tackle is the influence of Europe-based anarchist movements. Not only have Spanish anarchists been implicated in small-scale bomb attacks in Chile, but credit for a bomb at a Santiago subway station in July 2014 and for an explosion, causing several severe injuries, at a Santiago fast-food restaurant in the following September was claimed by the Conspiracy of Fire Nuclei, an extremist group that was founded in Greece.

Colombia

Impressively diverse in both its people and its terrain, Colombia has been cursed for half a century by conflicts – from civil war to localised assaults – that have featured various left-wing guerrilla groups and right-wing paramilitary forces. Their origins lie in a period known as *La Violencia*, sparked by the assassination in 1948 of Jorge Eliécer Gaitain, a Liberal Party presidential candidate. In the ensuing ten-year civil war the countryside became a battleground for the paramilitary forces of the Liberal Party and the Communist Party, both of whom fought against the paramilitaries of the Conservative Party and on occasion against each other. The death toll may have been as high as 200,000 and torture and rape were commonplace.

The social and political consequences of *La Violencia* have haunted the country ever since: the communist-inclined left claims to fight for social justice, equality and the rights of the peasantry; the pro-US, anti-communist right claims it defends stability, property rights and law and order.

Not all the various actors, however, have remained outside the law. The 19th of April Movement (Movimiento 19 de Abril, or M-19), a guerrilla force founded in 1970 that preached revolutionary socialism, forswore armed conflict in 1970 and became a legal political party, the Democratic Alliance M-19 (Alianza Democrática M-19, or AD/M-19). Similarly, the Quintin Lame Armed Movement (Movimiento Armado Quintin Lame, or MAQL), which was founded in 1984 and named after a dead leader of Colombia's indigenous people in Cauca province, renounced in 1991 its armed struggle against the state and the encroachments of wealthy landowners. Other left-wing or Marxist guerrilla groups that laid down their Kalashnikovs were the Peasant Student Workers Movement (Movimiento Obrero Estudiantil Campesino) in the 1960s and the People's Revolutionary Army (Ejército Revolucionario del Pueblo, or ERP) in 2007.

Yet, despite many efforts, often brokered by Cuba and neighbouring Latin American nations, to negotiate peace settlements, other left-wing guerrilla groups maintain their opposition to the state. One is the National Liberation Army (Ejército Nacional de Liberación, or ENL), founded in 1964 with a doctrine that combines Marxism with liberation theology and nationalism. The ENL, which was added to the US list of terrorist organisations in 1997, has probably fewer than 3,000 active fighters and sustains itself principally by extorting ransoms for kidnap victims and by imposing war taxes. Another group is the Popular Liberation Army (Ejército Popular de Liberación), founded in 1967 with a Marxist-Leninist ideology and now able to muster fewer than 200 members.

By far the most successful of the leftist guerrilla armies, with their ideological mix of Marxism and revolutionary socialism, has been the Revolutionary Armed Forces of Colombia–People's Army (Fuerzas Armadas Revolucionarias de Colombia–Ejército del Pueblo), better known simply as the FARC, founded in 1964 as the military wing of the Colombian Communist Party. The FARC gives an armed identity to many genuine grievances in Colombian society, especially rural poverty and the plight of peasants forced from much of their land by big agribusiness and powerful landowners.

In 1998 the US Defense Intelligence Agency worried that the FARC might seize power within five years and so succeed in turning Colombia into a narco state. This assessment had a basis in reality: in the mid-1990s the FARC had been able to capture hundreds of government soldiers, leading the state in 1999 to concede to guerrilla control an area the size of Switzerland in the southern provinces of Caqueta and Meta. But the FARC's threat was gradually blunted, with the organisation suffering severe losses in personnel and territory during the 2002–10 presidency of Alvaro Uribe, whose policy was to use military force to convince the FARC to come to the negotiation table – which they finally did in 2012 under President Uribe's successor, Juan Manuel Santos, with talks first in Oslo and later in Havana.

A question that in peace negotiations becomes diplomatically important but is irrelevant on the ground is the status of the FARC. Colombia, Canada, Chile, the EU, New Zealand and the US all consider it to be a terrorist organisation; Argentina, Brazil, Ecuador, Nicaragua and Venezuela recognise it as a legitimate political and military force. Such contrasting opinions aside, the reality is that the FARC has several thousand men, and women, under arms: the FARC in 2007 claimed 18,000; the Colombian government's figure in 2011, taking note of those who had laid down their weapons, was fewer than 10,000. This decline mirrors the loss of territory controlled by the FARC.

But even as the number of its guerrillas and its command of territory dwindle, the FARC remains a force to be reckoned with, having a significant presence in 25 of the country's 32 provinces. In 2011 President Santos said that the previous year the FARC had killed 460 government soldiers and wounded 2,000. In subsequent years, with both the guerrillas and the government showing a commitment to negotiation, the level of violence has fallen. Foreign governments such as Canada in 2015 still warned their citizens to "exercise a high degree of caution due to the unpredictable security situation", but Colombia was clearly no longer as dangerous as in 1996–2005 when a kidnapping took place every eight hours and every day someone was victim of a landmine. Yet if the FARC has reduced its military activity it has maintained non-military ones: kidnapping, both for ransom and for political leverage; extortion (especially from large landowners); bank robberies; and drug-trafficking – or the taxing of drug-traffickers.

Cocaine addiction

The relationship between the FARC and the illegal drug industry is a kind of symbiosis: the FARC needs money and drug-growers and traffickers need protection. Yet many of the biggest landowners and drug-traffickers believe in furnishing their own protection, so there has been a proliferation over the decades of paramilitary groups loosely preaching anti-communism (a political stance which has often brought them support from the US).

The paramilitary groups were founded, with US encouragement and covert aid, in the 1960s and were given what amounts to official approval in 1968 with Law 48 to allow "the organisation and tasking of all of the residents of the country and its natural resources ... to guarantee National Independence and institutional stability". Perhaps inevitably, as cocaine supplanted coffee as Colombia's main export, various paramilitary groups became the private armies of the drug cartels. In the early 1980s the Medellin drug cartel joined with the Colombian military, US and local businesses, wealthy landowners and Colombian politicians to form Muerte a Secuestadores or MAS (Death to Kidnappers), a well-equipped paramilitary force waging war against the FARC and the ENL. To provide legal support for the MAS and oppose the organising of workers and peasants, Colombian landowners – some of them drug-traffickers laundering their drug revenues – then formed the Asociación Campesina de Ganaderos y Agricultores del Magdalena Medio (Association of Middle Magdalena Ranchers and Farmers).

Both the leftist guerrillas and the paramilitary groups have been guilty of torture, kidnapping, murder and other abuses of human rights. In 1987 official statistics noted that the paramilitaries had killed more civilians than the guerrillas, and two years later the government issued decrees to combat "the armed groups, misnamed paramilitary groups, that have been formed into death squads, bands of hired assassins, self-defence groups, or groups that carry out their own justice". In practice, the decrees were circumvented, and in 1997 most of the paramilitary groups combined to become the Autodefensas Unidas de Colombia or AUC (United Self-Defence Forces of Colombia), which in 2001 then appeared on the US list of terrorist organisations. One AUC leader, Salvatore Mancuso, extradited to the US in 2008, said in 2012 that he had been contacted by Venezuelan opponents of Hugo Chavez to help overthrow the Venezuelan president.

Whereas the FARC continues its armed struggle – though at a minimal level since its declaration in December 2014 of a unilateral and indefinite ceasefire – the AUC has demobilised, wooed by legislation between 2003 and 2006 promising lenience to its combatants. However, paramilitarism has not gone away: there remain around a dozen *bandas criminales emergentes* or BACRIM (emerging criminal organisations), as the Colombian government terms them. Their purpose is not to wage war on the state or its opponents but rather to protect their share – perhaps 40% – of cocaine exports.

Despite the efforts of the government and the US to eliminate the drug trade, those exports continue to fuel not just the violence and human-rights abuses of the FARC and the paramilitaries but also the country's widespread corruption (Transparency International, an organisation that monitors and publicises corporate and political corruption in international development, notes that 93% of company directors in a 2012 sample said they paid bribes in the course of their business). By the mid-1990s a combination of Colombian police and army action, spurred by sustained pressure from the US, had managed to dismantle the powerful Medellin and Cali drug cartels; and yet cocaine production remained as high as ever, prompting many observers to deride as counterproductive the Plan Colombia, in which between 2000 and 2010 the US gave military and economic aid of $7.3 billion to combat coca production and the traffickers.

Sadly, even if Colombia's conflicts were to end tomorrow (talks in September 2015 promised a peace accord in March 2016), the effects of their violence would continue. Both the FARC and the ENL have used landmines to protect their territory or deter raids on coca fields. In 2012 these landmines and other explosive remnants of war killed 75 and wounded 421. The toll on Colombia's innocent is far from over.

Ecuador

After the military governments of the 1970s, democracy now appears firmly rooted in Ecuador, despite its having seven presidents in the decade before Rafael Correa began his first term in 2006. As a leftist president, the US-educated Correa (he has a PhD in economics from Illinois University) joined Latin American peers such as Evo Morales of Bolivia, Daniel Ortega of Nicaragua and the late Hugo Chavez of Venezuela in provoking the wrath of the US; and in 2012 he heightened tensions with the US still more by giving asylum to the Wikileaks founder, Julian Assange, in the Ecuadorean embassy in London.

Given this background, it is perhaps ironic that any armed threat to the government should come from the left. The Grupos de Combatientes Populares or GCP (Groups of Popular Combatants) declares:

> We have a great responsibility to educate, organise, mobilise and fight politically and militarily for the masses of the major urban centres ... We recognise ourselves as one of the organisations that seek to oppose the violence of the rich with the revolutionary armed struggle. We are an organisation by and for the revolution.

Its impact, however, has been small. In 2011 leaflet bombs, designed to sow through the air anti-government messages, exploded without injury in several cities, leading the government to accuse both the GCP and the previously unknown Armed Revolutionary Insurgent Forces of Ecuador (FAIRE in the Spanish acronym). In the so-called Red Sun (Sol Rojo) case, the state accused the GCP of planting its bombs to disrupt a forthcoming visit by the president of Colombia.

Red Sun refers to the Communist Party of Ecuador–Red Sun (Partido Comunista de Ecuador–Sol Rojo), a Maoist group close to the Shining Path guerrillas in Peru.

Red Sun, which also calls itself Puka Inti in the indigenous Quechua language, is one of several insurgent groups that emerged in the 1990s, among them the Alfarist Liberation Army and the Guerrilla Coordinator of Ecuador. None, however, has gathered any mass support or matched the now-demobilised Eloy Alfaro Popular Armed Forces, which was named after an early 20th-century revolutionary and was able to carry out kidnappings and bank robberies in the 1980s. This may not, of course, prevent them from trying. The greater problem for the state would be if the various militants were to collaborate with Colombia's FARC. The Colombian guerrillas have long had camps on Ecuadorean soil, with the government in Quito at one time turning a blind eye to their presence. This became impossible when Colombian jets in 2008 bombed a FARC camp within Ecuador, in the process killing the FARC's second-in-command, Raul Reyes. The attack led to Ecuador suspending its diplomatic relations with Colombia for two years – but it also brought a change of heart, encouraging the Correa government to take action against the FARC.

Mexico

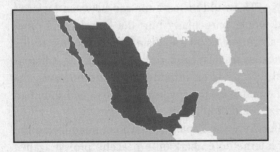

Rivalled only by Brazil, the United Mexican States – to give the country its official name – is Latin America's economic giant (and its output per head is greater than in more populous Brazil). More to the point, in terms of the conflict engendered by the US war on drugs, Mexico is the only Latin American country that shares a border with the US.

The geographical consequence is that Mexico is the main point of entry into the US for Latin America's seemingly unending supply of illegal migrants and drugs. The political and military consequence is a similarly unending battle by both the US and Mexican governments against the well-armed and wealthy Mexican gangs – often termed drug cartels and narco terrorists – which manage this supply. Meanwhile, the human consequence is a barely credible death toll: estimates range from around 60,000 to more than 100,000 fatalities during the 2006–12 presidency of Felipe Calderon, who deployed the country's military forces in a full-scale and sustained assault on the cartels. A great many of those deaths were the result of warfare between the cartels, rather than just with the forces of the federal state.

Happily, the government is no longer at war with the Zapatista Army of National Liberation (Ejército Zapatista de Liberación Nacional, or EZLN), a revolutionary movement preaching a kind of libertarian Marxism in Chiapas, Mexico's southernmost state. The Zapatistas, led by a mysterious figure under the *nom de guerre* Subcomandante Marcos, announced themselves to the world on January 1st 1994, the day on which the North American Free Trade Agreement (NAFTA) came into effect to promote increased commerce between Mexico, the US and Canada.

Believing that NAFTA would increase the gap between Mexico's rich and poor and would particularly hurt the Mayans and other indigenous peoples, around 3,000 Zapatista insurgents greeted the agreement by attacking military and police barracks in Chiapas and seizing several towns. As an armed insurgency, however, the Zapatistas proved no match for the government forces and soon had to retreat to the jungles and mountains.

Rather more effectively, the Zapatistas have commandeered the headlines and the internet to embark on a peaceful protest against globalisation and for the rights of Mexico's indigenous peoples and women. In the words of Subcomandante Marcos:

We don't want to impose our solutions by force, we want to create a democratic space. We don't see armed struggle in the classic sense of previous guerrilla wars, ie as the only way and the only

all-powerful truth around which everything is organiséd. In a war,
the decisive thing is not the military confrontation but the politics at
stake in the confrontation. We didn't go to war to kill or be killed.
We went to war in order to be heard.

Two decades after its formation, and having achieved considerable autonomy in Chiapas, the EZLN still exists but more as a symbol of the Mayan struggle for land reform and equality than as an armed rebellion against the federal government.

Meanwhile, the Mexican authorities must combat the far more dangerous threat from the narco gangs. This threat is at least as important to Mexico's powerful northern neighbour. As far back as 2009, the then director of the CIA, Michael Hayden, told the US Senate's Armed Services Committee:

Escalating violence along the US-Mexico border will pose the second
greatest threat to US security this year, second only to al-Qaeda.

US fear

The concern of the US is twofold. The long-standing fear, justified by the transnational scope of gangs such as Mexico's Los Zetas and El Salvador's Mara Salvatrucha (MS-13), is that the narco gangs of Latin America have established themselves north of the border, either directly or through affiliates, in cities such as Los Angeles and Houston. Prisons in California and Texas are full of inmates whose intricate tattoos testify to their membership of the narco gangs. The more recent fear is that the gangs will help al-Qaeda or others to carry out attacks within the US. In 2011, Iran's Quds Force (a special unit of the Revolutionary Guard) was said by the US attorney general to have plotted to assassinate the Saudi ambassador to the US, enlisting the help of the Los Zetas cartel (the plot was supposedly thwarted by agents in the US Drug Enforcement Agency).

US security experts also speak of the presence in Mexico, which has many families of Lebanese and Syrian origin, of Lebanon's Hizbullah, considered a terrorist organisation by the US government. Whether Hizbullah would want to mount attacks in the US is at best uncertain, but it seems clear that Hizbullah regards the narco gangs as a source of finance and as useful money-launderers. In 2012 the US indicted Ayman Joumaa, a Lebanese-Colombian, and three others of Lebanese origin for laundering the proceeds of drug-trafficking; all four, it said, were working for Hizbullah in Latin America.

Whatever their threat to the security of the US, it is obvious that the drug cartels pose a serious threat to the security of Mexico – despite the war waged against them by President Calderon and (less forcefully) by his successor Enrique Peña Nieto.

There are half-a-dozen major narco gangs with the ability and weaponry to maintain their challenge to the authority of the state. The most powerful is probably the Sinaloa cartel, at least until the capture in February 2014 of its leader, Joaquín Guzmán, nicknamed "El Chapo" (Shorty) because of his relatively small stature. Guzmán had been captured before, spending eight years in prison before bribing guards to allow his escape in a laundry basket in 2001. In July 2015, Guzmán again escaped (this time through a specially dug mile-long tunnel). The evidence is that he was perfectly able to control the cartel from his prison cell.

The Sinaloa cartel can trace its origins back to the 1960s and Pedro Avilés Pérez, the first man to use aircraft to traffic marijuana into the US. In the following decades Avilés Pérez's heirs have made the cartel the dominant exporter from Mexico of cocaine, marijuana and locally made illegal amphetamines. In the process they have used not just tunnels under the US border, aircraft and fast boats but even mini-submarines. They have also bribed numerous government officials, police and military personnel, and have used at least one international bank (HSBC pleaded guilty in 2012) to launder drug money. One characteristic of the cartel is its willingness to use extreme violence, on both rivals and the innocent. Headless corpses, often bearing signs of torture, have been a tragic feature of the frequent wars between the Sinaloa cartel and other gangs.

The members of the Los Zetas cartel are even more brutal and ruthless than their Sinaloa peers. The cartel was founded by members of the Mexican army's elite special forces who deserted in 1999 and began to work for the Gulf cartel, before breaking away in 2010 to form Los Zetas. Given that the original members had received training from the special forces of both Israel and the US, Los Zetas can still boast a military and technological expertise unmatched by rival cartels.

Though Mexico's narco gangs have demonstrated impressive commercial skills in maintaining their drug exports despite all the efforts of both the US and Mexican governments to suppress the trade, they have also suffered setbacks. One reason is the full-scale military and police assault on the gangs during the Calderon presidency; a second was the $1.6 billion Mérida Initiative (a subtler version of the Plan Colombia), signed into law by the US Congress in 2008. The idea was not just to disrupt the narco gangs and secure the border by providing helicopters and other hi-tech equipment but also to help Mexico build its institutions and civil society.

One sign of the damage wreaked on the cartels was an announcement by the police in 2011 that the Beltran-Leyva gang had been forced to disband (its second-in-command, Arnoldo Villa Sanchez, was finally captured in April 2014). Similarly, La Familia Michoacana, founded in the southern state of Michoacán in the 1980s as a vigilante organisation to secure law and order, was also said to have disbanded in 2011. La Familia, having swiftly moved into the drugs business, was distinguished not just by its brutality but also by its bizarre quasi-religious identity: its Bible-carrying leaders insisted that their followers should undergo two months of brain-washing scriptural study and meditation and should not themselves indulge in the drugs they trafficked.

Such religious indoctrination did not induce a tendency to grant mercy. Their killings – no matter how horrendous – were "divine justice". In one infamous incident in 2006 members of La Familia used bowie knives to cut off the heads of five men while they were still alive; the next day the killers entered the Sol y Sombra nightclub in the Michoacán town of Uruapan and threw the severed heads onto the dance floor. A note they left behind declared:

> The Family doesn't kill for money; it doesn't kill women; it doesn't kill innocent people; only those who deserve to die, die. Everyone should know ... this is divine justice.

But as La Familia declined, so another cartel – the Knights Templar (los Caballeros Templarios) – has assumed power in Michoacán, taking over the trafficking of marijuana and the production of amphetamines. The Knights, however, are in turn being threatened. By levying taxes (that is, protection money) on local businesses, they have spawned opposition in the form of the Consejo de Autodefensas Unidas de Michoacán (Council of United Self-Defence Groups of Michoacán), well-armed vigilante groups that had despaired of effective intervention by local authorities all too easily bribed or intimidated by the Knights.

The Autodefensas claim to be interested solely in ridding their state of the drug gangs. As a spokesman declared in 2014:

> Our main objective and the reason why we are fighting is to clean
> up the 103 municipalities of the state of Michoacán from the
> organised crime of the Caballeros Templarios. As soon as we clean
> up all organised crime from our state, we will turn in our weapons
> to whoever asks for them.

This seems unlikely, given the mistrust many, if not most, Mexicans feel for the probity of the authorities (Mexico was a dismal 103rd in Transparency International's 2014 corruption rankings). There are, in any case, rumours that the Autodefensas are actually working with the Jalisco cartel in its attempt to wrest power from the Knights.

Whatever the truth, the government will be hard-pressed to disarm the Autodefensas or win any permanent victories over the warring cartels. The fundamental reason is that Mexico is the main transit point for an illegal drugs market in the US that shows no signs of disappearing. Second, Mexico's institutions, at both the local and federal level, are corrupt and ineffective. Third, US gun laws allow an abundant supply of weaponry to the narco gangs: there are around 6,700 licensed firearms dealers on the northern side of the US–Mexico border and only one legal seller of firearms in Mexico, which is why the vast majority of guns captured by the Mexican authorities from the cartels can be traced back to the US. In short, the US is Mexico's main trading partner in more ways than one.

Paraguay

The landlocked Republic of Paraguay was once a byword first for political upheaval – it had 31 presidents between 1904 and 1954 – and then for stifling dictatorship, in the shape of Alfredo Stroessner, who as head of the Colorado Party ruled the country with a ruthless disregard for human rights from 1954 until his overthrow in a military coup in 1989.

The repression of the Stroessner years did at least provide a degree of political stability that the country had rarely experienced since gaining its independence from Spain in 1811. In the disastrous 1864–70 War of the Triple Alliance, pitting Paraguay against the allied countries of Argentina, Brazil and Uruguay, Paraguay's pre-war population of around 525,000 was reduced to some 221,000, of whom only 28,000 were male adults. That bloody toll was compounded by the loss of almost half of the country's territory (though in the Chaco war with Bolivia between 1932 and 1935 Paraguay managed to redress the balance by gaining part of the disputed lowland region of Chaco).

Happily, disputes over Paraguay's borders no longer provoke military action to worry the nation's 6.7 million people (95% of them *mestizo*, with mixed Spanish and Amerindian blood). Indeed, in 2009 Bolivia and Paraguay finally signed an agreement to settle their competing claims in the Chaco region. Less happily, Paraguay suffers violent dissent within its borders from the Paraguayan People's Army (Ejército del Pueblo Paraguayo, or EPP), a communist guerrilla group formed in 2005 after the demise of the Free Fatherland Party (Partido Patria Libre, or PPL), which was one of several radical left-wing parties to take advantage of the downfall of Stroessner and come into the open.

The EPP is tiny, with estimates of its guerrilla numbers ranging from 20 to 100, and that figure was reduced in August 2014 by the formation of a splinter faction known as the Armed Farmers Group (ACA), whose 13 fighters were within a month reduced to eight following a clash with the security forces. But whatever its size, the EPP cannot be ignored by the state. Operating mainly in the north of the country, its campaign of bombings, kidnappings, cattle-rustling and extortion had resulted in over 50 deaths by the summer of 2014. In January 2015 its fighters burned a farm in the Concepción Department and left a note demanding that the owner pay a fine of $300,000 and distribute beef free to local communities as a punishment for the deforestation of the area (the note had explained: "Nature is not ours; it is only borrowed from future generations."). A few days later a German couple, who had been kidnapped from their farm by the EPP only hours earlier, were found shot dead. In March 2015 the EPP continued its campaign of ecologically motivated intimidation, leaving a note beside the corpses of three farm workers warning farmers not to use pesticides or own weapons.

Whether the EPP can be eradicated by the state is an open question. The Paraguayan government claims that the guerrillas have been helped by the FARC of Colombia, which implies that any solution to the guerrilla war in Colombia could also help Paraguay. However, the factors that inspire armed radicals will remain: pervasive corruption; social inequality (60% of Paraguayans live in poverty); and agricultural commercialisation that has resulted in thousands of families becoming landless poor. Given the additional lure of drug-trafficking (in which the EPP is said to be implicated) and smuggling, Paraguay is unlikely to enjoy an entirely peaceful and virtuous future. It will also have to endure the mistrust of the US, which accuses Paraguay, with a large community of Arab origin, of being a source of money for Lebanon's Hizbullah and Gaza's Hamas, both designated by the US as foreign terrorist organisations.

Peru

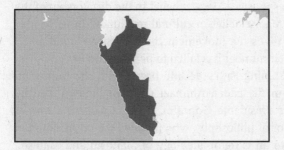

Since gaining its independence from Spain in 1821, Peru, in the Latin American fashion, has had periods of both military and democratic rule. It still hosts an insurgency that now ranks as the third-longest in the region's post-colonial history (the first is the FARC rebellion in Colombia and the second was the civil war in Guatemala that pitted various left-wing groups against the government from 1960 to 1996).

Most estimates of the Peruvian insurgency speak of a death toll between 1980, the start of the conflict, and 2000 of almost 70,000. But in the 21st century, the insurgency is a shadow of what it was. One reason is the defeat of the Tupac Amaru Revolutionary Movement (Movimiento Revolucionario Túpac Amaru, or MRTA), named after an 18th-century revolutionary, Tupac Amaru II (who himself took his name from Tupac Amaru, the last leader of the Incas).

The MRTA's first operation was a bank robbery in 1982 in the town of La Victoria; two years later it launched its armed struggle against the state. But the MRTA was weakened both by internecine conflict with the more extreme Shining Path (Sendero Luminoso) movement and by the pressure of the Peruvian military. Its last major action was the seizure in December 1996 of the Japanese embassy in Lima, when the MRTA held 72 hostages for the following four months until Peruvian forces stormed the building, rescuing all but one of the hostages. Since then, the MRTA has ceased to exist; and though some have attempted to infiltrate leftist organisations in Peru, the leaders are constantly under threat of arrest and prosecution.

By contrast, the Shining Path movement remains, though greatly diminished over the decades because of pressure from the

Peruvian military and popular revulsion over the ruthlessness of an organisation that espouses a Marxist belief in the dictatorship of the proletariat and a Maoist belief in cultural revolution. In its heyday in the 1980s and 1990s the movement could muster around 5,000 guerrillas; now their number has fallen to perhaps 200–500.

Much of the Shining Path's decline began with the capture in 1992 of its charismatic leader, Abimael Guzmán (known also by the *nom de guerre* Presidente Gonzalo). It was Guzmán, a former university professor of philosophy, who founded the organisation in the late 1960s with an extreme ideology of Marxism and Maoism. Its name refers to a slogan in the 1920s of the Peruvian Communist Party: "Marxism-Leninism will open the shining path to revolution." Taking the traditional Maoist line (ironically just as China under Deng Xiaoping was introducing its own version of capitalism), the Shining Path undertook the armed struggle in 1980, refusing to participate in the elections called by the state's military regime.

The result was a conflict of terrible brutality: by the guerrillas; by the paramilitary militias armed by the state to oppose the Shining Path; and by the state's own armed forces. The human-rights abuses by government forces were duplicated by those of the Shining Path, which even set up labour camps (basically slave encampments to work the fields) to punish those who had "betrayed the forces of the people". As a Shining Path document put it:

> For us, human rights are contradictory to the rights of the people, because we base rights in man as a social product, not man as an abstract with innate rights ... Our position is very clear. We reject and condemn human rights because they are bourgeois, reactionary, counterrevolutionary rights, and are today a weapon of revisionists and imperialists, principally Yankee imperialists.

In practice, this meant guerrilla war in the countryside, urban terrorism and the assassination of left-wing rivals who did not meet the organisation's ideological criteria (in retrospect it seems rather surprising that the US did not put the Shining Path on its list of terrorist organisations until 1997). Just how bloody the conflict has been for Peru was detailed by the Truth and Reconciliation Commission set up in 2001 after the fall of President Alberto Fujimori. Its final report in 2003 calculated that of the 69,280 people who had died or disappeared in the previous two decades, the Shining Path was responsible for 31,331. Perhaps as troubling for society, some 75% of the dead or disappeared spoke Quechua or another indigenous language – even though only a fifth of Peruvians speak an indigenous language as their first language.

Despite its setbacks after the 1992 capture of Guzmán (now condemned to spend the rest of his life in prison), the Shining Path is still capable of mounting attacks on government forces and strategic installations: for example, an attack in early 2014 on a work camp for a gas-pipeline company. At the same time, the government maintains its pressure: in April 2014 the authorities arrested on charges of terrorism and drug-trafficking 28 members of Movadef, which the government describes as the political wing of the Shining Path. Movadef, which has campaigned for the release from prison of Guzman and other Shining Path militants, called the arrests political persecution.

The remaining question is whether the Shining Path will survive in the years ahead. The likelihood is that its ideological principles will be a fig leaf for a future as a protector of Peru's coca-growers and cocaine producers, and as a drug-trafficker itself.

6 The United States: both superpower and vulnerable Goliath

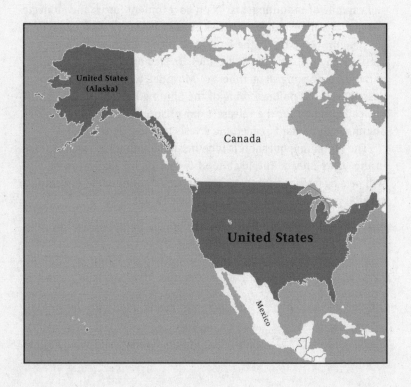

THE UNITED STATES OF AMERICA dominates the world. Its economic, military, technological and, indeed, cultural power (think of movies, pop music and McDonald's) is unequalled. As the 20th century ended, a French socialist foreign minister, Hubert Védrine, described it as an *hyperpuissance*: it was not just the world's sole superpower, following the collapse of the Soviet Union, but also its hyperpower.

Militarily the evidence is overwhelming: the US has the means to crush any enemy's conventional army, as it did in Iraq in 2003. Its special forces, namely the Green Berets, the Rangers, the Delta Force and the Navy Seals, can accomplish astounding acts of daring and skill, such as the 2011 killing of Osama bin Laden in his Pakistan hiding place. Its technological prowess means that no foreigner's e-mail or phone call is beyond its reach (as Edward Snowden, a former CIA systems administrator and contractor for the National Security Agency, revealed in 2013 when he leaked thousands of classified documents). Whether as the lead member of the North Atlantic Treaty Organisation (NATO) or acting on its own account, the United States is either involved in conflict or deterring conflict around the globe, from the Pacific to Latin America and from Central Asia to Africa. According to the Special Operations Command, during any given week in 2013 its personnel were active in 70 different countries, and in one week in March an extraordinary 92. In 2014 its special forces were deployed to 133 different countries, roughly 70% of the world's total, in missions ranging from night raids such as the killing of bin Laden to training exercises.

All this would surely have surprised the country's founding fathers. In his farewell address to the nation (actually printed in a newspaper rather than delivered in person), the first US president, George Washington, declared in 1796: "It is our true policy to steer clear of permanent alliances with any portion of the foreign world." Washington was warning his countrymen not to get involved in the perennial acrimony between Great Britain and France, but the usual paraphrase of his words is to "beware foreign entanglements".

This has been a futile quest throughout US history. Since economic and trade interests have to be protected, economic power and military power are bound to go hand in hand, especially in a world in which, as a result of globalisation, economies are increasingly interdependent.

In the 19th century this meant – among many armed conflicts – wars with Spain and China, and the occupation of the Philippines. In the 20th century the United States belatedly, but decisively, joined both the first and second world wars, as well as battling China and the Soviet Union in the Korean peninsula. Engraved in the memory of the US military, and of the country's politicians, is the humbling experience of the war in Vietnam, with the United States finally withdrawing its troops from all of Indochina in 1975.

But those major conflicts in the 20th century were accompanied by plenty of minor ones, from interventions in Lebanon and the invasion of Panama to the first Gulf war of 1990–91, pitting a US-led coalition against Saddam Hussein's Iraqi forces in Kuwait, or to the bombing of Serbian positions in the Balkan war of 1993–95. One ominous lesson for the US from those final decades of the century was that its overwhelming superiority in conventional warfare – so effective in the first Gulf war and in the Balkans – could become irrelevant in other theatres: in 1983 President Ronald Reagan had to withdraw American troops from Lebanon after suicide bombers first destroyed the US embassy in Beirut, killing 63 people, and six months later struck the barracks of the multinational peacekeeping force, killing 241 American and 58 French servicemen.

A similar, albeit lesser, humiliation occurred in Somalia in 1993 when rag-tag Somali militiamen shot down two American helicopters and dragged dead American servicemen through the streets of Mogadishu. The following year President Clinton ordered an end to the US's role in "Operation Restore Hope" and withdrew troops from Somalia. The cost had been $1.7 billion – and 43 dead and 153 wounded American soldiers.

The obvious message for US policymakers, and for its enemies, is that in the 21st century military might is not inevitably victorious. But there are other messages, too. One is that Iran, which had organised the Beirut bombings, had – and presumably still has – the capability to strike, at least indirectly, at American interests overseas. A second is that far too much of the Muslim world considers the US its enemy (Iran's Ayatollah Khomeini had famously described it as the "great Satan"). Meanwhile, the phrase asymmetric warfare has entered the military lexicon – and is here to stay.

The balance of power

Asymmetric warfare is hardly new: the biblical tale of David and Goliath or, indeed, the American war of independence from Great Britain are just two examples. Large disparities of military force will always compel the weaker belligerent to adopt unconventional weapons, be it David's slingshot or the improvised explosive devices (IEDs) triggered by mobile phones and used so effectively against the US and its allies in Iraq and Afghanistan.

In reality, the United States will always be the stronger belligerent, regardless of whether it is fighting a conventional army or a guerrilla insurgency. With an annual defence budget of around $700 billion (which is likely to fall somewhat with the winding down of the wars in Iraq and Afghanistan), it accounts for roughly 40% of the total military spending of the whole world, and spends almost seven times more than the next-biggest spender, China. Its armed forces total 1.4 million servicemen and women, with another 850,000 reserve personnel. It also has a far greater armed presence around the globe than any other country, friend or foe.

Just how great is a subject of some controversy. During his hopeless run for the US presidency, Ron Paul, an isolationist-inclined Republican member of the House of Representatives, boldly declared in 2011:

> We're under great threat, because we occupy so many countries. We're in 130 countries. We have 900 bases around the world. We're going broke. The purpose of al-Qaeda was to attack us, invite us over there, where they can target us. And they have been doing it. They have more attacks against us and the American interests per month than occurred in all the years before 9/11, but we're there occupying their land. And if we think that we can do that and not have retaliation, we're kidding ourselves. We have to be honest with ourselves. What would we do if another country, say, China, did to us what we do to all those countries over there?

Paul's figures may not be entirely accurate, and now that American troops have left Iraq and, by the end of 2016, Afghanistan it is hard to argue that the US is an occupying power anywhere. An unmanned radio relay tower is not what most people would consider a base, but it would count on the government's list of military facilities. The Pentagon lists well over 600 facilities in foreign countries outside active war zones (and those zones could include scores more). Moreover, Paul's account of 130 countries with a US military presence could well be an underestimate. When checking Paul's claims, the *Washington Post* managed to find 153 countries hosting US military personnel.

Whatever the precise details, the bottom line is that the United States is the world's sole military superpower and will remain so for some years to come, whatever the pretensions of Russia or China (the former cannot match US spending power and the latter – despite having armed forces numbering almost 2.3 million – is technologically far behind). The question then becomes how well US forces can cope with the conflicts in which they find themselves.

One answer in the first Gulf war has come to be known as the Powell doctrine. Spelled out by Colin Powell, at the time chairman of the joint chiefs of staff, the essence of the doctrine is that once all diplomatic attempts to avoid conflict have failed, the United States must use overwhelming force to minimise American casualties and accelerate the enemy's surrender.

In the first Gulf war, known as Desert Storm and lasting just 42 days, the doctrine clearly worked. Arguably, it worked also in the war with Iraq that broke out on March 19th 2003, since George W. Bush felt able to announce "mission accomplished" on May 1st 2003. But the aftermath of the US-led coalition victory was a literally bloody disaster, with American troops only able to withdraw from Iraq at the end of 2011 after an American death toll of almost 4,500 (all but 142 of them coming after the declaration of mission accomplished). As Powell had warned President Bush was possible, the United States had fallen victim to what he called the Pottery Barn rule: if you break it, you own it (which was, of course, an unwarranted slur on an American retail outfit renowned for its good customer service). What had been a conventional war against the armed forces of a state had become an exhausting struggle against myriad stubborn insurgencies.

That evolution has spawned, particularly during the presidency of Barack Obama, a different military tactic: the use of unmanned aerial vehicles, known to military types as UAVs and to the rest of us as drones. Obama's predecessor, George W. Bush, was also an advocate of drone attacks, but launched them with much less frequency. The first drone attack authorised by Obama came on January 23rd 2009, the third day of his first term, and destroyed a house in Pakistan's tribal regions. In the following years drone attacks have become a weapon of choice to strike targets in Pakistan, Afghanistan, Yemen and Somalia.

The attraction for any US commander-in-chief of a drone strike is obvious: it avoids the risk of American casualties, an especially important consideration for an electorate whose tolerance for foreign entanglements has been severely strained by the toll of American deaths and injuries in the protracted wars in Iraq and Afghanistan. The same is true of strikes by cruise missiles, such as those ordered by President Clinton in 1998 against al-Qaeda targets in Afghanistan and Sudan. In the 2011 assault on Libya that led to the toppling of Muammar Qaddafi, the US and the UK launched at least 161 Tomahawk cruise missiles to destroy Qaddafi's air defences. Those missile strikes and subsequent raids by British and French aircraft were in support of Libyan rebel groups, with Western politicians emphasising that they were not in the business of providing troops on the ground (though there were, in fact, a few special forces).

But the attraction has unintended consequences. The American military and the CIA say that they take great pains to be precise in their targeting, but no shiny missile coming literally out of the sky can be assured of hitting only the enemy (the "high-value target" in CIA-speak) and no innocent bystanders. Just how many innocent victims there have been is difficult to calculate. The Bureau of Investigative Journalism estimates that in his first six years in office, President Obama authorised nine times more drone attacks than in George W. Bush's two terms in office, killing at least 2,464 people, including 314 or more civilians, in Pakistan, Yemen and Somalia (countries outside the declared war zones of Iraq and Afghanistan). One well-attested incident, vouched for by a Yemeni government allied to the US, was the fatal targeting of a wedding convoy in 2013, mistakenly viewed by the distant drone operators as a convoy of al-Qaeda militants.

Regardless of the body-count arithmetic, the fact is that this form of remote computer-game warfare fosters huge anti-American resentment and, by extension, encourages local people to join the very organisations – be they al-Qaeda in Yemen, al-Shabab in Somalia or the Taliban in Afghanistan and Pakistan – that the United States is trying to destroy. As Donald Rumsfeld, then Bush's secretary of defence, asked in a 2005 memo in the context of Iraq:

> *Are we capturing, killing or deterring and dissuading more terrorists every day than the madrassas [Quranic schools] and the radical clerics are recruiting, training and deploying against us?*

The seeds of terror

It is always tempting to select single events that change the world. One example is the assassination in Serbia on June 28th 1914 of Archduke Franz Ferdinand of Austria, directly triggering the first world war. Another is the Japanese assault on Hawaii's Pearl Harbor on December 7th 1941, provoking the US to enter the second world war. The most notable so far in this century is undoubtedly September 11th 2001, the day on which two hijacked airliners flew deliberately into the Twin Towers of New York's World Trade Center and a third into the Pentagon building just outside Washington, DC (a planned attack by a fourth airliner was foiled by its passengers and ended with a crash in a Pennsylvania field). The death toll from these co-ordinated attacks was 2,996, including 19 hijackers bent on martyrdom in their extremist version of Islam.

Such events, however, do not really come out of nowhere: they are part of a context. The German Kaiser had been preparing for war well before the archduke's killing; tensions between the United States and Japan, which had been at war with China since 1937, had been growing for many years before the Pearl Harbor raid. The context of 9/11 (the US version of September 9th and also the nationwide emergency number) goes back to the 1980s when the United States supported with money and equipment Muslim *mujahideen* fighters in their efforts to drive Soviet troops out of Afghanistan. One of those *mujahideen* was Osama bin Laden, the scion of a Saudi family made extremely rich through their construction business.

Bin Laden's enmity towards the US stemmed not from Afghanistan

– after all he and the US government had a shared hostility towards the Soviet occupation of Afghanistan – but from the first Gulf war in 1990. Osama, who had returned from Afghanistan as a hero, offered to raise an army of *mujahideen* to oust Saddam Hussein's troops from Kuwait and to protect the Kingdom of Saudi Arabia. To his dismay – and then fury – the Saudi government rejected his offer and instead invited the US to base its troops in Saudi Arabia.

To bin Laden this amounted to an occupation of Muslim holy land by foreign crusaders, hence his decision to wage war on the US and its allies. In 1996 he issued a *fatwa* (a ruling by a Muslim religious authority, which he considered himself to be) calling for American troops to leave the Saudi kingdom. The following year he declared:

> For over seven years the United States has been occupying the lands of Islam in the holiest of places, the Arabian peninsula, plundering its riches, dictating to its rulers, humiliating its people, terrorising its neighbours, and turning its bases in the Peninsula into a spearhead through which to fight the neighbouring Muslim peoples.

In other words, 9/11 should not have been a surprise. Bin Laden had formed al-Qaeda ("the base" in Arabic) as long ago as 1988. It first targeted Americans – unavailingly, in this case – when in 1992 it exploded two bombs in Aden in an attempt to strike at American soldiers en route to Somalia. In 1996 some 19 American servicemen were killed in an attack on the Khobar Towers, a housing complex for 2,000 US military personnel, in eastern Saudi Arabia. Initially, the United States blamed Iran for the attack, but later accused al-Qaeda of responsibility. In 1998 al-Qaeda suicide bombers destroyed the US embassies in Tanzania and Kenya, killing 11 in Dar es Salaam and 213 in Nairobi. Thousands were also wounded, and almost all of the dead and injured in both blasts were non-Americans.

Even the targeting of the World Trade Center – an obvious symbol of Western capitalism – should not have been a surprise: in 1993 Ramzi Yousef, born in Kuwait to Pakistani parents, was responsible for a huge car bomb in the centre's garage, which failed to destroy the towers but still killed six and injured just over 1,000. Whether Yousef was a member of al-Qaeda is not clear, but his maternal uncle is Khalid Sheikh Mohammad, an organiser of 9/11. Yousef's career in terrorism lasted until his arrest in Pakistan in 1995, and at his trial in New York he defiantly asserted:

> Yes, I am a terrorist and proud of it as long as it is against the US government and against Israel, because you are more than terrorists; you are the one who invented terrorism and using it every day. You are butchers, liars and hypocrites.

That, of course, is not how the country sees itself. The thesis of the George W. Bush administration was that the United States, not least by virtue of its declaration of independence guaranteeing to all men "life, liberty and the pursuit of happiness", is a force for good with both a self-interest and a global responsibility in spreading democracy. Beginning his second term in January 2005, President Bush declared:

> It is the policy of the United States to seek and support the growth of democratic movements and institutions in every nation and culture, with the ultimate goal of ending tyranny in our world.

In a reference to 9/11 he added:

> We have seen our vulnerability, and we have seen its deepest source. For as long as whole regions of the world simmer in resentment and tyranny – prone to ideologies that feed hatred and excuse murder – violence will gather, and multiply in destructive power, and cross the most defended borders, and raise a mortal threat.

Given the country's past involvement in supporting anti-communist dictators in Latin America and the Middle East and in ousting democratically elected leaders such as Salvador Allende in Chile or Mohammad Mossadegh in Iran, cynics might well have raised an eyebrow at Bush's claim. But it is clear that the neoconservatives in and around the Bush administration did feel that overthrowing Saddam Hussein would bring democracy first to Iraq and then to its Arab neighbours. On the basis that democracies do not fight each other, democratic Israel – for which the United States has always pledged its full support – would then finally be an accepted part of the Middle East.

Harsh reality has stripped the US of that particular delusion. Its most determined enemies are in the Muslim world, convinced by the wars in Iraq and Afghanistan and by its unfailing support for Israel that the US is waging a war on Islam. Protestations that its military and diplomatic might saved Bosnian and other Muslims from Serbian tyranny (and atrocities) in the Balkan wars of the 1990s apparently count for nothing to the followers of al-Qaeda and similar Islamist groups. Instead, the US faces a continuing *jihad*, a word conveniently – albeit loosely – translated in the West as holy war.

Global war on terror

The question confronting any American president is how to respond to this challenge from Islamist extremism. In his January 2002 State of the Union message (the first after 9/11), George W. Bush famously described an "axis of evil", linking North Korea, Iraq and Iran as countries involved in terrorism and sharing a common quest for weapons of mass destruction (WMD) such as nuclear bombs or chemical armaments. A year later that definition provided the basis for the invasion of Iraq, on the mistaken grounds that Saddam had WMD and was planning to produce more.

The axis of evil speech explicitly targeted foreign governments, but 9/11 and the earlier attacks on US embassies were the product of non-state actors – and for them President Bush had devised a different slogan. On September 20th 2001, in a televised address to the joint houses of Congress, the president said:

> Our "war on terror" begins with al-Qaeda, but it does not end there. It will not end until every terrorist group of global reach has been found, stopped and defeated.

It was a powerful message, and "war on terror" quickly became "global war on terror", complete with a new medal, the Global War on Terrorism Service Medal, for military personnel.

Almost from the beginning the global war on terror attracted a certain amount of ridicule, especially from the US's European allies. How could you wage war against an abstract noun, and how could you ever declare victory? In 2007 the British government, which had followed the US's lead in both Iraq and Afghanistan, announced that it would no longer use the phrase war on terror (the then head of MI5 said later that 9/11 was "a crime, not an act of war" and "so I never found it helpful to refer to a war on terror").

The same view was taken by Barack Obama, who has rarely used his predecessor's dramatic phrase, and in 2009 the Department of Defense officially eschewed the phrase, replacing it with the undramatic "overseas contingency operation". Part of the linguistic shift was the notion that al-Qaeda was on the run, with its operations disrupted by the intelligence operations of the US and its allies. Indeed, in December 2012 one senior defence department official declared that al-Qaeda had been "effectively destroyed". Six months later President Obama defined his goal as "to dismantle specific networks of violent extremists that threaten America" – language that coincided with the dumping of "overseas contingency operations" in favour of "countering violent extremism".

But is it sensible to treat the threats from al-Qaeda and other Islamist groups as policing matters, as crimes rather than acts of war? In terms of attacks within the US, possibly yes. The two Chechen Muslim brothers who exploded two pressure-cooker bombs at the Boston marathon in 2013 were apparently self-radicalised, with no connection to Islamist groups but motivated by what one brother called a desire for "retribution for US military action in Afghanistan and Iraq". Moreover, the Federal Bureau of Investigation (FBI) had already been alerted by Russia's FSB intelligence agency that the elder brother was "a follower of radical Islam". In other words, the Boston bombings – whether to forestall them or to investigate them – were very much the responsibility of the FBI and the police.

Beyond the country's borders, however, the issue is very different. Attacks on Americans by the Taliban in Afghanistan or by al-Qaeda and the Islamic State in the Arab world and Africa demand the kind of response that only the CIA and the military can provide.

That response is rarely by the United States in isolation. In almost all its modern-day conflicts it has preferred to act in coalition with its allies. The second world war is an obvious example, but so too is the first Gulf war, when American forces in "Operation Desert Storm" were part of a coalition of 34 countries – including some

Arab nations such as Syria – operating with the backing of the United Nations. Similarly, the US invasions and occupations of Afghanistan and Iraq were accompanied by allies: in the case of Afghanistan, which American and British troops invaded in October 2001 under the slogan "Operation Enduring Freedom", the American troops were operating after 2003 as part of a NATO coalition; in the Iraq war the United States claimed a "coalition of the willing" with 48 members, though only British, Australian and Polish troops joined their American counterparts in the actual invasion.

Whatever the cute names given to its various forays abroad, and whatever the size of the coalitions, the reality is that it is the US that is the determining player. Even in the 2011 toppling of Qaddafi in Libya, where there was no acknowledged involvement of American "boots on the ground", US air and naval power were vital support for the lead roles taken by France and the UK in operating no-fly zones and a naval blockade to deny Qaddafi the ability to crush his opponents in Cyrenaica.

There is, however, a desire to have the political cover of a coalition (especially, as in the 2003 invasion of Iraq, when there is no UN approval); and, after the protracted and painful experiences of the Iraq and Afghanistan wars, there is also a deep reluctance to commit ground troops. This was particularly obvious in 2013, when the Syrian regime of Bashar al-Assad used chemical weapons against Syrian rebels and so crossed red lines set by President Obama. The assumption was that Obama would at least launch a missile attack on Syrian facilities; but at the last moment, perhaps swayed by a decision by the UK Parliament not to get involved, Obama satisfied himself with a Russian-brokered agreement that Syria would give up its chemical weapons. His decision was heavily criticised by many armchair warriors in Congress, but was widely welcomed by an American populace wearied of constant war in faraway places.

But since the US can hardly cut itself off from its interests in the rest of the world, its populace has to realise that it will still be targeted, directly or indirectly, in those faraway places. The result is the depressing reality that every US embassy is now a heavily guarded fortress, with its diplomats often isolated from the local populations that they are supposed to contact and understand.

If attacks on US targets are constant threats, the obvious response is to try to forestall them: "prevention is better than cure" might well be the motto now for the CIA and the US military. The means is a plethora of US-manned programmes, ranging from assisting foreign forces with training and equipment – as in Mexico, Colombia and other Latin American countries – to the deployment of American personnel, as in Afghanistan. One scheme, the Anti-Terrorism Assistance programme, has been in existence since 1983; has delivered counter-terrorism training to more than 90,000 law-enforcement personnel from 154 countries; and has active partnerships with 53 countries.

The programmes move with the times: in 2005 the US government founded (and funded) the Trans-Sahara Counterterrorism Partnership (TSCPT). In the words of the State Department:

> The core goals are to enhance the indigenous capacities of governments in the pan-Sahel (Mauritania, Mali, Chad, Niger, Nigeria, Senegal, and Burkina Faso) to confront the challenge posed by terrorist organisations in the trans-Sahara; and to facilitate co-operation between those countries and US partners in the Maghreb (Morocco, Algeria, and Tunisia).

Those goals are more easily defined than achieved. The State Department handout goes on to say:

> TSCTP has been successful in slowly building capacity and co-operation despite political setbacks over the years caused by coups d'états, ethnic rebellions, and extra-constitutional actions that have interrupted work and progress with select partner countries.

In other words, the counter-terrorism programme has not, in reality and despite the optimistic gloss of the State Department, been particularly effective. One reason is the corruption and inefficiency endemic in the partner countries; another is the spillover of weapons and manpower from the downfall of Qaddafi, which has left Libya in violent turmoil. A third reason is the ease with which Islamist extremists, such as al-Qaeda in the Islamic Maghreb (AQIM) and Ansar Din, have crossed the porous frontiers of the colonial era and filled what amounts to a security vacuum. The result has been a spate of kidnappings; a deadly assault on a gas facility in the Algerian desert in 2012; and a civil war in Mali, beginning in 2012, in which Islamist extremists effectively hijacked a Tuareg quest for the secession of the north of the country. In none of these were American interests directly involved, but it is the potential indirect repercussions that worry the government.

For that reason, since 2013 US special operations troops, including the army's Delta Force, have been stepping up their training of elite counter-terrorism groups in Libya, Niger, Mauritania and Mali. But good intentions can go awry: in Libya in 2013 a local militia overpowered the Libyan guard at a training base outside Tripoli and stole the weapons, night-vision goggles and vehicles provided by the US to train the putative Libyan elite force. In a similar setback, some US-trained commanders of the elite Malian army units have defected to the Islamist insurgents.

Global policeman?

Behind all such programmes lurks the perennial question of the hyperpower's role in the world. Political scientists love to coin phrases such as "the world's sheriff" or the "global policeman" (the first suggests the need for a posse – which is essentially what the US has achieved with its coalitions of allies – and the second implies that the world looks to the US to keep it in order).

But perhaps the best description is the "indispensable nation", ambiguous enough to meet most requirements and first coined in 1998 by Bill Clinton's secretary of state, Madeleine Albright. In reference to Saddam Hussein's Iraq she said:

> It is the threat of the use of force and our line-up there that is going to put force behind the diplomacy. But if we have to use force, it is because we are America; we are the indispensable nation. We stand tall and we see further than other countries into the future, and we see the danger here to all of us.

President George W. Bush's strategy was for the indispensable nation to be aggressive, hence the wars in Afghanistan and Iraq. President Obama's strategy has been to end those wars and to avoid others, hence his preference for drone strikes and cyber-warfare. But he still defines the US as indispensable. In a speech in May 2014 to cadets at the US Military Academy at West Point, he declared:

> Here's my bottom line: America must always lead on the world stage. If we don't, no one else will. The military that you have joined is, and always will be, the backbone of that leadership. But US military action cannot be the only – or even primary – component of our leadership in every instance. Just because we have the best hammer does not mean that every problem is a nail.

That last sentence was surely an oblique criticism of his predecessor's military adventurism. After all, Obama's message to the cadets, and by extension to the nation and to his critics, was clear enough:

> I believe that a world of greater freedom and tolerance is not only a moral imperative; it also helps keep us safe. But to say that we have an interest in pursuing peace and freedom beyond our borders is not to say that every problem has a military solution. Since World War II, some of our most costly mistakes came not from our restraint but from our willingness to rush into military adventures without thinking through the consequences, without building international support and legitimacy for our action, without levelling with the American people about the sacrifices required. Tough talk often draws headlines, but war rarely conforms to slogans. As General Eisenhower, someone with hard-earned knowledge on this subject, said at this ceremony in 1947, "War is mankind's most tragic and stupid folly; to seek or advise its deliberate provocation is a black crime against all men."

Obama makes a good point: wars are costly, in both lives and treasure, and often lead to unintended consequences – as the turbulent and bloody aftermaths in both Iraq and Libya demonstrate. He opposed the war in Iraq, but he has no such excuse for Libya.

Should the US, as Ron Paul would argue, therefore heed George Washington and steer clear of foreign entanglements? President Obama, in his speech to the next generation of American troops, answered that in the 21st century isolationism cannot be an option:

We don't have a choice to ignore what happens beyond our borders. If nuclear materials are not secure, that poses a danger to American cities. As the Syrian civil war spills across borders, the capacity of battle-hardened extremist groups to come after us only increases. Regional aggression that goes unchecked – whether in southern Ukraine or the South China Sea, or anywhere else in the world – will ultimately impact our allies and could draw in our military. We can't ignore what happens beyond our boundaries.

Indeed so, but Obama argues:

The odds of a direct threat against us by any nation are low and do not come close to the dangers we faced during the Cold War.

In other words, and despite Western alarm over Russia's annexation in 2014 of Crimea and its support for the secessionists of eastern Ukraine, the US's conflicts are with non-state actors, and in particular with al-Qaeda and other extreme Islamists. But what sort of al-Qaeda? As an organisation directed from the centre, first by Osama bin Laden and after his death by Ayman al-Zawahiri, al-Qaeda has been grievously weakened. But its franchise, with al-Qaeda offshoots in the Middle East and Africa, is – if anything – growing in power. So, too, is the influence of ISIS (the Islamic State in Iraq and Sham), which declared its Islamic State in 2014 and has since inspired allegiance from extreme Islamists from Algeria to Yemen.

The risks to US installations and personnel abroad were painfully illustrated by the 2012 assault on the American consulate in Benghazi, Libya. The attack, which led to the deaths of four Americans, including the ambassador, was probably carried out by Ansar al-Sharia (Supporters of Islamic Law), an extremist militia espousing al-Qaeda's aims.

But franchising extreme Islamism also brings risks to Americans within their own country. By mid-2015 the Syrian civil war had attracted perhaps 4,000 foreigners from the West – mostly of Muslim origin – to fight against the regime of Bashar al-Assad, and a great many of them were bearing arms for extreme Islamist groups such as the al-Qaeda-aligned Jabhat al-Nusra. The largest foreign contingents come from the UK and France, but it seems that the US contingent could have grown to perhaps 100, including one young man who in May 2014 carried out a suicide bombing. By definition, a foreign suicide bomber will not return to his homeland, but presumably some of the American fighters will. Might they then carry out the same kind of attacks that the two Chechen brothers launched in Boston?

The threat within

A nation that gives its citizens a constitutional right to bear arms and jealously guards their freedom of speech might well seem to be fertile soil for violent conflict between the people and their government. After all, there are reckoned to be anywhere up to 310 million guns in private hands, basically one gun for every American (though, of course, a majority do not own guns). There are also, according to a 2012 report by the Southern Poverty Law Center (a reputable civil-rights advocacy group), some 1,360 armed militias and other anti-government groups, sharing the belief that the federal government seeks to restrict their liberties. This total of 1,360 compares with just 149 such groups counted by the centre in 2008 – the year when Obama was elected president.

Are such groups and the national government therefore on a collision course towards armed conflict? Not necessarily. Despite the Boston bombings, terrorism against the state in the US occurs much less often than in Europe. Some Texans may joke about secession but the last serious attempt to leave the embrace of Uncle Sam was from Puerto Rico's Armed Forces of National Liberation (Fuerzas Armadas de Liberación Nacional, or FALN). Between 1974 and 1983 this small Marxist-Leninist group claimed responsibility for 120 bombings in US cities such as Washington, Chicago and New York and in Puerto Rico itself, killing six and injuring more than 100. The FALN has long been extinct and more peaceful calls for independence for the island from the United States fall on deaf ears: in a 2012 referendum on Puerto Rico's status, only 5.5% of the island voters chose independence.

Just as the FALN has faded from memory, so too have the radical groups seeking to overthrow the US status quo in the 1970s: for example, the Symbionese Liberation Army; the Weathermen; the Black Panthers and the Black Liberation Army; and the United Freedom

Front. The FBI can count plenty of other groups using terrorist tactics – from the Ku Klux Klan and the Aryan Nations to the Jewish Defense League and the Animal Liberation Front – but their motive is not to topple the federal government, no matter how much they might disagree with it on various issues. Most violence in recent times has been focused on single issues, such as attacks on abortion clinics by pro-life groups. Ted Kaczynski, the Unabomber, whose bombs killed three and injured 23 between 1978 and 1995, was attacking not the US but industrialisation and modern technology. The last home-grown terrorists of note were Timothy McVeigh and Terry Nichols: their bombing of a federal building in Oklahoma City in 1995 killed 168 and injured more than 680. Their motive was apparently revenge for the dozens of deaths caused by the federal authorities' clumsy and deadly handling of the 1992 Ruby Ridge incident, involving a family trying to escape from the world and the allegedly imminent apocalypse, and the 1993 Waco siege, when federal agents clashed with a bizarre religious group.

As those events disappear into the history books, Americans might well relax. Their chance of being killed in a terrorist attack – whether at home or abroad – are now about one in 20 million, a much better level of safety than for the citizens of Latin America, Africa or Europe. But it would be foolish for the authorities to let down their guard: there is always the risk that an armed militia might act on its paranoia about government control, and there is certainly the risk that US actions in the Middle East will rebound on its interests at home.

The Boston bombings of 2013 were one example of this. But another was the fatal shooting in 2009 of 13 servicemen and wounding of more than 30 others at the Fort Hood army base in Texas by Major Nidal Hasan, an army psychiatrist. Ominously in retrospect, Major Hasan had for several months been in e-mail contact with Anwar al-Awlaqi, an American member of al-Qaeda who was subsequently killed by a CIA drone strike in Yemen in 2011. As Védrine reminded the world, the United States is indeed a hyperpower, but, as al-Qaeda and others have shown, power does not automatically convey impunity.

7 Asia: people and potential – for both peace and war

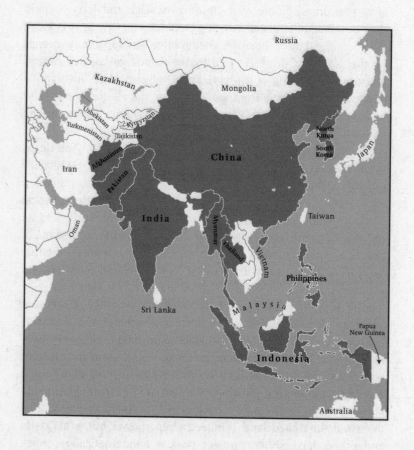

THE AREA BETWEEN the Ural Mountains and the Pacific Ocean – one conventional definition of Asia – is too vast for all-encompassing adjectives. Yet some generalisations are hard to dismiss: north-east Asia, with Russia (an Asian as well as a European power), China and North Korea all possessing nuclear arms, is a potential flashpoint with ominous repercussions for the whole world; south Asia is a perennial source of conflict, notably pitting nuclear-armed India (now almost as populous as China) against nuclear-armed Pakistan; Afghanistan and Pakistan are close to the status of failed states, constantly threatening to export Islamist terrorism to the rest of the world; and the states of South-East Asia find themselves at odds with an increasingly muscle-flexing China in disputes over their maritime borders.

One comfort is that the present is far more benign than the past. Japan's invasion of China in the 1930s led to perhaps as many as 10–20 million Chinese deaths (Japanese troops in their rape of Nanking in 1937 killed some 300,000 Chinese and raped 80,000 women). The Korean war of 1950–53 – still technically unfinished – claimed the lives of at least 1.6 million civilians, along with 36,000 American troops and 600,000 Chinese troops (some estimates for these and other nations' troops and civilians are much higher). The death toll in the Vietnam war, pitting the communist north against the US-supported south and involving neighbouring Laos and Cambodia, has been estimated at almost 3.5 million – including over 58,000 American servicemen – between 1969 and 1975.

By contrast, the continuing conflict in Afghanistan has been far less bloody: from the US invasion of 2001 to the departure of American combat troops in 2014 perhaps 20,000 civilians had been killed and almost 3,500 American troops and their foreign allies had died. The civil war in Sri Lanka, as the Tamil Tigers (Liberation Tigers of Tamil Eelam, to use their full title) sought independence for the north of the island, lasted from 1983 to 2009 – and was notable for the introduction by the Tamil Tigers of the suicide bomber as a weapon of war. Yet the death toll compared with the much shorter Korean war was low: some 27,639 Tamil fighters, 21,066 Sri Lankan government troops and 1,000 Sri Lankan police. Even though tens of thousands of civilians (mostly Tamil) were killed, especially in the final months of the war, the full total for the conflict is thought to be around 130,000 dead.

One explanation for this reduction in the harm that people do to one another is that wars between states have more or less disappeared (in the Afghanistan conflict the US-led coalition was assembled to overthrow a Taliban government but stayed in order to support its successors in their civil war with the Taliban). A second, related, explanation is the end of the cold war, during which the United States, China and the Soviet Union were committed to supporting their client states – hence the role of China and the Soviet Union in siding with the north in the Korean war and the role of the US in defending South Vietnam against the communist Viet Cong from North Vietnam.

Ironically, though, the cold war helped to foster the Islamist violence that has become such a feature in Asia in the 21st century. The religiously motivated and US-backed *mujahideen*, who in the 1980s fought to dislodge Soviet troops from Afghanistan, have evolved into an array of jihadist groups in central Asia. The East Turkestan Islamic Movement (ETIM), the Islamic Movement of Uzbekistan (IMU), the Hizb ut-Tahrir (Party of Liberation) and other militant groups, including the Tajik Jamaat Ansarullah (Assembly of the Helpers of Allah), have more or less been silenced by the dictatorial regimes of Turkmenistan, Uzbekistan, Tajikistan, Kyrgyzstan and Kazakhstan; now they mount their operations in perennially unstable Afghanistan, Pakistan and Kashmir (ETIM has always seen its base as China's Xinjiang province, which is East Turkestan in ETIM's terminology and home to the region's Uighur Muslim minority).

Given the enduring influence in the region of al-Qaeda (which has close links with IMU and possibly ETIM), and the attraction to young men of the Islamic State in Iraq and Sham (the Kyrgyz authorities said in 2014 that at least 50 Kyrgyz citizens were fighting for the self-proclaimed caliphate of the Islamic State), violent jihadism will surely remain a leading source of conflict in Asia, from Kabul all the way to Beijing.

However, it would be naive to suppose that wars between Asia's states will always be a matter for the history books. Economic power is often backed by military power and a willingness to use it. In 2015 China overtook the US as the world's biggest economy on a purchasing-power-parity basis, and within a couple of decades will overtake it in military spending, too. Meanwhile, other Asian nations are also increasing their defence budgets (by one calculation Asia-Pacific nations excluding China surpassed military spending by Europe in 2015). Fear of a hegemonic and aggressive China is the reason so many Asia-Pacific states, from Singapore and Indonesia to the Philippines, Taiwan and Japan, view their various alliances with the United States as a security guarantee – a guarantee made all the more necessary by the absence of regional defence alliances. For the moment, however, the conflicts that preoccupy Asia's governments are mostly internally generated, whether by ideology, race, religion or all three.

Afghanistan

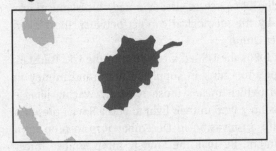

> *May God keep you away from the venom of the cobra, the teeth of the tiger, and the revenge of the Afghans.*

Sadly, plenty of foreign powers have ignored this salutary warning by Alexander the Great in the 4th century BC. A British invasion in the 19th century ended in massacre and a humiliating rout; the occupation of Afghanistan by Soviet troops in the late 20th century ended with their embarrassed withdrawal; and the invasion of the country in this century by American troops and the subsequent US-led NATO occupation have ended with little to show for all the money spent and lives lost other than a continuing civil war and rampant corruption.

Underlying the foreign fascination with Afghanistan is what Rudyard Kipling, a British writer, popularised as "the Great Game": the strategic rivalry in the 19th and early 20th centuries between the Russian and British empires for control of central Asia and its access to British India. The updated version of the great game was the cold war: Afghanistan, as a client state of the Soviet Union, was a threat to the US's alliance with Pakistan, which was constantly – and at times militarily – at odds with pro-Soviet India. Add to that the proximity of oil-rich Iran and, across the Arabian Sea, the oil reserves of the Arabian peninsula, and perhaps it is not surprising that outside powers have been unable to resist involvement in the aptly named "graveyard of empires".

Some of this geopolitical thinking, despite the ending of the cold war, still holds true. But the immediate reason for foreign involvement now is the struggle to contain extreme Islamism, a struggle complicated by the use of Afghanistan as a proxy battlefield by Pakistan and India. Of course, as already noted, this Islamism was originally fostered by the ideological conflict between the United States and the Soviet Union.

Throughout the 1980s the US led a coalition of the UK, Pakistan, Saudi Arabia, Egypt and China in supplying arms and money to various *mujahideen* (which means those who are waging *jihad* – loosely translated as holy war) in their fight to end a Soviet presence that had begun with an invasion in December 1979 to prop up a communist government. By 1988 the Soviet Union, whose forces in Afghanistan had risen to 120,000, was willing to sign a peace deal with Afghanistan, the US and Pakistan, and by mid-February the following year the last Soviet soldier had left the country after a decade that had claimed the lives of around 15,000 Soviet troops killed in action, with several hundred thousand of their comrades wounded and many thousands dead from disease.

What has followed has been a classic example of "be careful what you wish for". The *jihad* against the Soviet occupation attracted as many as 25,000 fighters from the Arab world, many, if not most, of them wedded to a fundamentalist interpretation of Islam. One such *mujahid* was Osama bin Laden, whose al-Qaeda network was later responsible not just for the killing of American soldiers in Somalia in 1993 and the bloody attacks in 1998 on US embassies in Kenya and Tanzania but most famously for the September 11th 2001 attacks on New York and Washington, DC. Having first been an ally of convenience for the United States, bin Laden had become its sworn enemy.

In the meantime, Afghanistan, a country of some 33 million, had descended after the Soviet withdrawal into a vicious civil war between rival *mujahideen* groups. Much of the rivalry was ethnically based, pitting Pashtuns (some two-fifths of the population), Uzbeks, Tajiks, Hazara and other still smaller minorities against each other. Some of the rivalry was religious: though most Afghans are Sunni, perhaps as many as 19% – principally Hazara – are Shia. Eventually, in 1996 the capital, Kabul, fell to the Pashtun-dominated Taliban.

The Taliban (the word is the Persian plural of the Arabic *talib*, meaning student) owed their existence, and their success, to Pakistan's Inter-Services Intelligence (ISI) agency, the most powerful institution in a country that has never enjoyed stable civilian rule. Pakistan's aim was to provide itself with strategic depth to its north, an idea first entertained by President Zia ul-Haq in the 1980s when he feared that the Soviet Union might move from Afghanistan south into Pakistan. The ISI is believed to have trained around 90,000 Afghan fighters during the 1980s.

For a brief period after the fall of Kabul, the West seemed prepared to collaborate with the Taliban: they were providing order and – echoing the "Great Game" – perhaps they could facilitate the transmission of natural gas from Turkmenistan to Pakistan. But the Taliban, followers of the fundamentalist Deobandi school of Sunni Islam, soon proved themselves far too extreme for any such accommodation. The brutal imposition of strict *sharia* law, including stoning for adultery, and a ban on female education horrified those foreigners who had cheered the defeat of the Soviet army. When the Taliban in 1996 declared the Islamic Emirate of Afghanistan, it was recognised only by Pakistan, Saudi Arabia and the United Arab Emirates.

Conceivably, the Taliban could have stayed in power, confining the country – or at least the two-thirds of Afghanistan under their control – to a medieval and brutal obscurantism. Their mistake, however, was to have afforded asylum in 1996 to Osama bin Laden, who had just been expelled from Sudan. The subsequent al-Qaeda attacks on the US embassies in Kenya and Tanzania then provoked American missile strikes in 1998 against al-Qaeda camps in Afghanistan. The following year the US stepped up pressure on the Taliban to surrender bin Laden by imposing financial sanctions and an air embargo.

Neither managed to persuade the one-eyed Taliban leader, Mullah Muhammad Omar, to revoke his Muslim duty to protect a guest – that is, bin Laden. Worse, from a US perspective, was the assassination on September 9th 2001 of Ahmad Shah Massoud, the US-supported Tajik commander of the Tajik and Uzbek-dominated Northern Alliance of *mujahideen* groups opposed to the Taliban. Two days later, bin Laden launched the worst attack on the United States since Pearl Harbor. When Mullah Omar refused to expel bin Laden on the grounds that the US had not provided evidence of his guilt, President George W. Bush on October 7th 2001 began "Operation Enduring Freedom", with US and British air strikes on Afghanistan, supported by their special forces and by *mujahideen* from the Northern Alliance. By December the Taliban government had fallen; an interim government had taken office under Hamid Karzai, a Pashtun previously in exile in the US; and the UN-authorised International Security Assistance Force (ISAF – under NATO command from August 2003) had arrived to consolidate the victory over the Taliban.

A positive view of Afghanistan at the end of 2014, when the US withdrew its combat troops and ISAF switched to a training role for the Afghan National Security Forces, is that much had been achieved. President Karzai won successive elections in 2004 and 2009 – the two terms allowed by the constitution – and Ashraf Ghani was elected president in 2014; girls have gone to school in increasing numbers; and improved health care has, according to some UN statisticians, raised life expectancy for today's 33 million population (double the number at the start of the 1980s) to perhaps 62, compared with 55 at the start of the century.

A more realistic view is that the Taliban are far from defeated. The number of their fighters has been generously estimated at 25,000, confronting a NATO force that at its peak in 2011 numbered 140,000 (including 101,000 American troops), and Afghan security forces that numbered 94,000 and were supported by an equivalent number of Afghan police. The arithmetic comes out at a ratio of around 12:1 in favour of the US and its allies, and yet the overwhelming might of ISAF, equipped with helicopter gunships and all kinds of sophisticated weaponry, has failed to end the Taliban's control of much – if not most – of the territory outside the main cities.

One explanation is the Taliban's effective use of the weaponry of asymmetric warfare, notably improvised explosive devices (IEDs) that can be ignited remotely by mobile phones and religiously motivated suicide bombers. A second is the sanctuary across the border in Pakistan available to the Afghan Taliban (for example, Mullah Omar, despite a $10 million US bounty on his head). A third has been popular resentment of the corruption of the Karzai regime and its alliance with the country's various warlords. In a NATO military engagement more than twice as long as the second world war, several NATO states – for example, France, Canada and the Netherlands – withdrew their soldiers from Afghanistan earlier than planned, conscious that they were losing support at home and winning precious little for their efforts. An added, psychologically damaging factor was the number of "green on blue" killings, when Afghan government soldiers turned their fire on ISAF soldiers. Some 60 NATO personnel were killed in this way in 2012.

One justification for the $100 billion in aid (most of it from the US) spent on Afghanistan since 2001 is that it has stopped the export of terrorism from the country. In the absence of a second 9/11, perhaps so. But the counter-argument is that the years of war and occupation have reinforced the view of many in the Muslim world that the US in particular and the West in general are waging a war on Islam. Meanwhile, attempts to curtail Afghanistan's opium production (the US has spent $7.6 billion on eradication programmes since 2001) were mocked by a record harvest in 2014.

The obvious question for the electorates in NATO countries is whether the gains in Afghanistan have been worth the casualties: for example, more than 2,300 American and 450 British deaths out of a NATO total of almost 3,500. The more pressing question for Afghans themselves is whether the Taliban will return to power. It may seem unlikely that the Taliban will retake the cities, yet – given the level of corruption throughout the country – it is hard to be confident that the Afghan armed forces, theoretically some 200,000-strong and helped by some 13,000 NATO troops in non-combat roles, will be effective in controlling the countryside. It is also possible that government forces will have to face not just the Taliban but militants pledging loyalty to the Islamic State, the new caliphate proclaimed in 2014 by Iraq's Abu Bakr al-Baghdadi. In May 2015 the governor of the north-eastern province of Kunduz claimed that foreigners trained by ISIS were fighting alongside the Taliban. In the same month, the US commander of NATO's 13,000-strong "Resolute Support Mission", advising and training Afghanistan's security forces, said ISIS was trying to recruit Afghans – and was also at times clashing with the Taliban in its quest for men and territory.

There will surely be renewed attempts to find a settlement between the government and the Taliban, building on the sporadic negotiations that took place in the Karzai era and were encouraged by President Barack Obama. But the willingness of the Taliban to compromise is by no means certain: in September 2011 Burhanuddin Rabbani, a respected Tajik warlord negotiating at the time with the Taliban as chairman of the Afghan High Peace Council, was killed by a suicide bomber in Kabul, probably by Taliban elements opposed to reconciliation. Equally uncertain is the willingness of Pakistan to promote a settlement: the ISI seems wedded to the idea that the Taliban serve Pakistan's strategic interest, whatever the resulting instability in Afghanistan.

China

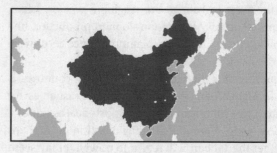

With a population of more than 1.3 billion the People's Republic of China (PRC) is the world's most populous nation (although India will overtake it within the next two decades). On the basis of purchasing-power parity it also now boasts the world's biggest economy. Put the two together, add some well-attested expertise in cyber-warfare (in 2014 the FBI accused China of cyber-attacks on American companies) and China is a power to be reckoned with. The People's Liberation Army (PLA), which includes the navy and air force, has 2.3 million frontline personnel, with another 2.3 million in the active reserve of the armed forces and police; there are more than 9,000 tanks and around 900 fighter jets; and the navy, with more than 60 submarines, one aircraft carrier (with more to come) and around 70 destroyers and frigates, can deploy its might throughout the Pacific Ocean and beyond. When its status as a nuclear-weapons power with a permanent seat on the UN Security Council is also taken into account, China can clearly inspire the respect of all in the Asia-Pacific region and of Russia and the United States, both of which are keen to preserve their Pacific interests.

It also inspires a certain amount of fear among its lesser Pacific neighbours, even technologically advanced Japan. Competing territorial and maritime claims mean that China is in dispute with Japan over the Senkaku islands (Diaoyu or Diaoyutai, in Chinese); with Vietnam over the Paracel islands; with the Philippines over the Scarborough Shoal; and with Malaysia, the Philippines, Vietnam and Brunei over the Spratly islands (where China, ratcheting up the tension, in early 2015 began "island building" by reclaiming land in defiance of protests by the US and its regional allies). To add still more complexity, the PRC's claims are also made by Taiwan, which calls itself the Republic of China (ROC) and considers itself to be the legitimate government of all China.

China's claims are not limited to the Pacific region. It has a long-standing dispute with India over the Aksai Chin border region in the Himalayas, claims most of the Indian state of Arunachal Pradesh and has an ill-defined (and therefore potentially contentious) border with Bhutan.

Against such a background, it is remarkable how seldom the PRC – founded in 1949 when Mao Zedong's communist legions expelled the US-backed Kuomintang government of Chiang Kai-shek to exile in Taiwan – has resorted to military action.

In the Korean war of 1950–53 it intervened in support of communist North Korea, fighting South Korea and the US-led UN troops to a stalemate.

In 1959 Chinese troops were deployed to crush a rebellion in Tibet, which had declared its independence from China in 1913 but had been formally forced ("liberated" was the word used by Mao) into the PRC in 1950.

In 1962, following several border clashes with India following India's reception of the Dalai Lama and his followers from Tibet, China sent troops to resolve its disputed mountain frontier with India around Kashmir. After a month of fighting along the Aksai Chin plateau in one of the world's most inhospitable regions, China emerged with de facto control of Aksai Chin, leaving the rest of Kashmir divided between India and Pakistan.

In March 1969, when tensions between China and the Soviet Union were at their highest, fighting broke out between the PLA and Soviet forces along the Ussuri river, marking the ill-defined border between the two countries. As the clashes continued into the summer, there seemed a real prospect of full-scale, even nuclear, war between communism's two leading powers. Happily, in September 1969 high-level diplomacy was able to lower the temperature (though a full settlement of the Russia–China border was not reached until 2008).

The final full-scale exercise of Chinese military power in the 20th century was its invasion of Vietnam in February 1979. This was in retaliation for the occupation by Vietnam of neighbouring Cambodia in a successful bid to topple the genocidal Khmer Rouge regime of Pol Pot, an ally of China. The Chinese action was also motivated by anger at Vietnam's mistreatment of its ethnic Chinese minority and by a desire to diminish the influence of the Soviet Union, an ally of Vietnam, as a rival power in the communist world. In the event, though both sides claimed victory in the month-long war, it is clear that the PLA – only just emerging from the turmoil of the Cultural Revolution – had suffered relative humiliation at the hands of the battle-hardened Vietnamese. Border skirmishes with Vietnam continued through the 1980s, ending only with Vietnam's 1989 withdrawal from Cambodia, but it was not until 2009 that the dispute over the Sino–Vietnam land border was eventually settled.

At least according to China's own rhetoric, even as its military might grows its neighbours will have nothing to fear. In 2014 President Xi Jinping pledged to settle China's territorial disputes peacefully:

China stays committed to seeking peaceful settlement of disputes with other countries over territorial sovereignty and maritime rights and interests.

Xi's words confirm China's long-standing view that no country should interfere in another's internal affairs. This stance conveniently ignores China's willingness to employ its economic power, whether through politically influential investments in Africa or through its creation in October 2014 of the Asia Infrastructure Investment Bank (AIIB), an obvious competitor to the US-dominated World Bank. The stance also allows it to stay aloof from conflicts in the Middle East while attacking any outsider who dares to criticise the abuse of human rights within China – or, indeed, any action by Chinese citizens against the state. The most famous recent example of dissent in China was the student-led occupation of Beijing's Tiananmen Square in April 1989, culminating in the brutal clearing of the demonstrators by the PLA on June 4th with a death toll estimated to range from 200 to more than 2,000.

In contrast to the peaceful tactics of the Tiananmen students, China's Muslim Uighur minority have a proven willingness to use violence to secure their goal of independence for the Xinjiang Autonomous Region in the far north-west of the country. Though China recognises some 56 distinct ethnic groups, more than 90% of the population are Han Chinese; and the Han are the majority everywhere except in Tibet and Xinjiang, which is home to some 10 million Uighurs, a Turkic people present also in neighbouring Kazakhstan, Kyrgyzstan and Uzbekistan.

Xinjiang has been fought over by rival powers, notably the Mongols and the Chinese, for millennia, and part of it enjoyed a brief independence from China from 1944 to 1949 as the Soviet-backed East Turkestan Republic. The Uighur cause was cynically exploited by the Soviet Union after the so-called Sino–Soviet split in 1960, an ideological schism finally healed in 1989 with Mikhail Gorbachev's visit to Beijing (where his policy of openness was applauded by the Tiananmen students). Soviet support included funding for the East Turkestan People's Revolutionary Party (ETPRF) and the United Revolutionary Front of East Turkestan (URFET). When Soviet troops in

1979 invaded Afghanistan, China felt it was being squeezed by Soviet power – hence its decision, in company with the United States, to support the Afghan *mujahideen*.

The geopolitical calculations have long since changed, with the China of Xi Jinping increasingly comfortable with the Russia of Vladimir Putin. What has not changed is the opposition to the Chinese state of the Uighurs, who often use tactics of terrorism to strike beyond Xinjiang. In 1997, for example, the Turkey-based Organisation for Turkestan Freedom claimed responsibility for the bombing of a bus in Beijing, injuring some 30 people. Five years earlier, the East Turkestan Islamic Party was said to be responsible for two bus bombs in the Xinjiang capital, Urumqi, that killed at least three and injured 23. Most active has been the East Turkestan Islamic Movement (ETIM), responsible, for example, for a 2008 operation in which ETIM militants drove a truck into a column of jogging policemen in Kashgar, killing at least 16.

One worry for the Chinese government is that Uighur militants will inspire similar actions by Tibetan militants (in 2002 two Tibetans were accused of setting off a bomb in Chengdu, the capital of Sichuan province, causing several casualties). A greater worry, perhaps, is that the Uighur dissidents – some of whom have trained in Afghanistan and may have forged links there with al-Qaeda – will refine their tactics to create more havoc (at least two aircraft hijackings have been foiled). With deliberate symbolism, in October 2013 three ETIM militants in an apparent suicide attack drove a car into a crowd in Tiananmen Square, near the portrait of Mao Zedong, killing themselves and two tourists and injuring some 38 others. Clearly, Uighur dissent, fuelled by growing Islamic extremism, is not about to be defeated.

India

With almost 1.3 billion people the Republic of India can justly claim to be the world's largest democracy, and – in sharp contrast to the military dictatorships so common in neighbouring Pakistan after the bloody partition of British India in 1947 – it can also boast that it has always been ruled by civilian politicians.

That should not imply a tradition of pacifism, despite the tactics of non-violence famously used by Mahatma Gandhi to wrest India's freedom from the UK. Independent India has so far fought three wars with Pakistan and one with China. As far back as 1974 India conducted an underground nuclear-weapons test, and then more nuclear tests in 1998 (prompting Pakistan to develop its own nuclear capability). Today India probably has more than 90 nuclear warheads, and Pakistan 100 or so. Doomsayers worry that although neither country has signed the Nuclear Non-Proliferation Treaty, at least India has a no-first-use policy whereas Pakistan does not.

From Pakistan's point of view this is logical enough, since India is by far the stronger nation in conventional military terms. With 1.3 million active frontline personnel, India's armed forces are double Pakistan's, as is the number of its combat aircraft and submarines. In the years 2007–14 India was the world's biggest arms importer, and by 2020 it will probably have the world's fourth-biggest defence budget, overtaking Japan, France and the UK. In the modern version of "the Great Game", India feels a need to counter not just Pakistan but also a nuclear-armed China that is sending its navy into the Indian Ocean and developing facilities for its ships in Pakistan, Bangladesh, Sri Lanka and Myanmar – a "string of pearls" in a metaphor first used by the US defence department and then adopted by the Indian press. Furthermore, with the Soviet Union, traditionally an ally of India, now gone, the balance of power in Afghanistan has shifted to Pakistan's advantage rather than India's.

To many outsiders the perennial tensions in the Indian subcontinent appear absurd. After all, though Pakistan separated from India in order to be a majority Muslim state, India has more than 100 million Muslim citizens and both countries share the same history of British India (and, of course, the same passion for cricket). The cause of their mutual hostility is the status of Kashmir, a Muslim-majority state in British India whose Hindu maharajah, Hari Singh, dithered about whether it should join India or Pakistan on partition in August 1947. This led to an invasion by Muslim Pashtun tribesmen from newly created Pakistan in October 1947, which in turn led to the maharajah calling on Indian troops for help.

The result was the first Indo-Pakistan war. After some 14 months and a death toll of perhaps 1,500 on each side (estimates vary considerably), Pakistan occupied the northern third of the state, naming it Azad Kashmir (Free Kashmir), and India incorporated the rest of the state (comprising the Muslim-majority Kashmir Valley, the Hindu-dominated Jammu at the south of the valley and Buddhist Ladakh in the east) into the Indian Federation, naming it Jammu and Kashmir. Ever since, troops from both countries have eyed each other – and frequently confronted each other – across the "line of control", with Pakistan governing around 4.5 million Kashmiris in Azad Kashmir and India counting 10 million inhabitants of Jammu and Kashmir as Indian citizens.

The second Indo-Pakistan war, in 1965, occurred when Pakistan sent troops in disguise into Jammu and Kashmir in the hope of provoking a general Kashmiri uprising against India. After six weeks of fighting, the two sides withdrew to their previous positions under a ceasefire negotiated by the Soviet Union, each claiming to have won (India more convincingly than Pakistan).

The confrontations with Pakistan in the 1960s were not the only military challenge for India. In 1962 it proved to be the weaker adversary when China's People's Liberation Army attacked along the disputed Sino-Indian border, gaining control of the Aksai Chin plateau in a month-long war that left hundreds dead on both sides – often because of the extreme cold in battles that took place 4,000 metres above sea level. One fundamental cause of the Sino–Indian war was sloppy work by British colonial cartographers in defining the border in the 19th century. More proximate causes were China's anger at the sanctuary given in India to Tibet's Dalai Lama; Indian anger at China's claim to the Indian state of Arunachal Pradesh (South Tibet in some Chinese formulations); and the impact of the cold war, with China, following its ideological split in 1960 with the Soviet Union, keen to rebuff any territorial claims by pro-Soviet India.

Though the border issues between India and China remain unresolved, tensions have relaxed to such an extent that since 2007 the two nations have held several joint military exercises, concentrating on counter-terrorism programmes.

The same relaxation cannot be claimed for India's relationship with Pakistan, despite the occasional diplomatic overture by one side or the other. The third Indo–Pakistan war, which for once had nothing to do with Kashmir, broke out in 1971 when India sided with the Bengalis of East Pakistan in their war of liberation to create the new country of Bangladesh. The East Pakistanis had announced their secession in March, provoking brutal retaliation by the authorities in West Pakistan. Fearing that India would become involved, Pakistan launched pre-emptive air strikes in December on targets in north-west India, including Agra (the home of a quickly camouflaged Taj Mahal). This was a huge mistake: India reacted with its own air strikes on both parts of Pakistan and sent its troops to support the Bengalis. After just 13 days Pakistan surrendered. The eastern half of the country was now Bangladesh and more than 90,000 Pakistani troops were prisoners of war in India.

In retrospect, a bifurcated Pakistan united only by Islam was never likely to last, given the ethnic and cultural differences between West and East Pakistan. By contrast, resolving the conflict between India and Pakistan over Kashmir too often seems a permanent impossibility. In 1999 the two countries clashed in the so-called Kargil war – a three-month conflict beginning in the Kargil district of Kashmir that could reasonably be called a fourth Indo–Pakistan war.

The cause of the war, according to India, was the infiltration of

Pakistani troops and Kashmiri militants across the line of control (Pakistan claimed that the combatants were all Kashmiri freedom fighters seeking to liberate Kashmir from Indian control). The consequences were Indian air strikes, relentless artillery exchanges, hundreds killed on both sides and waves of refugees. A ceasefire and the withdrawal of Pakistani troops were eventually agreed as a result of US pressure on the Pakistani government and military high command. Given that in the previous year Pakistan had conducted its first nuclear test (24 years after India's), this was surely just as well: the Kargil war remains the only conflict fought between two nuclear powers using just conventional weapons.

In theory, the conflict over Kashmir should be conducted by diplomatic means following a ceasefire agreement signed by India and Pakistan in 2003. In practice, the ceasefire has been flouted on an almost routine basis. For example, India accused Pakistan of more than 550 violations in 2014, leading to deaths on both sides.

Even more worrying, perhaps, is the apparent willingness of Pakistan (or certainly its Inter-Services Intelligence agency, or ISI) to condone terror attacks from Pakistan on targets in India. One such was the assault in December 2001 on the Indian parliament in New Delhi by militants from Lashkar-e-Taiba (LeT, or Army of the Pure) and Jaish-e-Mohammad (JeM, or Army of Muhammad), Islamist groups dedicated to ending India's rule in Jammu and Kashmir. The attack killed 14, including five militants, and led to the official banning of the groups in Pakistan the following year (India says they nonetheless have the continued protection of the ISI). Another attack, blamed on the LeT, was the explosion of twin car bombs in Mumbai in 2003, apparently in revenge for the killing in Gujarat the previous year of hundreds of Muslims by Hindu rioters. More than 50 people were killed and almost 250 injured.

By far the worst such attack, however, was the 2008 assault by Pakistani members of the LeT on India's financial centre, Mumbai. Co-ordinated attacks struck a dozen targets, most notably the Taj Hotel. In a four-day battle with Indian security forces some 166 people, including ten LeT militants, died and more than 600 were wounded. The surviving attacker (later executed) confessed to his interrogators that the ISI had supported the assault, the most deadly in Mumbai since 13 car bombs (allegedly also involving the ISI) in 1993 claimed at least 250 lives and injured more than 700.

One extremist Muslim group, the Indian Mujahideen (IM), has ambitions that go far beyond Kashmir. Its stated goal is to establish an Islamic caliphate in south Asia and punish India for its alleged oppression of Muslims. The Indian authorities argue that the group is a front for the LeT. The US State Department, which added the group to its list of foreign terrorist organisations in 2011, agrees that the IM "has significant links to Pakistan-based terrorist organisations". Whatever the strength of those links, it is clear, the State Department concludes, that the IM, with several hundred militants, "has been responsible for dozens of bomb attacks throughout India since 2005, and has caused the deaths of hundreds of civilians".

The IM is by no means the only group in armed conflict with the Indian government. Around 200 of the country's 626 districts are prone to attacks by insurgent groups, most notably the Naxalites. These are fighters from the Communist Party of India (Maoist) and other communist parties, who take their name from Naxalbari, a village in West Bengal. Beginning their operations in the 1960s, the Naxalites have long since spread their revolt throughout east and central India and even down to the far south. Their strength, which ultimately derives from the grievances felt by the impoverished tribal inhabitants of states such as Chhattisgarh, is estimated as high as 40,000 fighters. Of the 400 or so deaths from terrorism in India in 2013, around half were attributed to the Naxalites, making them the country's greatest threat to internal security in the eyes of the Indian authorities.

The Naxalites are not the only rebels originating in north-east India. The so-called "seven sisters" – Arunachal Pradesh, Assam, Meghalaya, Tripura, Nagaland, Mizoram and Manipur – are connected to the rest of the country only by the Siliguri corridor, a strip of land as narrow as 14 miles (23 kilometres). Their sense of isolation, coupled with the large numbers of tribal peoples outside the caste system, has for decades fostered a secessionist spirit. The United Liberation Front of Assam (ULFA), for example, has been seeking independence for Assam through armed struggle since 1979; the Naga Federal Army, allegedly having benefited from training in China, has been active for half a century; and Manipur is host to four insurgent groups. There are even demands for entirely new states: in Assam, for instance, the mainly Muslim ULFA clashes with the National Democratic Front of Bodoland (NDFB), which was formed in 1998 and wants to carve out a distinct state for the aboriginal Bodo people.

Whether the Indian authorities employ the right tactics against threats to the country's internal security is a matter of constant debate. There are far too many religiously motivated riots that occur despite the security forces: for example, the 2002 riots in Gujarat in which, according to the government, at least 790 Muslims and 254 Hindus were killed, though others claim 2,000 Muslims died. There is, too, the latent demand for Khalistan, a separate homeland for India's Sikhs (the army's bloody removal of Sikh separatists from the Golden Temple in Amritsar in 1984 led to the assassination of the prime minister, Indira Gandhi, by her Sikh bodyguards). And military operations in the north-east have singularly failed to end the multiple insurgencies there.

Yet despite all this, India's messy democracy continues to command the loyalty of the great mass of the population. Even in the north-east, popular protests took place in December 2014 denouncing the NDFB for co-ordinated attacks that killed 76 tea-plantation workers, Hindus and Christians from the Adivasi tribe. Over time, the hope is that economic growth will reduce the incentives for violence and so disarm the insurgents. But before that happy day the best remedy for the problems associated with Kashmir would be a genuine reconciliation between India and Pakistan.

Indonesia

With a population of more than 250 million spread over literally thousands of islands and speaking several hundred languages, the Republic of Indonesia has an obvious need to create some kind of national cohesion in its extraordinary ethnic mosaic – hence the national motto, *Bhinneka Tunggal Ika* (Unity in Diversity in Javanese), and the ideology of *pancasila* (five principles), formulated by General Sukarno in his four-year guerrilla war to achieve independence in 1949 from the Netherlands.

Pancasila emphasises belief in one God; just and civilised humanity; the unity of the country; democracy based on consultation; and social justice for all. Such admirable ideas have arguably been crucial in guiding independent Indonesia through decades of dictatorship under Generals Sukarno and Suharto through to democracy under freely elected presidents (the latest being Joko Widodo, elected in July 2014).

Yet the process has hardly been trouble-free (quite apart from the hundreds of thousands killed during a purge of communists after a failed coup in 1965). Even as Sukarno (who had been in detention under the Dutch until released by Japanese invaders in the second world war) finally won independence for Indonesia, the Maluku islands (the Moluccas) attempted an armed secession. There have been similar secession movements elsewhere in the Indonesian archipelago, from Aceh in northern Sumatra to the western half of New Guinea, first incorporated into Indonesia in 1969 as Irian Jaya. And, whatever the compulsory teaching of *pancasila*, there have been outbreaks of communal and ethnic violence, such as the 1999–2002

Muslim–Christian conflict in the Maluku islands that cost 5,000 or more lives.

The secessionist impulse was fed by the influx (the *transmigrasi*) of migrants from Java to other islands, but it may now have been blunted by the less dictatorial stance of the authorities in Jakarta. The Free Aceh Movement (Gerakan Aceh Merdeka, or GAM), espousing a stricter form of Islam than usual in 87% Muslim Indonesia, began its armed struggle in 1976, helped by funds and training from Libya. Finally, after 28 years and the loss of 15,000 lives, the government and the GAM in 2005 signed a peace agreement that has granted special autonomy to Aceh, an amnesty for the GAM's 3,000 or so fighters, the granting to local government of 70% of the province's income from petroleum and other natural resources, and a pledge by the GAM to abandon demands for independence. Furthermore, the Jakarta government has not interfered with Aceh's adoption of *sharia* as its legal code.

A similarly protracted independence struggle was that of the people of overwhelmingly Christian East Timor, a Portuguese colony that had been granted its independence by Lisbon in 1975 only to be invaded by Indonesia in 1976. The impulse for Indonesia's invasion was its fear that Fretilin (Frente Revolucionária de Timor-Leste Independente, or the Revolutionary Front for an Independent East Timor) would establish a communist state within the Indonesian archipelago. The result was more than two decades of brutal occupation by Indonesian troops in conflict with the 20,000 or so militants (including those with only minimal training) of Fretilin's military wing, Falintil (Forças Armadas da Libertação Nacional de Timor-Leste, or the Armed Forces for the National Liberation of East Timor).

Significantly, even though Indonesia had incorporated East Timor as its 27th province, the UN continued to define the territory as a non-self-governing territory under Portuguese administration. As violence continued (at least 100,000 died between 1974 and 1999, including the 1991 massacre of more than 250 mourners at a funeral procession in Dili of a Fretilin supporter), it was the gathering force of democratic protest in all Indonesia that produced a solution. President Suharto was toppled in 1998 and succeeded by his deputy, B.J. Habibie, who agreed that the UN should sponsor a referendum in East Timor in 1999 offering special autonomy within Indonesia. The result was a

78.5% no vote – and so a vote for independence. This was a signal for pro-autonomy militants to go on a deadly rampage, killing some 1,400 civilians, yet Indonesia allowed the transfer of East Timor to UN control and in May 2002 East Timor finally achieved its independence and became the first new sovereign nation of the 21st century.

The question is whether East Timor's secession will be a model elsewhere in the sprawl of Indonesia's islands. The most pressing problem is in Irian Jaya (Victorious Irian), as Indonesia used to term the former Dutch New Guinea, the western half of the huge island of New Guinea. The Netherlands, retreating from its overseas possessions, attempted in 1961 to introduce self-government for the territory known also as West Papua. The following year Indonesian troops invaded, only to be rebuffed by Dutch troops helped by the indigenous population. The outcome was a UN-administered phased transfer of the territory to Indonesian rule in 1963, subject to approval in a future plebiscite. The subsequent "Act of Free Choice" (the vote was limited to 1,026 Papuan representatives) supposedly unanimously approved Indonesia's formal annexation of the territory in 1969, despite a vigorous guerrilla movement by the Free Papua Movement (Organisasi Papua Merdeka, or OPM), established in 1965 to fight for West Papuan independence (though some would prefer union with neighbouring Papua New Guinea).

The low-level conflict has led to human-rights abuses by both sides, especially by Indonesian troops, leading by some accounts to around 500,000 Papuan deaths over the past half century. However, the OPM's dream of secession looks implausible: one reason is that Indonesia would be loth to relinquish the mineral wealth of the area; a second is that almost half of the territory's 2.4 million population are now Javanese immigrants, unlikely to support any Melanesian Papuan demand for independence; and a third is that the government in Jakarta is softening its approach. In 2001 Irian Jaya was given special autonomy status and in 2003 was divided into two new provinces, Papua and West Papua.

Just three years later, in mid-2006, the OPM announced a unilateral ceasefire and pledged to continue its struggle by political means alone. In practice, however, the armed conflict has not stopped. In 2015 the British Foreign Office advised:

Clashes in late July 2014 resulted in the death of security service personnel and civilians in the Lanny Jaya regency of Papua province. If you're travelling in the region you should exercise extreme caution.

In purely military terms no secession movement in Indonesia will succeed: the Indonesia armed forces number 476,000 frontline personnel, with another 400,000 in the active reserve. By contrast, anti-government guerrillas probably number no more now than a few thousand. The same arithmetic applies to what is probably a greater threat – at least psychologically – to the country's internal security: violent Islamism.

By both cultural and political tradition Indonesia has always been religiously tolerant: *pancasila* was preached to the young and the regimes of both Sukarno and Suharto were determinedly secular; and the Darul Islam (House of Islam) movement, founded in the 1940s to establish an Islamic state, complete with *sharia* law, was crushed by Sukarno in 1962. However, in recent years Indonesia has been unable to avoid the impact of violence in the Middle East and the influence of Saudi money in promoting a Salafist version of Islam (as in Aceh).

The consequence has been a chain of terrorist incidents carried out by several extremist groups whose founders share Arab origins: for example, the Majelis Mujahidin Indonesia (Council of Indonesian Jihadists); the Front Pembela Islam (Front of Islam Defenders); the Jema'ah Islamiyah (Islamic Congregation) and its splinter group Jamaah Ansharut Tauhid (Congregation of Supporters of Monotheism); and the now-disbanded Laskar Jihad (Warriors of Jihad). The most prominent group has been Jema'ah Islamiyah, which in collaboration with al-Qaeda launched co-ordinated bomb attacks against 11 churches on Christmas Eve 2000, killing 19. The most notorious incident was the 2002 bombing of a nightclub in a tourist resort in Bali, killing 202, most of them foreign tourists. In 2009 Jema'ah Islamiyah killed seven and injured more than 50 in almost simultaneous suicide-bomb attacks on the Marriott and Ritz-Carlton hotels in Jakarta. The targets of Islamist extremists have not, however, been confined to Christians, foreigners and the state: in 2011 three members of the Ahmadiya sect of Islam were bludgeoned to death in West Java as heretics.

While the Middle East remains in turmoil, Islamist violence in Indonesia will doubtless continue too, despite the success of Densus 88 (Special Detachment 88, or Detasemen Khusus 88), a special counter-terrorism squad financed by the US and trained by the CIA, the FBI and the US Secret Service, in tracking down extremists and nipping many attacks in the bud. According to the head of Indonesia's National Counter-terrorism Agency (BNPT), some 86 Indonesians had left the country in June 2014 to fight for ISIS and its Islamic State in the Middle East; and in October the number had more than tripled to 264. This compares with about 300 who left to join the *mujahideen* in Afghanistan between 1985 and 1994. As the BNPT head pointed out:

> *Because Indonesia has the world's largest Muslim population, the country will always be at the centre of recruitment. It's time for other stakeholders to bolster their efforts to prevent the proliferation of ISIS ideology, as it will pose a risk to our security once the ISIS fighters return home.*

Korea (North and South)

The world has several "frozen conflicts" – for example, between India and Pakistan over Kashmir, between Morocco and Polisario in the Western Sahara, and between Cyprus and the Turkey-backed Turkish Republic of Northern Cyprus. But none has such potential for widespread war as the six-decade armed stalemate between the

Democratic People's Republic of Korea (DPRK, or North Korea) and the Republic of Korea (ROK, or South Korea).

The impoverished and communist North Korea, home to around 25 million, is now a nuclear-weapons power, with a history of extremism; the wealthy and capitalist South Korea, with a population of 49 million, is protected by a defence treaty with the US that involves the presence on ROK soil of 29,000 American troops (with another 49,000 army and naval troops available from neighbouring Japan). Given that China, North Korea's one constant ally, Russia and the US are all nuclear-weapons powers, the risk is always that the occasional clashes between the north and the south will get out of control and drag outside powers into a conflict spreading far beyond the Korean peninsula.

One such incident was the 2010 sinking in the Yellow Sea of the *Cheonan*, a South Korean navy corvette, with the loss of 46 South Korean sailors. Despite denials by the DPRK government in Pyongyang, international experts agreed with South Korea that the cause was a torpedo fired from a North Korean submarine. The sinking of the *Cheonan* was not without precedent: in 1967 DPRK artillery destroyed another ROK vessel, this time with the loss of 39 lives, and there have been many minor clashes – usually damaging the ROK more than the DPRK – over the years.

One factor in the maritime clashes is that the maritime border – the northern limit line (NLL) between the two countries – was not part of the armistice of July 1953 to end the 1950–53 Korean war but was unilaterally drawn the following month by the US-led UN forces (ironically, at a time when the DPRK had little sea power, the original aim of the line was to stop ROK ships moving north). Since 1999 the DPRK has drawn its own demilitarised line to the south of the NLL, and has frequently sent ships (often for the rich fishing prospects) south into what are disputed waters.

There is no such ambiguity in the land border between north and south. This is the demilitarised zone (DMZ) dividing the peninsula at the 38th parallel that was set by the armistice signed in July 1953 between the UN, North Korea and China. The 38th parallel had originally been drawn as a dividing line by US officials in 1945, as the United States and the Soviet Union apportioned the spoils from the second world war during which the Korean peninsula had been occupied by Japan. In 1948, as the north proclaimed itself the DPRK and the south the ROK, both the Soviet Union and the US withdrew their troops. Since both the DPRK and the ROK claimed to be the legitimate government of the whole Korean nation, tensions rose – until in June 1950 the DPRK mounted an invasion across the 38th parallel. This provoked an immediate condemnation at the UN and the dispatch of American troops from their bases in Japan to support the ROK.

At first the war went badly for South Korea, with North Korean troops in the first two months of the conflict pushing almost to the southern tip of the peninsula. However, counter-attacking UN troops – from some 21 countries, led by the US with some 88% of the force – managed by October 1950 to be within striking distance of the Chinese border. Indeed, General Douglas MacArthur, at the head of the UN force, argued strongly for an invasion of China to defeat international communism. Although President Harry Truman disagreed with MacArthur (and the following year sacked him), an alarmed China reacted by entering the war in June 1950 in support of North Korea.

Over the following three years there was brutal warfare, a military stalemate and, from July 1951, protracted peace talks until the exhausted combatants finally signed the 1953 armistice – an agreement that technically still leaves the DPRK and the ROK at war with each other. Historians note that the Korean war was the first proxy war in the cold war between the Soviet Union (which supplied aid to China and the DPRK) and the United States, and the first time that jet fighters were used against each other in combat.

The irony in the 21st century is that China, while still the DPRK's only significant ally, shares much the same view of the north–south conflict as the US and the ROK. One reason is that the People's Republic of China is communist more in name than in reality, and enjoys a valuable trading relationship with the ROK. A second is that the collapse of the DPRK regime would almost certainly lead to an uncontrolled flood of refugees into both China and the ROK.

A third reason to worry not just China, the ROK and the US but the whole world is the sheer unpredictability of the DPRK regime, under first Kim Il Sung (the "Great Leader" and now the "Eternal Leader", according to the DPRK's hagiography of the ruling dynasty), then his son Kim Jong Il (the "Dear Leader") and now his grandson Kim Jong Un (the "Outstanding Leader" and later the "Dear Leader").

Domestically, the regime's insistence on *juche* – self-reliance based on political independence, economic self-sufficiency and independence in defence – has condemned the population to frequent famine and terrible poverty, while also producing enough scientific expertise to develop nuclear weapons and to manufacture (and export) long-range missiles. In foreign policy, the regime has at times resorted to extremist tactics: in 1983, for example, its agents set off a bomb in a mausoleum in Myanmar that killed 21 people, including four ROK cabinet ministers and two senior advisers to the South Korean president; in 1987 agents planted a bomb on a Korean Airlines airliner that killed all 115 passengers and crew (the attack was apparently punishment for the ROK's refusal to invite DPRK athletes to the 1988 Seoul Olympics); and it has admitted kidnapping 13 Japanese citizens in the 1970s and 1980s to help train DPRK spies in Japanese customs.

Despite their common language and common ethnicity (the population of the peninsula is almost completely homogeneous), peace negotiations between north and south have made precious little progress over the decades. Whereas the DPRK retains its dictatorial personality cult, the ROK has long since moved from military rule to full-throated democracy – and enormous economic success. In 1998 the ROK president, Kim Dae-jung, offered economic and humanitarian aid to the DPRK, and this "sunshine policy" led to a summit meeting in 2000 with Kim Jong Il, the establishment of a tourism zone in the DPRK and the Kaesong industrial zone just north of the DMZ. Yet none of this prevented the sinking of the *Cheonan* or led to the abandonment of the DPRK's nuclear-weapons programme.

That goal depends on the six-party talks – the tortured and tortuous negotiations involving the US, China, Japan, Russia, South Korea and North Korea. They began in 2003 after the DPRK – described by President George W. Bush in 2002 as part of the axis of evil – had withdrawn from the Treaty on the Non-Proliferation of Nuclear Weapons and announced it would no longer abide by a

1992 agreement with the ROK to keep the peninsula free from nuclear weapons. In 2006 the DPRK test fired a long-range Taepodong-2 missile (it failed on that occasion) and conducted its first underground nuclear-weapons test. The following year it closed a nuclear reactor in exchange for aid agreed in the six-party talks, but by 2009 it was ready to conduct a second underground test and then in 2013 a third.

The optimists hope that economic and financial sanctions against the DPRK can influence its behaviour, as can the occasional carrot (for example, the US decision in 2008 to remove the DPRK from its terrorism blacklist after it promised to shut down the Yongbyon nuclear site). The pessimists say that any modifications to the DPRK's behaviour have been tactical and temporary (in 2010 it emerged that it had secretly built a new facility for enriching uranium at Yongbyon).

So far in the 21st century the pessimists seem to have more evidence in their favour, not just in terms of the DPRK's nuclear ambitions. They note also North Korea's cyber-expertise, pointing to America's accusation that the DPRK was responsible for the 2014 hacking of Sony Pictures in an attempt to stop the release of a comedy film about the assassination of Kim Jong Un. The US charge may or may not be justified, but no one doubts that North Korea has the cyber-capability – and this may yet prove more powerful than the possession of a few nuclear warheads. In the meantime, the situation is inherently tense: the DPRK has 1.1 million active military personnel and the ROK almost 700,000; both countries have more than 400 fighter aircraft; and both have dozens of submarines. Even without the nuclear threat, war by accident is horribly possible.

Myanmar

The Republic of the Union of Myanmar – Burma until the country's ruling military junta began a series of name changes in 1989 – was for decades a pariah nation. After gaining its independence from the UK in 1948, the minerals- and forestry-rich country was isolated from the rest of the world first by General Ne Win and his Burma Socialist Programme Party, who seized power in 1962, and then from 1988 by the ominously named State Law and Order Restoration Council (renamed in 1997 the less ominous State Peace and Development Council).

Throughout the decades the regime has had to cope not just with several bouts of popular unrest (government forces killed thousands of demonstrators during riots in 1988) but also with separatist insurgencies by Myanmar's minorities, notably in the Shan and Kachin states in Myanmar's eastern and northern regions but also in the Rakhine (formerly Arakan) region bordering Bangladesh.

The country's pariah status has eased since 2011, when President (previously general) Thein Sein agreed that the National League for Democracy (NLD) and its leader, Aung San Suu Kyi (who had been released in 2010 from her latest period of 15 years of house arrest), would be welcome participants in the political process. Thein Sein's relative loosening of the regime's grip on power has coincided not just with warmer relations with the United States but also with a succession of ceasefires with Myanmar's plethora of insurgent groups as the government prepared for elections in 2015. For example, the United Wa State Army (UWSA) signed a ceasefire agreement in 2011, and the New Mon State Party (NMSP) signed an accord in 2012.

The problem is consolidating the ceasefires. Talks between the government and some 16 guerrilla groups assembled in the optimistically named National Ceasefire Coordination Team (NCCT) were held in 2013. Of the 56 million population of Myanmar around two-thirds are ethnically Burman, and the government has always been loth to share power with ethnic minorities, which range from the Shan and Karen (around 8% each) in the east and centre of the country to the Mons (around 2%) in the south. Some 13 insurgent groups signed ceasefires in 2011 and 2012, but not all have held. The Shan State Army/Restoration Council of Shan State (SSA/RCSS), for example, agreed a ceasefire for its 6,000 fighters in January 2012 which was soon broken; and the Kachin Independence Army (KIA), with 5,000 guerrillas fighting in the north of the country, resumed its armed struggle in 2011 after a 17-year truce. Another challenge for the government is to pacify the Myanmar National Democratic Alliance Army (MNDAA), a force of around 1,000 guerrillas drawn from the Kokang people – part of the country's Han Chinese minority – in the east of Myanmar. After several years of calm, the MNDAA clashed with government forces in February 2015, perhaps striving to protect its drug-trafficking activities.

With more than 400,000 active personnel in the *tatmadaw*, Myanmar's armed forces, the government has obvious numerical superiority over its foes – and has been prepared to exercise it, with horrific abuses of human rights, including sexual violence by the military. Some of those who have suffered worst have been the Rohingya, a Sunni Muslim minority of around 1.3 million living in what was Arakan state and is now officially termed Rakhine. As far as the authorities are concerned, the Rohingya – regardless of how many generations they may have been in Myanmar – are illegal immigrants from Bangladesh. Since 1982 the government has rendered the Rohingya stateless, not including them on its list of 135 ethnic groups. Meanwhile, there are frequent sectarian clashes between the Rohingya and the state's Buddhist Rakhine majority. And the Arakan Army, whose 400–500 combatants (a figure that may well be grossly exaggerated) fight alongside the KIA, is a Buddhist organisation with no apparent love for the Rohingya.

Conceivably, Thein Shein's desire to claim an acceptable role for

Myanmar in the world and improve its relations with the United States will bring not just new waves of foreign investment but also domestic tranquillity. But much will depend on ending ethnic conflicts and alleviating the plight of the Rohingya, hundreds of thousands of whom have fled to squalid camps in Bangladesh and Thailand: Aung San Suu Kyi, a Nobel peace-prize laureate, has been notably silent on the issue.

The prospects are not particularly promising. The ethnic insurgencies are often connected – as in Shan state – with opium production and smuggling, which both finance the rebellions and give them a reason to continue. At the same time, the country's topography is perfect for guerrilla warfare.

As for harmony between Myanmar's Buddhist majority and Muslim minority, this is surely unlikely while Ashin Wirathu, a Buddhist monk, leads the extremist 969 Movement, responsible for several cases of lynching Muslims and burning their homes. In a nation that has long been obsessed with numerology, 969 refers to the nine attributes of the Buddha, the six attributes of his teachings and the nine attributes of the *Sangha*, or monastic order; it stands in contrast to the 786 used by many South Asian Muslims as the numerical total of the letters used in the opening phrase of the Quran. Wirathu is often described as a Buddhist bin Laden, and he will doubtless be aware that bin Laden's successor at the head of al-Qaeda, Ayman al-Zawahiri, vowed in September 2014 that al-Qaeda will protect Myanmar's Muslims.

Pakistan

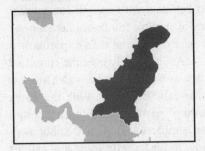

From its very birth, emerging from the partition of British India in 1947, Pakistan (land of the pure in Urdu) has had a violent, blood-stained existence. The Islamic Republic of Pakistan, to use its full title, has fought three wars (and by some definitions a fourth) with neighbouring India; lost half its territory with the 1971 secession of East Pakistan to become Bangladesh; suffered frequent bouts of sectarian violence; and alternated between corrupt democratic rule and military dictatorships.

Along the border with Afghanistan, huge swathes of the country – from Baluchistan northwards through the Federally Administered Tribal Areas to the North-West Frontier – ignore the writ of the central government in Islamabad and offer sanctuary to extreme Islamist bodies such as al-Qaeda and the Taliban. Given the belief held by many Western and Indian officials that the country's Inter-Services Intelligence (ISI) agency is complicit with such organisations and ready to export their terrorism, the accusation is often levied that Pakistan is almost a failed state, but one that also has nuclear weapons.

From Pakistan's point of view its nuclear capacity is a necessary protection against the threat of India, which conducted its first underground nuclear-weapons test in 1974. By contrast, Pakistan carried out its first nuclear tests in 1998, just a month after India had tested five nuclear weapons. In terms of the military balance between the two neighbours, Pakistan carries far less weight: its population of 196 million provides 617,000 active frontline personnel, half the number India gets from its 1.3 billion population. In terms of military aircraft and naval ships Pakistan is at a similar disadvantage, which explains why India can afford to preach a no-first-use policy for its 90 or so nuclear warheads whereas Pakistan, with around 100 nuclear warheads, takes refuge in a policy of credible minimum deterrence.

Although the imbalance has existed since the days of partition, it has singularly failed to keep the peace, especially over the contested sovereignty of Kashmir, a princely state in British India with a Muslim majority but a Hindu ruler, Maharajah Hari Singh. With the status of Kashmir undecided at the time of partition, Pashtun tribesmen from the newly created Pakistan simply invaded in October 1947, prompting the maharajah to throw in his lot with India and call for India to send troops.

This first Indo-Pakistan war lasted for 14 months and ended with Pakistan in control of the northern third of the state, naming it Azad Kashmir (Free Kashmir), and India in possession of the rest, now called Jammu and Kashmir. It left both armies facing each other across the so-called line of control, with Pakistan in charge of around 4.5 million people in Azad Kashmir and India around 10 million in Jammu and Kashmir.

With neither country able to agree on the plebiscite for Kashmir recommended by the UN, the scene was set for the second Indo-Pakistan war, in 1965, when Pakistan sent troops in disguise across the line of control in the hope of provoking a general Kashmiri uprising against India. After several weeks of fighting, which included incursions by Indian troops into the Pakistani province of Punjab as far as the outskirts of Lahore, the two sides withdrew to their previous positions, each claiming to have won (India more convincingly than Pakistan).

Kashmir, however, was not the only point of friction with India in the 20th century. In 1970 General Yahya Khan, intending to move from military rule to civilian rule, ordered Pakistan's first democratic elections since independence. However, in what was then the mainly Bengali East Pakistan all but two seats were won by Sheikh Mujibur Rahman's Awami League, which thereby gained a majority in the country's National Assembly without having won a single seat in West Pakistan. The idea of a Bengali-led government was unacceptable to Pakistan's military elite, which reacted by sending troops to East Pakistan in March 1971 to regain control of the province. This led to a declaration of independence for Bangladesh by Rahman and a war of liberation by the Mukti Bahini (Liberation Army).

As some 10 million Bengalis sought refuge in India, and after pre-emptive strikes in December by the Pakistani air force on targets in India, the Indian government sent troops in support of the Mukti Bahini. The butchery by Pakistan's forces in their attempt to stop East Pakistan's secession cost hundreds of thousands of Bengali lives – estimates range from 300,000 to a Bangladesh government claim of 3 million – over a nine-month period. The two weeks of the third Indo-Pakistan war resulted in the humiliating surrender by 90,000 Pakistani troops, the resignation of Yahya Kahn and the ascendancy to the presidency of Zulfikar Ali Bhutto, leader of the Pakistan People's Party (PPP).

The return to civilian rule was marked by the Simla agreement in 1972 in which Bhutto and India's prime minister, Indira Gandhi, pledged to respect the line of control in Kashmir and seek a negotiated settlement of the two countries' differences. So much for good intentions: in 1977 Bhutto, now serving as prime minister rather than president, was ousted in a military coup by General Muhammad Zia ul-Haq, put on trial for authorising the murder of a political opponent and, in 1979, executed. In a decision whose repercussions are still felt today, Zia proceeded to Islamise Pakistan by introducing many features of *sharia* law – for example, the *hudood* ordinance of 1979, which allowed punishments such as flogging, amputation and stoning for offences such as adultery – and by strengthening laws against blasphemy (to the detriment in recent years of Christians and the small Ahmadiyyah minority, which is not considered Muslim by the majority Sunni population).

Regardless of the ever-increasing emphasis on Pakistan's Muslim identity, the issue of Kashmir strikes a chord of nationalist rather than religious pride for both Pakistan and India. In May 1999, during the first civilian government of Nawaz Sharif and his Pakistan Muslim League party, the two countries came to blows yet again when Pakistani troops and Kashmiri freedom fighters seeking to liberate Kashmir from Indian control crossed the line of control, provoking an Indian naval blockade of Pakistan and air strikes on Pakistani positions. Fought in the Kargil district of Ladakh, with some of

Kashmir's highest mountains, the Kargil war, lasting three months, could equally be termed a fourth Indo-Pakistan war, characterised by heavy artillery battles and the loss of hundreds of lives on both sides before US pressure on Pakistan brought a ceasefire and the withdrawal of its troops. A political victim of the war was Nawaz Sharif, ousted in October 1999 in a military coup led by General (later president) Pervez Musharraf.

In the 21st century, as in the 20th, Pakistan's political power has gone back and forth between military dictatorships and civilian rule. President Musharraf, for example, was forced to resign in 2008 and was replaced by a civilian government under Asif Ali Zardari, whose wife Benazir Bhutto (daughter of Zulfikar Ali Bhutto and herself prime minister in the late 1980s and again in the mid-1990s) had been assassinated in 2007.

One constant has been Pakistan's involvement in the affairs of Afghanistan. Both countries are Islamic republics and both have strong ethnic links: the Pashtun make up around 40% of Afghanistan's population and around 15% of Pakistan's. They also share a common (disputed) border, marked by Mortimer Durand, a civil servant of colonial British India, in 1883 and known as the Durand Line. Afghanistan prefers not formally to accept the Durand Line as the border lest it divide the Pashtun people; Pakistan regards the border as fixed but fears a revolt by the Pashtun tribes. When Afghanistan's friendships in the 20th century with the Soviet Union and India were added into the mix, Pakistan perhaps had reason to feel nervous and develop what it called a policy of "strategic depth" in Afghanistan to counter the influence of Soviet-backed India – hence its alliance with the US during the cold war, its supply of training and sanctuary for thousands of foreign *mujahideen*, and the supply of its own *mujahideen* in their war to end the Soviet occupation of Afghanistan that began in 1979. Pakistan has also provided a safe refuge for some 3 million Afghans fleeing the conflict in their homeland.

However, the new version of Kipling's "Great Game" has led to an ambiguous relationship between Pakistan and the US. The US has lavished huge amounts of aid on Pakistan (according to some estimates, around $83 billion between 1948 and 2014 in inflation-adjusted dollars), interrupted only by brief spats over Pakistan's nuclear programme or the 2011 killing by American special forces in Pakistan of Osama bin Laden. But Pakistan's ISI has frequently worked against US interests, notably in aiding the Afghan Taliban – even as Taliban fighters, including the Pakistan-based Haqqani network, were using suicide bombers and improvised explosive devices to attack US and other NATO forces in Afghanistan.

The fact that the ISI, with some 10,000–25,000 active personnel, operates as a state within a state is a reality of Pakistani politics that the US finds hard to accept. As Admiral Mike Mullen, chairman of the joint chiefs of staff, put it in 2011:

> In choosing to use violent extremism as an instrument of policy, the government of Pakistan, and most especially the Pakistani army and ISI, jeopardises not only the prospect of our strategic partnership but Pakistan's opportunity to be a respected nation with legitimate regional influence. They may believe that by using these proxies, they are hedging their bets or redressing what they feel is an imbalance in regional power. But in reality, they have already lost that bet.

The bet has included giving sanctuary (always officially denied) to Mullah Muhammad Omar, the leader of the Afghan Taliban, and to Osama bin Laden, leader of al-Qaeda. US officials find it hard to believe that bin Laden, killed on May 2nd 2011 by American special forces in a daring raid on a house in Abbottabad in north-eastern Pakistan, was not in some way protected by the ISI. The bet has also allowed extremist groups such as Lashkar-e-Taiba (LeT, or Army of the Pure) to carry out attacks on India, notably the assault by a small LeT commando group in November 2008 on targets in Mumbai that led to more than 160 deaths.

The LeT was formally banned by Pakistan in 2002, a year after being designated a terrorist organisation by both the US and the UK, but credible accusations continue of links with the ISI. The same is true for others in an array of radical groups, ranging from the Tehreek-e-Taliban Pakistan (TTP), better known as the Pakistan Taliban, to the Harkat-ul-Mujahideen, operating mainly in Kashmir, and the Jaish-e-Mohammad (JeM, or Army of Muhammad).

But the bet has costs, not least if the ISI cannot fully control the extremist groups, or if it is at odds with its own government. In 2007 the Red Mosque (Lal Masjid) in Islamabad was the scene of a bloody confrontation between militant Islamist students, including many young women, and the security forces. The students, mainly from the North-West Frontier Province, were protesting against the support given by President Musharraf to George W. Bush's war on terror – support that had led to assassination attempts on Musharraf by the JeM. After an eight-day siege the security forces stormed the mosque, with the loss of scores of lives.

Another cost is the US policy, under both George W. Bush and Barack Obama, of using drone attacks to kill Islamist extremists, regardless of their protection – or otherwise – by the ISI. According to the Bureau of Investigative Journalism, based in the UK, in the first five years of the Obama presidency American drones killed between 416 and 951 Pakistani civilians, including up to 200 children. No matter how many of the civilians were militants (and no matter that, at least under President Musharraf, the Pakistan government had tacitly approved the drone policy), the popular reaction in Pakistan has been a huge increase in anti-Americanism.

A third cost is the loss of Pakistani lives from the contradictory policy of giving succour to Islamist groups while simultaneously fighting them as part of the alliance with the United States. Mariyam Aurangzeb, the parliamentary secretary for the interior, told a Pakistani television channel in December 2014 that at least 50,000 Pakistani lives (military and civilian) had been lost in the war on terror after the September 11th 2001 attacks on the US: "Pakistan has given unprecedented sacrifices against the war on terrorism." Many of those sacrifices have been made in the Federally Administered Tribal Areas and the Khyber Pakhtunkhwa Province, where the Pakistan Taliban (or TTP) – essentially an alliance of militant groups against the Pakistan military – have for years been trying to assert a de facto, sharia-imposing independence from Islamabad's authority.

Although the TTP and its 25,000 fighters can count on plenty of supporters in the regions that border Afghanistan, it may well have lost many with an attack in December 2014 on an army school in Peshawar, capital of the Khyber Pakhtunkhwa Province. More than

130 schoolchildren were slaughtered in what the TTP said was revenge for the deaths of innocent tribesmen and children in a recent army offensive. Certainly one consequence (immediately after a visit by the US secretary of state, John Kerry) was a decision by the Pakistan government in January 2015 to outlaw the Haqqani Network, a 10,000-strong Afghan group allied to the Taliban and operating from bases in the Waziristan tribal area of Pakistan (the US has offered a $5 million bounty for the capture of Sirajuddin Haqqani). As one government official commented, in an implicit admission of Pakistan's aid to Islamist groups

> *The military and the government are on the same page on how to tackle militancy. There is no more "good" or "bad" Taliban.*

Nonetheless, it would be naive to conclude that the ISI will abandon all its clients or that Pakistan's strategists will suddenly lose interest in the fate of Afghanistan. Despite their honeyed words in occasional meetings with the leaders of Afghanistan and India, Pakistan's leaders – be they military or civilian – are not fully in command of their own country. The TTP, which claimed responsibility for a failed bomb attack in New York's Times Square in 2010, will remain a force to be reckoned with, and it seems unlikely that al-Qaeda, which has links with the TTP and other Islamist groups in Pakistan, will disappear from the country. Indeed, it is entirely possible that the Islamic State in Iraq and Sham (ISIS) will seek to expand into Afghanistan and Pakistan. In December 2014 a video was released showing female students at Islamabad's Red Mosque sitting beneath an Islamic State flag and pledging allegiance to Abu Bakr al-Baghdadi, the self-proclaimed caliph.

Pakistan may mean the land of the pure, but until Afghanistan finds lasting peace and until a settlement is found for the Kashmir dispute with India, Pakistan will remain a dangerously fragile state – vulnerable to extremism and armed with nuclear weapons.

Philippines

A Pacific archipelago of more than 7,000 islands, the Philippines were occupied first by the Spanish in 1542 and then by the US in 1898 at the end of the Spanish–American war. This history has left the Republic of the Philippines (its independence, after occupation by the Japanese during part of the second world war, came in 1946) with the comic tag of "three centuries in a convent and half a century in Hollywood". More seriously, it has left the country with a deep friendship for the US and, from 1951, a mutual defence treaty. Until 1992 this alliance took concrete form in the shape of the giant Clark Air Base (actually abandoned in 1991 after a volcanic eruption) and the Subic Bay naval base.

The US bases may officially be gone, but in 2014 a ten-year agreement was reached to give American forces access to several Philippine bases, and also to "pre-position" in those bases American fighter jets and ships. For the Philippines, which has a maritime dispute with China over the Spratly islands (also claimed by Malaysia, Taiwan and Vietnam) and the Scarborough Shoal, the US is an indispensable guarantor of security. The Armed Forces of the Philippines (AFP), with some 220,000 active frontline personnel from a population of 108 million, are a tenth the size of China's, and have minimal naval assets compared with China's. In 2014 China and the Philippines came perilously close to blows in the South China Sea and the obvious risk is that water cannons – used by Chinese coastguard ships in February 2014 against Philippine fishing boats – will be followed by more lethal weapons.

While the Philippines' maritime and territorial disputes (there is a dormant claim to the Malaysian state of Sabah) are potential causes of conflict, actual conflict bedevils the Manila government from two sources: the New People's Army (NPA), which is the armed wing of the Maoist Communist Party of the Philippines (CPP), and various Muslim separatists – from the Moro National Liberation Front (MNLF) to the brutally extreme Abu Sayyaf Group – in the southern part of the archipelago.

Although more than 80% of Filipinos are Roman Catholic, the appeal of the supposedly godless NPA, formed in 1969, is clear enough. Despite a promising start after independence, when the Philippines had better economic prospects than South Korea, the country became a byword for social inequality, corruption and repression during the 1965–86 quasi-dictatorship of President Ferdinand Marcos, who in 1972 imposed martial law lasting for almost a decade, purportedly to counter the threat of communism and Muslim separatism. The NPA's roots were in the Huk peasant movement, which had fought the Japanese in the second world war and then waged rebellion against the new Philippine republic; its armed struggle could similarly be justified as a battle for the poor against the rich (especially when Marcos's land reforms benefited the landowners more than the peasantry). By contrast, Marcos viewed combat against the NPA as part of the cold-war fight against communism, and thus a way of sustaining support from the United States (Marcos also sent Philippine troops to fight alongside Americans in the Vietnam war).

The power of the NPA, which in the 1980s could command perhaps 26,000 fighters, has waned, largely because of sustained pressure from the AFP in concert with American special forces. By 2015 NPA guerrillas, financing themselves by extorting taxes from local businesses, were said by the government to number around 4,000. Their targets are government agents or officials and US interests in the Philippines (hence the killings of several American soldiers in the late 1980s). In 2004 President Gloria Macapagal Arroyo authorised talks in Norway with the National Democratic Front (NDF), which represented both the CPP and the NPA. Yet frequent ceasefires, both formal and informal, have been interrupted by clashes between the NPA and the AFP (which in the process gained a reputation for human-rights abuses). The government and the NPA declared a truce in January 2015 for the duration of the visit to the Philippines by Pope Francis, and then declared their truce over once he had departed.

Although violence from the NPA cannot be discounted, the Philippines faces a more serious threat from Muslim separatists in the southern islands of Mindanao, home to most of the Philippines' 5 million Muslim minority, and the Sulu archipelago. The Moro National Liberation Front (MNLF) was founded in 1972 by renaming the Mindanao Independence Movement, created in 1969 by Nur Misuari, a university professor, to protest against the 1968 massacre by the AFP of Muslim recruits who were attempting to escape a mysterious bid by the Philippines to reclaim part of the Malaysian state of Sabah. Misuari's ambition was to create a Bangsamoro Republik (*bangsa* meaning nation and *moro* meaning moor, or Muslim).

On paper, Misuari fulfilled his aim in August 2013 by announcing an independent Bangsamoro Republik covering all of Mindanao and the provinces of Sulu and Pawanan. In reality, the announcement seems to have been prompted by fears of being sidelined in the government's negotiations with the Moro Islamic Liberation Front (MILF), which split from the MNLF in 1977 on the grounds that the MNLF was too moderate. Ten years later, when the MNLF accepted an offer of autonomy for Mindanao rather than independence, the MILF, comprising around 3,000 (some estimates say 12,000) fighters, rejected the proposal and resumed the armed struggle.

The question for the Philippine government is whether the call of Muslim separatism will ever be silenced. Over the decades there have been several apparently successful accords: in 1976, for example, Muammar Qaddafi of Libya brokered the Tripoli agreement between the MNLF and the Marcos government giving autonomy to part of Mindanao; ten years later President Corazon Aquino held talks with Misuari and in 1989 signed a law setting up the Autonomous Region in Muslim Mindanao (ARMM). Aquino's successor, Fidel Ramos, in 1996 signed a peace agreement with the MNLF that allowed Misuari to become governor of the ARMM, only for Misuari to lead a renewed rebellion in 2001. The government has had similar dealings with the MILF, notably with President Arroyo in 2008 agreeing the outlines of a Muslim homeland (the accord was later deemed unconstitutional) and then with talks in Tokyo agreed by Arroyo's successor, Benigno

Aquino (son of Corazon). The eventual result of those negotiations was the signing in March 2014 by the government and the MILF of the Comprehensive Agreement on the Bangsamoro (CAB), aiming to establish by 2016 a new and better-funded autonomous entity to replace the ARMM.

The MNLF and then the MILF were originally the most effective – or at least most threatening – guerrilla movements, but that characteristic has now moved to the Abu Sayyaf Group or ASG (*abu sayyaf* means father of the swordmaker in Arabic), a radical Islamist group founded in 1991 by Abdurajak Janjalani, a former MNLF member who had fought against Soviet troops in Afghanistan. There have been various leaders in subsequent years (Abdurajak Janjalani was killed in 1998 and replaced by his brother, Khadaffy, who was killed in a clash with government troops in 2006), but the Afghanistan experience appears to have created an enduring link with al-Qaeda. Though the ASG's numbers are thought to be 200–500, down from a peak of 1,300 in 2000, the group has punched above its weight this century with a series of bombings (such as an attack on a ferry in Manila Bay in 2004 causing 116 deaths) and kidnappings. The kidnappings help to finance the group and are often accompanied by extreme brutality: for example, the beheading of an American hostage in 2001 and the beheading of two Filipino Jehovah's Witnesses in 2002.

In contrast to other Muslim groups, the ASG is happy to carry out attacks beyond the Philippines, kidnapping foreigners in the Malaysian state of Sabah in both 2013 and 2014. It also sees itself as part of a worldwide Islamist movement: in 2000 it kidnapped a visiting American Muslim and demanded as his ransom the release of Sheikh Omar Abdel Rahman and Ramzi Yousef, imprisoned in New York for their role in the 1993 bombing of the World Trade Center. Further evidence is the link with both al-Qaeda (initial funding for the group is said to have come from Muhammad Jamal Khalifa, a brother-in-law of Osama bin Laden) and Indonesia's Jemaa al-Islamiyah, which has strong ties to al-Qaeda. One question is whether the ASG will develop links to ISIS in preference to al-Qaeda. In July 2014 a senior ASG leader pledged his allegiance to ISIS, and in September the group said its release of two German hostages would depend on Germany stopping its support for the campaign against ISIS. A similar pledge of allegiance came from the Bangsamoro Islamic Freedom Fighters (BIFF), a small group that broke away from the MILF in 2008 and which the British Foreign Office notes carried out several attacks in 2014 on the Philippine security forces.

Over the decades thousands have died in the struggle by the Armed Forces of the Philippines – increasingly successful but not yet complete – to suppress both the NPA and the Muslim separatists, and there will surely be more victims in the future. One reason, whatever the peace agreements, is that the economic pressure of the growing Catholic majority in Mindanao will increase Muslim feelings of resentment. Another is that the endemic corruption of Philippine politics, the yawning divide between rich and poor, and the quasi-feudal role of local warlords with their own private armies are bound to breed violence. At the same time, being an outlaw group with easily acquired weaponry is an obvious way in a poor country to make money through kidnapping, extortion and drug-trafficking. All a group needs is a political or religious slogan to give a fig leaf of ideological respectability.

Thailand

The Kingdom of Thailand – or Siam, until its change of name in 1939 – is the only South-East Asian nation never to have been colonised (indeed, Thailand can be translated as land of the free). This unique distinction has much to do with a history of pragmatism in foreign policy: the country was an ally of the UK in the first world war, of Japan in the second world war and of the United States in the Vietnam war. As a country whose military leaders at the time feared the potential spread of communism in Asia, Thailand was also the first in Asia in 1950 to send troops in support of South Korea in the Korean war. Communism survives today in neighbouring Laos and Cambodia, but is hardly a threat in much more powerful and prosperous Thailand (though Thai forces have occasionally clashed with Cambodian troops this century over a disputed section of their land border).

A second distinction, however, is the nation's taste for coups d'état by armed forces who now number 306,000 active frontline personnel: following the replacement of the absolute monarchy in 1932 by a constitutional monarchy, by 2014 Thailand had had 25 general elections and 19 coups, of which 12 were successful. There is a social and economic divide between urban Thais and less prosperous rural Thais which was reflected in widespread, often violent riots in recent years before the military deposed the civilian government of Yingluck Shinawatra in 2014. But regardless of the tensions between the "red shirt" supporters of Yingluck and the "yellow shirt" opponents of the political movement founded by her exiled brother, Thaksin, almost all of the country's 68 million inhabitants share a reverence for the monarchy (*lèse majesté* is a serious crime). They also share an ethnic and religious identity: 95% are Thai and Buddhist, though at least half of them have at least some Chinese blood in their ancestry.

However, the far south of the country – the provinces of Pattani, Yala, Narathiwat and parts of Songkhla – is an exception to this ethnic coherence, with the region forming the ancient Muslim sultanate of Pattani (which is often spelt Patani). The region, dominated by a Malay rather than purely Thai ethnicity, had for centuries paid tribute to Siam and was confirmed as part of Thailand by the Anglo-Siamese treaty of 1909. But following the second world war the idea of Muslim separatism took hold and increased over the decades because of the corruption and maladministration of the Thai officials sent to govern the provinces.

The result has been decades of a low-level insurgency which has claimed from a population of 1.8 million an accumulated death toll of more than 6,000, shared between the Thai security forces (in recent years around 30,000 troops have been stationed in the south), the various rebel groups and local civilians. The first armed insurgent group was the now-defunct Barisan Nasional Pembebasan Pattani (BNPP, or National Liberation Front of Pattani), which sprang from a 1947 uprising in Narathiwat. A second was the Barisan Revolusi Nasional (BRN, or Revolutionary National Front), founded in 1960 to form through armed struggle a Malay–Muslim socialist nation in South-East Asia. A third group was the Pattani United Liberation Organisation (PULO), founded in 1968 and active in the 1970s and 1980s, thanks in part to support from Libya. The PULO's approach has been to use both violent and non-violent tactics, a choice that in 1995 led to the defection from the PULO of New PULO dissidents, who were convinced that violent tactics – such as bombings and arson – would be the sole route to success.

Other militant groups formed in the late 20th century: for example, the Islamic Mujahideen Movement of Patani (GMIP) was founded in 1995 by a veteran from the anti-Soviet war in Afghanistan; and the United Front for the Independence of Patani, known as Bersatu (united, in Malay), was an amalgam of fighters from the Barisan Islam Pembebsan Patani (the Islamic Front for the Liberation of Patani), the PULO and the BRN. But in the late 1990s a hearts-and-minds effort by the Thai authorities meant a lessening of unrest in the south and the near-disappearance of both the PULO and the New PULO, though not of the Barisan Revolusi Nasional–Coordinate (BRN–C), the only active faction of the original BRN.

Sadly for the victims of the insurgency, the hearts-and-minds approach did not carry on into the 21st century under the government of Thaksin Shinawatra, and the consequence was an immediate escalation of the conflict between the Muslim groups and the security forces. In 2001 five policemen and one village defence volunteer were killed in co-ordinated attacks on police posts in Pattani, Yala and Narathiwat; in 2002 there were 75 violent incidents, and 119 the following year. In January 2004 an unidentified group of around 100 guerrillas raided an army camp and seized assault rifles, machine guns and rocket-propelled grenades. From that month through to the end of August 2007, the authorities recorded 7,743 violent incidents, from drive-by shootings to improvised explosive devices, leading to a toll of 2,566 deaths and 4,187 wounded. By 2015 most estimates put the death toll at over 6,000.

Just how many are active in the insurgency in the 21st century is hard to assess: estimates range from 5,000 to a highly improbable 30,000, with recruits organised in small cells independent of any central body. What is clear is that in the past decade the insurgency has been increasingly influenced by the radical, jihadist Islam fostered in the wake of the wars in Iraq and Afghanistan. Another factor has been the return from jobs in Saudi Arabia and the Gulf states of Thai Muslim workers who have been influenced by the fundamentalist interpretation of Islam in the Arabian peninsula. At the same time, both the security forces and the insurgents – notably the Pejuang Kemerdekaan Patani (Patani Independence Fighters) from the loose coalition of the BRN–C movement – have frequently been guilty of human-rights violations. In one incident in 2004 around 80 Muslims arrested at an anti-government demonstration died of suffocation while in the army's custody. For its part, the insurgency has increasingly targeted Buddhist civilians: during the first few weeks of 2014, for example, Muslim militants killed five Thai Buddhist women, and proceeded to burn some and behead others.

A peaceful settlement of the conflict in the south of Thailand is not impossible. Neighbouring Malaysia, which has no wish for the conflict to spill over into its territory, hosted several rounds of talks in 2013 between the Thai government and the BRN – but then in May 2014 the government was turfed out of office and replaced by the army. With the turmoil in Bangkok having subsided, the army can turn its attention to securing a settlement in the south: in November 2014 the defence minister promised peace within a year. Whether that would be by force or negotiation was unclear. Malaysia's prime minister, Najib Razak, said in December that if the various factions of the insurgency halted their attacks and approached talks with a common policy, the Thai government would respond:

All parties need to respect the law and the Thailand prime minister has agreed that the army could reduce its presence.

Maybe so, but after half a century of conflict, no one is holding their breath.

8   War without end?

GEORGE SANTAYANA, a novelist and philosopher, famously declared in 1922: "Only the dead have seen the end of war." Given the content of this book, Santayana was clearly right: the world in the 21st century remains scarred and bleeding from violent conflict in or between dozens of its nations; refugees from its war zones number in the millions; and its scientists and military men devise ever more devastating weaponry, from the American drones that hunt down al-Qaeda and Islamic State fighters to the bunker-busting bombs that can destroy any hidden Iranian nuclear reactor. In short, mankind's propensity and capacity for violence seem both innate and permanent.

Yet in many ways the world is becoming less violent. Joshua Goldstein, an American political scientist, has used data from Oslo's Peace Research Institute to argue that in the first decade of the 21st century there were fewer war-related deaths than in any decade in the previous 100 years. Deaths averaged around 55,000 a year in 2000–10, compared with 100,000 a year in the 1990s, 180,000 during the 1950–89 cold war; and over 10 million a year during the second world war.

Arguably, the decline in violence has been a process going back through the millennia. Steven Pinker, a Harvard professor and a leading experimental psychologist and linguist, identifies six major declines of violence. The first was when humans forsook hunting for their food in favour of the kind of settled existence that leads to cities, governments and empires such as Rome – a transition, according to some ambitious forensic archaeology, in which the rate of violent death fell from 15% of the population in the pre-state era to 3% in the earliest states.

The second decline, beginning in medieval Europe, came when kingdoms centralised their control over feudal territories:

Criminal justice was nationalised, and zero-sum plunder gave way to positive-sum trade. People increasingly controlled their impulses and sought to co-operate with their neighbours.

The third was the humanitarian revolution that accompanied the Enlightenment (also known as the Age of Reason) in 18th-century Europe. The nasty punishments, from disembowelment to burning at the stake, that governments and the religious establishment liked to impose on those who dared to dissent were gradually abolished. The eighth amendment to the US constitution forbade "cruel and unusual punishment" (though this still does not, in contrast to the view in modern Europe, include capital punishment).

So far, so less violent – but it is worth noting that Pinker's third explanation has rather less to do with war, as opposed to the treatment of individuals, than his first two. By contrast, his fourth decline in violence is the long peace that followed the second world war:

Today we take it for granted that Italy and Austria will not come to blows, nor will Britain and Russia. But centuries ago, the great powers were almost always at war, and until quite recently, Western European countries tended to initiate two or three new wars every year. The cliché that the 20th century was "the most violent in history" ignores the second half of the century (and may not even be true of the first half, if one calculates violent deaths as a proportion of the world's population).

Whether this long peace has been the result of NATO, the European Union (garlanded with its 2012 Nobel peace prize) or the deterrent effect of nuclear weapons and their mutually assured destruction is a matter of debate. It has not stopped NATO and Russia from flaunting their military might over the crisis in Ukraine – Vladimir Putin in early 2015 allegedly threatened to use nuclear weapons if NATO tried to bring Crimea back into Ukraine or moved its forces to the Baltic states of Lithuania, Latvia and Estonia, whose Russian minorities Putin has pledged to defend.

But the long peace moves smoothly into what Pinker calls the new peace, a condition in which globalisation has produced so many shared interests in trade and finance that states prefer to go to arbitration rather than war. There are now remarkably few wars between states, and though – as the previous chapters show – there are plenty of civil wars, these conflicts within states tend to kill fewer people than wars between states. And the new peace coincides with Pinker's sixth reason for declining violence: the rights revolution, in which aggression becomes an unacceptable reaction in a world that values civil rights, human rights, women's rights and so on.

The statistics seem to support Goldstein and Pinker: the world's population in the 50 years to 2010 more than doubled, rising from 3 billion to 7 billion, but the number of deaths in battle plummeted to levels lower than the murder rate of the world's most peaceful societies.

As the cliché variously attributed to Benjamin Disraeli and Mark Twain puts it, there are "lies, damned lies and statistics"; so perhaps the decline in the casualties of war deserves a closer look. Though the second world war was an era of massive death and destruction, Pinker maintains that relative to the world's population it was only the ninth-deadliest era in recorded history. Perhaps so, but if the figures are recast to record annual fatalities per 100,000 people, the second world war becomes the deadliest episode of mass violence in a thousand years – at least according to researchers from Canada's Human Security Report Project.

But whatever the second world war's position in the rankings of human carnage, it ended decades before most of people in today's world were born, and it is demonstrably true that in comparison the casualties from today's wars are minuscule. In 2011, for example, the world's three deadliest conflicts were in Iraq, Afghanistan and Sudan, but the deaths in those conflicts were far fewer than the murders carried out by the drug cartels in Mexico; and Mexico's murder rate was much lower than the rates in Honduras, Guatemala, Belize and El Salvador.

Even so, if modern weaponry has become more effective – from fighter aircraft firing guided missiles to rapid-firing assault rifles in the hands of guerrilla armies – why have the casualties from any given conflict not matched the body count of previous wars? One answer is that today's warriors, especially government soldiers, are better protected, with the kind of body armour that previous generations could only dream of.

But the bigger answer is the advance in medical science. At one level this is as simple as vaccination programmes, proper sanitation and decent nutrition: these elements of developed societies mean that soldiers from advanced economies are far less prone to battlefield infections and far more likely to survive their wounds. The real advance, however, is in instant and expert treatment on the battlefield and extraordinarily rapid evacuation to well-equipped hospitals. The consequence can be seen in the numbers of American and coalition amputees (at least 1,550 from the American armed forces) from the wars in Iraq and Afghanistan: they have survived improvised explosive devices (IEDs) that would in earlier times have caused their deaths. If the wounded are lumped in with the dead in the casualties of war, the 50% decline in battlefield fatalities since the end of the second world war becomes a less impressive – though still significant – 20%.

The media and the message

The world's conflicts have always attracted the attention of the media. The reports in the *Times* of London of the Crimean war by William Howard Russell made him a household name in the 19th century. In the 20th century American TV reporters became network stars by covering the Vietnam war, and in the process became politically influential. When Walter Cronkite, a CBS anchorman, returned from a reporting trip to Vietnam in 1968 and punctured the bubble of optimism favoured by US generals, President Lyndon Johnson said, "If I've lost Cronkite, I've lost middle America" – and soon decided not to run for re-election.

Today's politicians may often have a poor sense of history (failing, for example, to learn the lessons of previous invasions of Afghanistan), but they are all too well aware of the "CNN effect". They are adept at using, or indeed manipulating, television to popularise themselves and their policies, but when TV footage of dreadful famines or exhausted refugees is beamed into their voters' living rooms, it is they who are manipulated: the inevitable demand from their voters is that "something must be done", regardless of whether the something turns out to be for the worse rather than the better.

A prime example is arguably the European and American assault on Libya that led to the toppling of Muammar Qaddafi in 2011. To see the protesters in Cyrenaica slaughtered in their thousands by Qaddafi's forces was too horrific to be allowed, yet preventing that fate has been followed by Libya's slide into failed-state chaos and by flotillas of desperate migrants from Africa and the Middle East setting off from the Libyan shore in the hope of a better life in Europe. The CNN effect can have other perverse results. The relentless broadcasting of the horrors of conflict in Iraq and Afghanistan has led to an almost ubiquitous compassion fatigue in the US and its European allies – hence the refusal to put Western boots on the ground not just in Libya but also against the Islamic State fighters in Iraq and Syria.

Increasingly in today's conflicts the CNN effect is waning for purely practical reasons. Whereas in the early days of the Lebanese civil war journalists would wear T-shirts that identified them as "press", knowing that this would give them a degree of protection, by the mid-1980s they had become targets for kidnapping and ransom. That status has since become commonplace, and not just in the Middle East. In far too many of the conflicts of the 21st century journalists enter at their individual peril: few media organisations can insure them, which means they will not send their staff correspondents to cover the conflict, and any American and British journalists taken hostage will not be ransomed by their governments (instead, in the hands of the Islamic State, they are likely to be beheaded on camera).

One consequence is that even as news-gathering technology evolves to provide a level of immediacy that Russell could never have imagined, it becomes ever harder for the TV viewer or newspaper reader to be properly informed. The outside world's picture of the Islamic State is one created by ISIS's own cameramen, sound recordists, video editors and computer technicians. To say that the filmed beheadings, slickly edited and uploaded to the internet, are horrifically barbaric is obviously true. But it misses the point, which is that the kind of psychological warfare – intimidating opponents and terrifying civilians – that Genghis Khan would have recognised serves also to seduce impressionable young minds far beyond the borders of the Islamic State. Thousands of European Muslims, including many young women aspiring to be "jihadist brides", have joined the ranks of ISIS.

Meanwhile, it is wrong to assume that the CNN effect has shortened the wars in which the West has involved itself. American combat troops left Iraq in December 2011, eight years after the invasion. American troops entered Afghanistan to overthrow the Taliban government in October 2001, and the date set by President Barack Obama for the last of them to leave is December 2016. In comparison, the world wars of the 20th century begin to look relatively short. The real difference is the level of pain. Voters in democracies are willing to tolerate prolonged conflict, becoming so bored that they pay scant attention to the latest news. But they are unwilling to sacrifice many lives in the cause of that conflict. It is simply unimaginable that the population of any developed country – including Russia – would today accept the 27 million deaths suffered by the Soviet Union in the second world war. It is similarly hard to believe that modern cities would be as steadfast as Stalingrad in 1942–43, defeating the German army in a battle lasting 200 days.

None of this will worry a guerrilla commander. As Henry Kissinger said of the Vietnam war: "The guerrilla wins if he does not lose. The conventional army loses if it does not win." This truism of asymmetric warfare – pitting the numerically or technologically weak against the strong – is being emphasised in the 21st century everywhere from Nigeria to the Philippines. The world's most powerful and effective armed forces, be they the Americans fighting the Taliban or the Israelis fighting the Palestinians, almost never manage to claim total triumph. It only takes a resilient and resourceful handful of militants to sustain a conflict, as the British government has found in Northern Ireland and the Chinese government has found in Xinjiang.

By this measure it will be almost impossible for modern states to eradicate movements such as al-Qaeda and ISIS, which care not a fig for the Geneva Conventions and the rules of war. The same was true of the extreme left-wing movements of the 1960s and 1970s, but those that have not been crushed by government security forces are mostly a shadow of their former selves, unable to compete with the attractions of greater democracy and popular affluence in Latin America, for example. Conceivably, the same will eventually be true of the extreme Islamist groups that have arisen in this century. In the meantime, as this book makes clear, their violence causes havoc not just in the Arab world but in Africa and Asia, too, and its tentacles stretch into the US and Europe – as illustrated by the September 11th 2001 attacks in the US, the bombings in Madrid, London and Moscow, and the slaughter in Paris of *Charlie Hebdo*'s editors.

Islam's mixed message

It is tempting to invoke the memory of Samuel Huntington and talk of a clash of civilisations between Islam and the West, but it is just as plausible to posit a clash between tradition and modernity. Today's Islamist extremism has many roots: Soviet and then Western invasions of Afghanistan; unemployed youth in Arab countries blessed with oil; the plight of the Palestinians and Western support for Israel; ethnic and tribal tensions in the Horn of Africa; corruption and economic inequality in Nigeria; competition for minerals, water and land in a swathe of countries across the African continent; social exclusion in western Europe. All these play a part in persuading some Muslims to resort to violence. But what gives them an apparent cohesion, allowing Boko Haram in Nigeria or Abu Sayyaf in the Philippines or jihadists in Libya to declare allegiance to the Islamic State, is a fundamentalist interpretation of Islam that aspires to recreate the Muslim society of the 7th century.

Cynics may say much of what they want already exists in Wahhabi and Salafist Saudi Arabia, with its *sharia* law, *hudud* punishments (criminal penalties, such as stoning, lashing and amputation, prescribed in the Quran and in the sayings of the Prophet) and restrictions on women. And it is true that Saudi Arabia, the guardian of Islam's holiest shrines, has an antipathy towards Shia Islam, and regards Iran, the bastion of the Shia, as a regional competitor whose influence must be checked.

However, in contrast to the beliefs of al-Qaeda and the Islamic State, Saudi Arabia is not a *takfiri* state: it does not declare that Shia

Muslims are apostates who must be executed – indeed, it welcomes Shia Muslims in their thousands to make the *hajj* pilgrimage to Mecca. This alone would put Saudi Arabia at odds with groups such as al-Qaeda and ISIS, but what makes the kingdom their enemy is the corruption and un-Islamic behaviour of so many of the ruling Saud family (such as their well-publicised excesses in the fleshpots of the West). The irony is that Saudi Arabia has helped create its own Islamist enemy by funding so many Salafist-inclined mosques and *madrassas* (Islamic schools) in both the Muslim world and in the West.

Saudi Arabia has a long-established, and seemingly effective, programme to rehabilitate (rather than torture) its jihadists. By the spring of 2015 some 2,800 extremists, including 120 former prisoners in Guantanamo Bay, had passed through rehabilitation centres in Riyadh and Jeddah, with 87% of them, according to the authorities, returning to normal life. But for every Saudi success there will be many, many more Muslims being radicalised in the prisons of the Arab world and in Europe (60% of France's 70,000 prisoners are Muslim, and some will surely be converted to fundamentalist extremism).

One way to reduce Islamist violence would be to eliminate the factors that help it to flourish. Economic growth and more jobs for the young would work wonders in Egypt, Algeria and Tunisia (a nation of just 11 million that by the end of 2014 had provided around 3,000 recruits for ISIS and al-Qaeda). An end to bad governance and corruption would work wonders everywhere. But none of this is likely to happen in the near future. Somehow Islam as a religion has to show that it can cope with the process of modernisation.

That need not be difficult. There are critics who decry Islam as theocratic, and therefore, in its dealings with the modern world, lacking in the flexibility afforded by Christianity's injunction to "render unto Caesar the things that are Caesar's; render under God the things that are God's". The criticism is surely misplaced: Turkey, Indonesia and Malaysia all show that Islam can coexist (albeit at times imperfectly) with the trappings of democracy such as free elections, parliaments and an independent judiciary; innovations such as *sukuk* bonds show Islam's prohibition of usury is hardly any obstacle in the world of finance.

Moreover, traditional Islamic jurisprudence allowed for *ijtihad* – loosely translated as effort or diligence, but really meaning the original or independent interpretation of problems not precisely solved by the Quran or the *hadith* (the Prophet Muhammad's sayings). The problem is that Sunni Islam decided after its first three centuries that, because of the accumulation of case law and precedent, *ijtihad* was no longer needed. By contrast, Shia Islam has always kept open the gates of *ijtihad*. If, as reformist movements in Islam have often demanded, Sunni theologians were to reopen those gates, fundamentalist interpreters of Islam would face a challenge from within their religion. Ironically, some Islamists favour *ijtihad*, believing that autocratic regimes such as Saudi Arabia use *taqlid* (the unquestioning acceptance of precedent) as a means of oppressing them.

The weapons lobby: willing sellers and willing buyers

Whatever the subtleties of Islamic jurisprudence, it is clear that governments in much of the world will have to counter Islamist violence for years to come, especially if – as seems depressingly likely – Libya and Somalia remain as failed states. But will they have to counter each other? Dwight Eisenhower, in his farewell speech as president on January 17th 1961, warned Americans:

> In the councils of government, we must guard against the
> acquisition of unwarranted influence, whether sought or unsought,
> by the military-industrial complex. The potential for the disastrous
> rise of misplaced power exists and will persist.

Eisenhower's sobering words are relevant throughout the developed world. Arms manufacturers employ hundreds of thousands of people, fund political parties, lobby vigorously for their own interests and amass export earning by selling their wares to the developing world. Excluding China, the world's arms producers made sales totalling $402 billion in 2013, with six American companies in the top ten (the UK's BAE Systems came in at number three, Europe's EADS at number seven, Italy's Finmeccanica at number nine and France's Thales at number ten). That was a year in which defence spending fell slightly. But now, given the tensions with Russia over Ukraine and the ambitions of China in the Pacific, defence spending is likely to rise. In 2015 defence spending by Asia-Pacific countries, excluding China and the Middle East, was expected to be greater than Europe's, and military budgets were sharply increased in Russia (by 60% on arms, as part of a defence budget rising by 15%) and in the Baltic states that fear Russia's intentions.

The underlying question is whether the possession of weapons increases the likelihood of using them, or whether – as with nuclear weapons – they deter. The argument can go either way: the armed forces of the US, whose defence spending accounts for roughly half of the world's total, have seen active service in every decade since the second world war. But such involvement is inevitable given US commercial links around the globe and the role of the US as the world's policeman, despite the isolationist instincts of many Americans and President Obama's wish to share with others the US's global role. By 2040 it seems likely that China's defence spending will overtake the US's, and the US's Pacific allies worry that it will no longer be an effective or sufficient guarantor of their security against an increasingly powerful China. Their fears are understandable, especially given the rise in Chinese nationalism, but China always maintains it has no expansionist ambition – and it has not fired a shot in anger against another state since its brief war with Vietnam in 1979.

The evidence of history is that a tendency to violence is a human characteristic. For all the passive resistance of Gandhi or the conscientious objections to military service of the Quakers, men – and often women – have constantly resorted to violence, in attack or in defence, to achieve their goals. Their weapons have ranged from the swords and trebuchets of the Middle Ages to the cluster bombs and multiple-warhead cruise missiles of modern times. The romantic notion of war by single combat, with the outcome decided not by armies but by single warriors, goes back to the *Iliad*. This has rarely occurred in reality, though Thai history celebrates the combat, mounted on their elephants, between Siam's King Naresuan and the Burmese crown prince Mingyi Swa in 1593 (the king won and went on to conquer much of South-East Asia by more conventional means).

If war by single combat is mostly a myth, it nonetheless promises a real benefit: the minimising of bloodshed. Sadly, the guerrilla conflicts and civil wars of the 21st century are likely to use their increased firepower to promise more rather than fewer casualties and more rather than less destruction. Yet there is a real prospect that in conflicts between states bloodshed will be avoided by a new form of battle: cyberwar. Given that all modern economies rely on computers to operate everything from their electricity grids to their banking systems, all are potentially or actually vulnerable to a clever hacker or a smart piece of computer coding (such as the Stuxnet worm that damaged Iran's nuclear programme in 2009 and 2010). In 2015 the United States, which has been both a victim and an agent of cyber-attacks, announced it was updating its cyber-warfare strategy, naming China, Russia, Iran and North Korea as the greatest threats to its cyber-security.

This may be so. But all governments are aware that cyber-warfare is not something that will necessarily be confined to conflicts between states; it is just as likely that it will be a tactic of asymmetric warfare, too, with even the most powerful nations liable to be attacked by small groups or even individuals. As Eugene Kaspersky, the founder of a leading internet security firm, commented in 2012 at a conference in Israel:

> With today's attacks, you are clueless about who did it or when they will strike again. It's not cyber-war, but cyber-terrorism.

In which case, Pinker's view of a less violent world may be physically true, but it will need to be balanced by the argument of General Martin Dempsey, chairman of the US joint chiefs of staff. In 2012 he declared:

> I can't impress upon you [enough] that in my personal military judgment, formed over 38 years, we are living in the most dangerous time in my lifetime, right now.

Appendices

1 From terrorism to respectability: time and triumph change everything

Gerry Adams Sinn Fein leader against British rule in Northern Ireland, often accused of IRA membership; then a principal actor in the peace process leading to the Good Friday Agreement

Yasser Arafat Fatah and Palestine Liberation Organisation guerrilla leader against Israel; honoured as Nobel peace laureate for recognising Israel, renouncing violence and signing the Oslo accords with Yitzhak Rabin

Menachem Begin Irgun guerrilla leader against the British in Palestine; Nobel peace laureate as prime minister of Israel

Fidel Castro Leader of the communist revolution against the US-supported Batista regime in Cuba; later, as Cuba's president, revered by much of the developing world but not by the United States

Raul Castro Rebel commander against US-supported Batista regime in Cuba; now president (following brother Fidel) as Cuba and the United States normalise their relations

Agim Ceku Accused by Serbia of committing war crimes as commander of the Kosovo Liberation Army in the late 1990s; later, government minister in independent Kosovo

Daniel Cohn-Bendit	Known as Danny the Red during his days as an anarchist luminary in the May 1968 riots in Paris; now a respected Franco-German member of the European Parliament
Angela Davis	As a communist in the US with close links to the Black Panther Party, she was accused, and acquitted, of conspiracy in a 1970 attack in a California courtroom in which four died; now admired as a feminist leader and retired University of California professor
Joschka Fischer	As a member of Germany's Proletarian Union for Terror and Destruction led several street battles in the early 1970s against the police; later admired as a prominent member of the Green Party and as Germany's foreign minister 1998–2005
Ernesto "Che" Guevara	Latin American anti-imperialist and guerrilla leader executed in Bolivia in 1967; now posthumously revered by Western students as a symbol of freedom
Jomo Kenyatta	Mau Mau leader in war against British in Kenya; honoured first prime minister and president of independent Kenya
Martin McGuinness	Leader of Provisional IRA war against British rule in Northern Ireland; now deputy first minister of Northern Ireland
Nelson Mandela	Imprisoned for 27 years as leader of the anti-apartheid struggle of the African National Congress; then Nobel peace laureate and first president of post-apartheid South Africa
Muammar Qaddafi	Revolutionary hero who financed liberation movements and terrorist attacks around the world; then praised by the West for abandoning weapons of mass destruction; later denounced by the West for his tyrannical practices, leading to his overthrow

Dilma Rousseff   Imprisoned as a Marxist urban guerrilla against Brazil's military dictatorship; now president of democratic Brazil

Hashim Thaci   Accused of drug- and organ-trafficking as leader of Kosovo independence movement; later, first prime minister of independent Kosovo (though still accused by a report to the Council of Europe of criminal activity)

2 Terrorist organisations: to designate and to proscribe

WHEN GOVERNMENTS – most, but not all, Western – describe organisations such as al-Qaeda, ISIS or Boko Haram as terrorists, their official action is more than symbolic. The US talks of "designated" organisations; the UK of "proscribed" organisations; and the European Union, in a triumph of legalese, of "persons, groups and entities on the list to the effect that they have been involved in terrorist acts within the meaning of Article 1(2) and (3)" of a "common position" adopted by EU member states in the immediate aftermath of the September 11th 2001 terrorist attacks in the US.

The UK government explains what is common to all:

> It is a criminal offence for a person to belong to or invite support for a proscribed organisation. It is also a criminal offence to arrange a meeting to support a proscribed organisation or to wear clothing or to carry articles in public which arouse reasonable suspicion that an individual is a member or supporter of the proscribed organisation. Proscription means that the financial assets of the organisation become terrorist property and can be subject to freezing and seizure.

At least in theory, the seizure of financial assets should be a powerful weapon in the hands of governments. After all, it costs money for an organisation to arm and pay its militants, and many a jobless young man has joined an insurgency simply to get regular pay. In practice, most terrorist organisations – al-Qaeda and ISIS are good examples – sustain themselves regardless of financial sanctions.

In which case, perhaps it is the symbolism that counts most. A UK government minister declared in January 2000:

There are three principal reasons why we think proscription is important. First, it has been, and remains, a powerful deterrent to people to engage in terrorist activity. Secondly, related offences are a way of tackling some of the lower-level support for terrorist organisations ... Thirdly, proscription acts as a powerful signal of rejection by Government – and indeed by society as a whole – of organisations' claims to legitimacy.

Yet political considerations are never far away. When Hillary Clinton was the US secretary of state, she resisted pressure from her own department, from the Justice Department and from the FBI to designate Boko Haram as a terrorist organisation, preferring instead to accept the Bureau of African Affairs' argument that to do so would raise Boko Haram's status and encourage the Nigerian army to adopt excessive brutality against any opposition. Her compromise was to designate three Boko Haram leaders as terrorists, rather than the whole organisation (which was finally declared a terrorist organisation in November 2013 by Clinton's successor, John Kerry).

US politics, influenced by the domestic debate over how to deal with Iran's nuclear ambitions, were also at play in the 2012 delisting of the Mujahedin-e Khalq, a radical leftist organisation opposed to the Islamic regime in Iran. Cynics (or realists) will note, too, that in its desire to roll back the so-called Islamic State, the US has co-ordinated its efforts with those of Kurdish forces linked to the PKK (Partiya Karkerên Kurdistan, or Kurdistan Workers' Party), even though it has been a designated terrorist organisation since 1997.

Lists of terrorist organisations compiled by the US, the UK and the EU can be found at:

■ http://www.state.gov/j/ct/rls/other/des/123085.htm

■ https://www.gov.uk/government/uploads/system/uploads/attachment_data/file/417888/Proscription-20150327.pdf

■ http://eur-lex.europa.eu/legal-content/EN/TXT/PDF/?uri=OJ:JOL_2015_082_R_0009&from=EN

A list of terrorists sought by the US can be found at:

■ https://www.rewardsforjustice.net/english/most-wanted/all-regions.html

3   The Arabic challenge

ARABIC TRANSLITERATION is rarely straightforward: there are only three vowels in Arabic (*fatha*, *damma* and *kasra* – a, u and i), though each can be lengthened by the addition of a consonant. The vowels are normally not written down, except in the Quran or in cases where there would otherwise be confusion (*damma*, for example, is used to signal a passive verb). Given that English has five vowels, there is always the possibility of a transliteration mismatch.

Consonants are even more challenging. There are, for example, two different types of t, s, d and h. There are also some consonants for which there are no English equivalents (for example, the consonant *ain* – a kind of strangulated glottal stop – is normally represented by an apostrophe, as also is *hamza*, a barely noticeable glottal stop.

The Economist transliterates the name of the former leader of Libya as Qaddafi. A purist would write Qadhdhafi, though in Libyan pronunciation the name becomes Gadafi (with a long second a). A purist would always write Muhammad, but others may opt for Mohammad, Mohamed, and so on. The problem is compounded by the personal preferences of the people themselves: for example, Hosni Mubarak, rather than Husni (which would be more correct since there is no o vowel in Arabic). Accents, too, play their part. A purist would prefer Jamal Abd al-Nasir, but Egyptians in speech use a hard g rather than a j, and so the usual spelling is Gamal Abdul Nasser or Gamal Abdel Nasser.

Then there is *al*, as in al-Qaeda (which should really be al-Qa'ida), meaning simply the. But with a capital A the word means family, as in Al-Saud. And there are the sun letters, in which consonants elide, so that a purist might well transliterate jabhat al-nusra as jabhat an-nusra. Adding to the complex is the *ta marbuta* (a tied or joined t), which is written as a soft h in Arabic at the end of a word, so that a purist would transliterate nusra as nusrat.

Forgive us, therefore, our inconsistencies. We write of Bashar al-Assad, though the CIA correctly spells his family name as Asad (the lion). We call Qaddafi-era Libya a *jamahiriya*, because that is how the Libyans spelt what should properly be *jamahiriyya*. As for the various jihadist groups, some from countries such as Pakistan that use the Arabic script but not the language, consistency is an impossible dream.

Acknowledgements

THE INTERNET ALLOWS organisations as varied as government agencies and obscure militias to spread their messages to the world – and so is a marvellous aid in the 21st century to any author or researcher. This book owes much to dozens of websites and many authorities, from academic and political think-tanks to individuals. As a journalist I have experienced conflict first hand – be it outright war or seething and violent unrest – from Lebanon and the Western Sahara to Kashmir and the Philippines. The lesson is that good people do bad things, and sadly the chapters in this book suggest that they always will.

Those chapters would not exist without the encouragement and advice of Stephen Brough at Profile Books. I am particularly grateful for the insights on Africa of Xan Smiley, to the patience of my wife Hilary, watching me hunched for far too long over the keyboard, and to the ever-perceptive copy-editing of the indefatigable Penny Williams. Any mistakes are, of course, my own.

Index